The Next American Century

William Van Lear

UNIVERSITY PRESS OF AMERICA,® INC.
Lanham • Boulder • New York • Toronto • Plymouth, UK

Copyright © 2008 by
University Press of America,® Inc.
4501 Forbes Boulevard
Suite 200
Lanham, Maryland 20706
UPA Acquisitions Department (301) 459-3366

Estover Road
Plymouth PL6 7PY
United Kingdom

Library of Congress Control Number: 2007935044
ISBN-13: 978-0-7618-3906-4 (clothbound : alk. paper)
ISBN-10: 0-7618-3906-2 (clothbound : alk. paper)
ISBN-13: 978-0-7618-3907-1 (paperback : alk. paper)
ISBN-10: 0-7618-3907-0 (paperback : alk. paper)

Contents

Figures and Tables

Acknowledgments

The successful completion of this manuscript owes much to the constructive and critical input from colleagues. I thank Dr. Gary Williams for reading and critiquing much of the text. Dr. Peter Lodge, Dr. James Giermanski, and Dr. Bayster had helpful comments on distinct portions of the manuscript. The most substantive assistance came from Dr. John Plecnik who helped me to think through the financial and ethical consequences of globalization.

A second group facilitated the conceptual progress of the work. The students in my economics classes proved helpful by asking thoughtful questions and by getting me to think more deeply about issues and ideas. My employer, Belmont Abbey College, was instrumental by providing the financial support I required and the requisite time I needed to make this manuscript a contribution to the ongoing debate about economic evolution, ideas, and policymaking.

Inspiration for my work as an educator and as an author stems from two great economists of the twentieth century, John Maynard Keynes and John Kenneth Galbraith. Their rich and timeless insights and arguments have created in me a drive for knowledge and a hope for continued human progress. With admiration, I also apply in the manuscript the concepts of contemporary economists Paul Davidson, Randall Wray, and Tom Palley whose works standout in heterodox economic thinking.

A final word of appreciation goes to my parents and friends who have cultivated in me a love of learning and the discipline to follow through on whatever I elect to do.

Chapter One

Overview

This book is about understanding the historical context for today's globalization and America's important role in driving globalization. This undertaking is an effort to rather comprehensively address the varying and interrelated social, political, and economic dimensions of nation-state integration. A theory of globalization is established that centers on the core economic driving mechanisms of this phenomena. Important financial aspects of global capitalism are discussed. The text addresses the themes of wealth, power, class, and policy in an age of globalization, and this particular chapter provides an overview of the content and argument of the entire book. The text provides a balanced, analytical, and critical examination of current economic evolution.

The book begins with an historical overview of the three modern waves of world economic integration, followed by a chapter addressing the important political economic implications of the current era of globalization. The middle part of the book takes on the interrelated issues of global central banking, the international financial system, and cycles in commerce and finance. The final section addresses the discontents and challenges imposed by globalization; the broad concerns of global markets and growth, economic instability and employment, public policy, foreign policy, and the politics of globalization are covered. The manuscript concludes by summarizing the necessary policy responses to the attending problems of globalization.

The book establishes a context for comprehending globalization by providing an historical overview of three phases of modern globalization. The first era of globalization occurs in the 19th century, and is followed by the second wave after an interlude brought on by WWI. The second wave of globalization spans the 1945 to 1980 period, superseded by the contemporary phase running into the 21st century.

British foreign and economic policy, the London financial market, and the gold standard monetary system characterize the first globalization era. The expansive British Empire and technological change facilitate capital flows and global trade. Unregulated economies and little public policy intervention subject capitalist countries to business and financial cycle instability. Finance comes to dominate business decision-making and financial market speculation increases. Central banks arise to prevent financial fragility and illiquidity from impacting business investment. Nationalist aspirations and a drive to colonize create substantial conflict among major economic powers and between the powers and those they conquer.

The war and inter-war period witness the continued gradual erosion in British international preeminence and the rise of America to importance. Economic challenges impinge on Europe and the West. Economic distress in Europe and financial instability in the context of an investment boom in the U.S. create conditions for political extremism in parts of Europe and business depression throughout the capitalist world. Another world war and major efforts at domestic economic institutional overhaul continue to impede what had been a protracted move toward globalization.

The second era of globalization runs from the mid 1940s through to about 1980, and is noted for concerted efforts across capitalist societies to institutionalize and build on the reforms experimented within the prior forty years. Many of the reforms have a domestic focus intended to assure greater financial-economic and political stability. The Bretton Woods system is created to do the same internationally by ushering in a more stable yet expansive international economic order built to foster integrated international trade and investment. Domestic and international financial stability is sought and achieved. The core corporations of leading countries again push investment across borders and the firm itself is reconfigured to emphasize growth and stability. America is clearly preeminent in this stage, manifested in the importance of the dollar in international exchange and U.S. influence in Bretton Woods institutions. Socialist countries led by the Soviet Union form their own economic and political block, and compete with western democratic capitalist nations for allies and resources.

The 1970s is a period of transition from one kind of globalization to another. Domestic inflation and unemployment challenges revive interest in domestic policy preoccupied with inflation control and entrepreneurial incentive creation. A policy emphasis shift permitting more outcomes determined by private decisions and competition replaces a policy focus on income stability and high employment. The collapse of the Bretton Woods system, based on fixed exchange rates and capital controls, ushers in a more free market, deregulated international system based on flexible exchange rates and no capital controls. Competition between developed nations extends to competition among all.

Push and pull factors spread capitalism across the globe, manifested in increasing capital flows to emerging market countries and flows exiting high cost developed countries. Production location, employment markets, corporate supply chains, and finance become nearly global in the third phase of globalization. Consequently, employment instability, income distribution shifts, pressures for curricular change in education and structural changes in firms become intense. Government policy remains widely interventionist but heavily promotional of the internationalization of capital. Military deployments and foreign policy are directed at fighting terrorism, developing commercial connections, and maintaining safe conditions for economic interests. Finance becomes a relatively more important aspect of the economy, demonstrated in increased financial flows, borrowing and spending, mergers across fields of finance, and trading activity. International Money Manager Capitalism, not completely unlike the "Finance Capitalism" of the early 20th century, comes into its own.

The text moves on to chapter three where important political economic implications of the on-going globalization of nation-states are addressed. The themes of this section include (1) the driving mechanisms for globalization, (2) economic stability, employment and income effects, and some public policy issues, and (3) how public support for globalization may be undermined by the excesses of upper-class conduct. Colonization, conquest, and nationalism animate the first era of globalization. Cold War pressures and the revival of the European and Japanese economies drive the second era. The third era's driving force is centered on political confrontation between western culture and Islam and in Anglo-American efforts to expand capitalist institutions and democratic governance world-wide, partly to achieve political domination but also to open up many new, more profitable investment options than possible merely from domestic trade or commerce between developed nations. The particular mechanisms involve policy prescriptions delivered to non-integrated countries and U.S. current account deficits that bolster the performance of non-integrated economies. In a combined fashion, these mechanisms foster globalization American style, the former through economic and political pressure and example, and the latter by shifting domestic American resources and opportunities to developing economies, making them into "emerging market" economies. Reinvestment by these countries back into the U.S. and other established developed countries creates an interdependent relationship with momentum. Continued global prosperity and progress is predicated on the spreading of wealth and ownership across developed country populations who invest in developing countries and who in turn invest back into major world economies.

Despite the prominence of finance in the current era, the system appears to offer relative economic stability. Short run and longer term factors exist however that may bring economic challenge. Tension exists within developed nations over the new income and employment opportunities that arise from globalization and the two-fold effect of job churning and the system's inherent inability to ever provide full employment on its own. Capital mobility is expressed in cross-border money flows but also in the reconfiguring of business productive capital through restructurings, mergers, and relocations. Central banks have become the main means of public policy intervention, either to address inflation or growth problems. Classical leanings of policymakers and a misunderstanding concerning what a central bank can actually do could exacerbate difficult existing conditions or create economic problems when none had existed. Governments confront a policy conundrum of instilling entrepreneurial incentives and maintaining adequate income supports and stabilizers; central banking can run at cross purposes to the larger public purpose of the state. Controversy prevails over the extent to which national governments should engage in global regulatory efforts and contention exists over the degree to which global governance is to be performed by private economic interests.

If public servants and private capitalists are inattentive to the broad social needs of people, who are affected by change induced by the former group, they stand to confront negative reaction and opposition. Employment and business opportunities must avail themselves and upward pressure on people's wealth must continue in order to achieve the wide support necessary to permit globalization to go forward. The book enumerates many real world examples and experiences that work to undermine the legitimacy of current world economic development.

The middle parts of the book cover central banking, the international financial system, and business and financial cycles. These are importantly related issues because the operation of the financial system affects and is affected by economic cycles, all of which is influenced by central banks' monetary policies. The spread of globalization and prosperity necessarily require a resilient financial system and robust financial conditions that promote continued global investment, business opportunities, and job creation. Policymakers should not be lulled into monetary policy overreach. They should not succumb to thinking that dynamic, complex, globally interconnected economies can be fined tuned through short term interest rate adjustments or by unfettered free markets. Though the current system's evolution suggests increased financial stability relative to prior times, monetary policy makers should not therefore implement restrictive policies because the system can withstand greater restrictive measures. Promotion of financial stability is the more prudent approach to policy, regardless of the system's inherent proclivity to stability or expansion. Modern central banking is assessed and critiqued, and reforms are addressed.

Healthy and expansionary business conditions prevail generally in the current age. In part this comes from the extensive expansion of product, resource, and labor markets from globalization. These expanding markets provide more private demands to supply, and lower costs to produce that supply. Technology and the concomitant productivity increases help to further a favorable commercial climate. Public management of effective demand and regulation of commerce and finance assist in sustaining profitable, expansionary conditions for business. Financial conditions are usually robust and very accommodating to business and consumer needs. The "affluent society" and "ownership society" culture combine with international money manager capitalism to create a propitious symbiotic relationship between the financial and business sectors. America's drive as hegemon to globalize the world in its own image draws in and creates emerging market nations whose relationship with America is favorably symbiotic.

But nothing human is ever perfect. Negative economic outcomes arising from the very same forces promoting prosperity and stability are eminently possible. Too much risk taking, or employing overly complex financial strategies or derivative assets, or perhaps too many traders controlling overly concentrated wealth and all betting wrong simultaneously, could spark a global economic retrenchment or worse. Endlessly sustaining profitable business is not likely either. An undue dependence on strong consumption growth, financed by upward pressure on household net worth's and an ever growing supply of credit, suggests vulnerability to continued solid profit performance. Self interest can undermine the current system if private economic power is exploited too much to favor a small class of people or if the word "public" is essentially dropped from policy measures that, when implemented, are strongly class biased or too restrictive on effective demand.

Long run success of the current evolutionary transformation of the world requires that the benefits be adequately shared within and across nation-states. Contrary to the Age's philosophical rhetoric about public sector pull-backs on social programs and income supports, governments and central banks must play a supportive role in not only fostering effective demand but broadening the distribution of benefits from globalization. The book identifies and explicates five practical ways governments can succeed in policy-making.

The challenges and discontents of globalization are addressed in chapter seven. Following a summary of the main points found in the preceding chapters, various economic and political issues are discussed. Economic issues include markets, efficiency, stability and growth. Political issues involve addressing the regulatory foundation, security, peace and prosperity, and nationalism. Reflections on the politics of wealth, power, and class complete the chapter.

Understanding any economic system requires an understanding of power within the system to determine outcomes. Institutions are the locus of power and tend to reflect class interests. Economic outcomes are registered on markets, so power is exercised through institutions and observed on markets. Global corporations and finance, and global institutions of governments, affect the course and pace of development. Global economic efficiency depends on whether market prices reflect the underlying commercial fundamentals or whether those prices reflect speculative trading outcomes not closely linked to commercial fundamentals or needs.

International economic stability is supported by a confluence of forces, but interestingly the overall stability in country business conditions runs concurrently with industry level upheaval and change. Excitement arises from modernizing, dynamic economies brought on by globalization but angst prevails for millions whose jobs are eliminated or shifted elsewhere in the world. Economic success becomes more stratified producing optimism and progress along side dislocation and decline. World economic conditions are sufficiently healthy to maintain social comforts and political support for the policy-induced evolution underway, yet an underlying current of discontent pervades public sentiment.

Capitalist societies have a penchant for growth founded on material improvement aspirations and funded by new money creation. Debts fuel spending beyond current incomes, allowing future incomes to rise. Stability within this process of income expansion requires that by and large, those who go into debt can service their debt; in other words, they reap the income gains of economic growth. Even when financial asset prices remain elevated and interest expense modest, as is normal in today's capitalism, defaults and financial fragility can nevertheless undermine economic welfare.

Developed country cross-border spending makes emerging market country reliance on export led growth successful but simultaneously creates substantial churning within their own domestic business and employment sectors. By elevating costs, very buoyant domestic conditions entice MDC companies to expand foreign hiring and to accelerate world integration, in turn creating momentum for further integration as domestic labor markets become ever more flexible and affected by capital outflows. Fully successful emerging market growth policies require attention to developing strong internal markets for business and job creation. Whole sale opening to global economic pressures by developing economies does not necessarily lead to more rapid growth.

Public policy has a responsibility to address the potentials for financial fragility, insufficient total demand, and unemployment. It should also become ever more deeply involved in sustaining the material and social protections reminiscent of the 20th century period. The book promotes the ideas of a modern New Deal for, and policy coordination among, developed countries.

The book goes on to discuss issues of peace, prosperity, nationalism, and security. For globalization to succeed, the hegemon driving it must behave in a certain way. Constructive leadership entails building the basic economic and technological infrastructure of the world economy. It requires being open about the downsides to globalization and an active willingness to address these downsides, even if through multilateral or supranational organizations. Government and private economic leaders need to see their privileged status in world affairs commanding statesmanship directed at improving the current system and protecting people and communities from serious externally generated social negatives. And honesty about globalization's substantial transformative effects requires the hegemon to tread lightly on other cultures and allow lengthy integration periods as well as the possibility for countries to opt out of integration. Globalization can bring shared security and prosperity but if coercively driven and imposed on nonintegrated states, combative relations result.[1]

Wealth, power, class, and policy converge in the politics of globalization. Multinational economic interests tend to support an unbridled globalization, except when their immediate financial or property interests are threatened by the lack of legal protections. To get this kind of system necessitates dividing voting blocks or preventing voting coalitions from forming. The book uses immigration, unionization, and foreign policy to demonstrate how this is done. People are impacted differently from globalizing national economies, and therefore globalization is political. The question is whether and to what extent is this recognized by electorates? An enlightened and moral elite will not only attempt to address ill effects of the current system but be a conduit for popular political expression for reform.

The concluding chapter advocates pro-active regulatory and supervisory intervention by states and central banks. A summary table is provided that identifies on-going challenges created by integration with appropriate attending policy responses. One point made stresses the urgency of governments taking seriously income disparities generated through the manipulation of global business assets by considering proper corrective regulatory options and acknowledging the likely political outcomes to the process of globalization upon ignoring such disparities. A social responsibility exists, it is argued, to assist those negatively affected by asset redeployment and microeconomic instability engendered by globalization. While globalization is not reversible, it can be guided by policy and redirected in a socially beneficial way by a politically active and influential upper middle class. The twenty-first century is the next American century.

NOTE

1. This is particularly true in nonintegrated states that contend with deep seated historically conditioned in-fighting among factional interests.

Chapter Two

A History of Modern Globalization

INTRODUCTION

A society's institutions are what characterize and define that society, and institutions affect the performance of economies over time. Institutions shape relations among classes of people, influence private sector behavior, and define the role of the state. Institutions are simply the means employed by people to cooperate, who have like values and interests, to achieve common objectives. An economic system consists of a constellation of institutions which condition growth, profitability, and capital accumulation. Systems can be effective or ineffective at promoting economic growth and stability. If ineffective, problems arise and persist, often worsen, and create conflict in society. Growth stagnates, recession sets in, and the necessary process of accumulation is disrupted. Instability and discontent arise. Eventually, the severity of problems leads to crisis and institutional breakdown prompting construction of new institutions and policy, corrective of past problems.[1]

Understanding modern globalization requires an understanding of the historic evolution in institutional design and the gradual economic integration of national economic systems into an international political-economic order. Each era in globalization is institutionally unique and is characterized by distinctive traits. Modern globalization begins with the creation and expansion of colonial empires in the nineteenth century, progresses to a period of cold war contentions and spheres of hegemonic influence, followed by the spread of capitalism internationally, largely under the auspices of American political-economic leadership. Institutional design and public policy, economic self interest, and technological change combine to create three distinct waves of globalization.

GLOBALIZATION'S FIRST ERA: 1870–1914

The British dominate the first era of globalization. The pound operates as a world currency, readily exchangeable into gold. Pounds are held for means of payment and as a store of wealth. The financial center is located in London, where the "City," London's financial district, importantly influences British domestic and international economic policy. The global monetary system is built on a gold standard that fixes exchange rates among countries and determines the money supply available to finance economic activity. Balance of payments disequilibria are settled by either capital or gold flows between countries. The fixity of exchange rates lowers the uncertainty of foreign direct investment (FDI) but since gold supplies had no immediate connection to commercial needs, periodic financial crises and deflation beset nations that conduct international trade using the gold standard.

Falling transportation and communication costs, and falling tariffs, encourage global economic interconnection. Steam and petroleum fuel engines, better sailing ships, the telegraph, and railroads improve the efficiency, speed, and reliability of commerce. Lower tariffs reduce import costs, and thus increase trade among nations. Trade patterns are such that industrialized colonial powers import raw materials to support their manufacturing bases and then export finished products. Immigration, exports relative to world output, and capital flows relative to developing country output, all increase substantially. Global growth accelerates [King and King 2005, 209]. As the hegemonic power, Britain influences thinking on international political economic relations and enforces international trade and monetary rules. And due to such dominance, Britain pushes for global free trade and open markets, policies that provide substantial benefits to export and foreign investment oriented domestic enterprises.

In the years prior to WWI, goods, capital, and labor flowed across borders with the same ease as today. Foreign investment equaled one third of developing countries' GDP [Wynne 2005]. Keynes describes the accomplishments of and impact on life that this era afforded:

> What an extraordinary episode in the economic progress of man that age was which came to an end in August, 1914! The greater part of the population, it is true, worked hard and lived at a low standard of comfort, yet were, to all appearances, reasonably contented with this lot. But escape was possible, for any man of capacity or character at all exceeding the average, into the middle and upper classes, for whom life offered, at a low cost and with the least trouble, conveniences, comforts, and amenities beyond the compass of the richest and most powerful monarchs of other ages. The inhabitant of London could order by telephone, sipping his morning tea in bed, the various products of the whole

earth, in such quantity as he might see fit, and reasonably expect their early delivery upon his door-step; he could at the same moment and by the same means adventure his wealth in the natural resources and new enterprises of any quarter of the world, and share, without exertion or even trouble, in their prospective fruits and advantages; or he could decide to couple the security of his fortunes with the good faith of the townspeople of any substantial municipality in any continent that fancy or information might recommend. He could secure forthwith, if he wished it, cheap and comfortable means of transit to any country or climate without passport or other formality, could despatch his servant to the neighboring office of a bank for such supply of the precious metals as might seem convenient, and could then proceed abroad to foreign quarters, without knowledge of their religion, language, or customs, bearing coined wealth upon his person, and would consider himself greatly aggrieved and much surprised at the least interference. But, most important of all, he regarded this state of affairs as normal, certain, and permanent, except in the direction of further improvement, and any deviation from it as aberrant, scandalous, and avoidable. The projects and politics of militarism and imperialism, of racial and cultural rivalries, of monopolies, restrictions, and exclusion, which were to play the serpent to this paradise, were little more than the amusements of his daily newspaper, and appeared to exercise almost no influence at all on the ordinary course of social and economic life, the internationalization of which was nearly complete in practice [Keynes 1920, 10–12].

British hegemony shows signs of strain in the 19th century.[2] Maintaining a far-flung empire is costly in treasure and lives. But the two most important factors that precipitate hegemonic decline are WWI and the pound overhang. The economic consequences of war are catastrophic. Europe's economies are in ruins from four years of battles and stalemate. The debt structure created to finance the war became too burdensome to meet obligations, given the poor business conditions. The treaty of Versailles imposes unrealistically harsh reparations on the Central Powers. Poor continental economic conditions negatively affect British economic performance. In an effort to conduct war, countries focus on domestic production and go off the gold standard to more easily finance the war. The gold standard and trade collapse, along with British economic dominance, from war.

The second force to undermine British hegemony had to do with flaws in a fixed exchange rate gold standard system. British preeminence in the world economy led to a pound overhang whereby too many pounds circulated globally than could be comfortably backed by the available gold supply in London. Calls on gold drained gold supplies and increasingly made Britain's commitment to convert gold for paper currency suspect. War and the overhang prompt the British to go off the gold standard. Attempts in the 1920s to reestablish the gold standard ultimately fail. Marked differences in country inflation rates since 1914 make the old fixed rates inappropriate for balanced trade. Nevertheless, the British reset the pound at its prewar high value, undercutting the ability of its manufacturing firms to globally compete. The Great Depression destroys the gold standard as trade collapses.

The firm in the first era of globalization becomes much more outward looking and internationalist. A new ethic of accumulation, growth, and risk taking propels national industrial development and the extension of the firm across borders. Increasingly, businesses expand in size, and produce for national and international markets. Capital is invested into domestic manufacturing, and competitive price pressures and new technologies lead firms to exploit economies of scale, exporting some output or employing foreign resources in production. Transportation improvements and globally connected national capital markets finance the arrival of big business. The corporate form of business becomes the preferred accumulation devise, amassing ever larger amounts of people and capital. The factory and mass production are the mainstays of this period. While doing business remains "a way of life" for entrepreneurs, wealth accumulation becomes an end in itself for industrial and finance capitalists. Banks remain short-term providers of credit but retained earnings from operations and financial markets supply funds for expansion. Professional management and founding owners operate corporations for the long run success and viability of the business, but rentiers gain influence as industrial wealth is passed down through the generations and accumulates in financial institutions.

This period is one of high investment and growth, but capitalist economies are increasingly subject to business cycles and financial panics. The 19th century is full of examples of speculative excesses, financial crises, and consequent crashes. The typical story is that a "displacement" opens up new profit opportunities that are financed by credit creation. Certain industries undergo substantial growth, exhibited by rising investment and profit, and this growth feeds back onto the need for more finance. Some asset, such as stocks, companies, currencies, or commodities, becomes a source of speculation, where eventually an asset bubble develops.[3] The speculative boom ends when the high prices are seen as unsustainable, given the underlying economic fundamentals of the economy. Traders and businesses rush for liquidity as asset owners sell off their holdings of the overvalued asset. Capital losses lead to loan defaults, and the distress in the financial sector brings an end to commercial expansion. Booms and panics in one country propagate world-wide through psychological, commercial, and financial linkages [Kindleberger 1978].

The first wave of globalization is noted for the internationalization and integration of capital markets, of increased capital mobility, and for the powerful influence of investment bankers in corporate affairs. Leading financial institutions promote the allocation of capital based on competitive rates of return as opposed to the funding of local endeavors via personal relationships. Industrial fortunes, created by the advent of corporate enterprise in the nineteenth century, provide significant savings pools to tap into. Improvements in financial intermediation contribute to increased levels of saving and investment. Life insurance companies and most importantly investment banks provide increased long term funding and occupy important positions on transnational corporate boards. Money capital flows from the relatively low return Old World to fund higher return New World frontier development [Lenin 1974 (1916) ; O'Rourke 2000, 209–212, 214–215, 225–231].[4]

Finance capital assists in overseeing the development of the modern large corporation. As size and scope of corporate activity increase so do corporate bureaucracies, necessitating two important innovations. First, professional management teams come to administer operations. They employ management science to foster efficiency and profitability in large organizations. Second, firms are restructured along divisional lines. Distinct product lines become profit centers, each employing the various business skills of marketing, finance, and management to produce and increase returns to the overall enterprise. Consolidation of America's most economically important firms occurs through two major merger waves, one around 1900 and the other in the 1920s. Industry concentration arises through bankruptcies and mergers of competitors, and vertical integration occurs as firms buy-out suppliers and distributors. By the end of the 1920s, much of corporate America operates in more stable, less competitive, oligopolistic industries.

Four important institutional changes affecting investment and the corporation arise in this period. First, within major businesses, ownership separates from control. Increasingly large, diverse, and complex enterprises require professional management teams to administer operations. Stockholders become larger in number and less influential in company affairs as their knowledge about operations is inadequate and their holdings represent a small fraction of the outstanding equities. Separation brings about a divergence of interest between owners and management. Through the capital markets, bond—and stock—holders provide finance and speculate on financial asset prices. Investment and enterprise become solely an executive function. This development splits the financing-speculation process from the investment-enterprise process. The return on financial assets becomes a preoccupation of financiers, and this leads to a second development. Conflict arises between the economic interests of the financial and industrial sectors over the distribution of profit. Industrial capitalists are rewarded with profit for investing and risk-taking, but financiers demand a claim to the firm's earnings given their role in providing external finance and fostering corporate consolidations.

A third institutional change facilitates the above, namely the rise of organized stock exchanges. Participants in the exchanges are interested in trading and speculation with a focus on capital gains based on short-term economic developments. Stock prices at times fluctuate significantly due to shifting stockholder expectations and confidence concerning corporate earnings, and because Exchanges offer liquidity and easily revocable commitments. Fickle assessments of corporate profitability, as expressed in stock markets' continuous reevaluation of firms, substitutes for long run, more stable assessments produced by business insiders.[5] The stock exchange becomes an arena for trading financial assets and therefore facilitates the speculation unleashed by the separation of ownership from control in major corporations. This era of globalization is consequently marked by intensified periods of financial instability, severe economic downturns, and income inequality. As an acute observer of early globalization, Keynes' own words are informative:

> . . . the professional investor is forced to concern himself with the anticipation of impending changes . . . of the kind by which experience shows that the mass psychology of the market is most influenced. Of the maxims of orthodox finance none . . . is more anti-social than the fetish of liquidity, . . . there are . . . such serious minded individuals and that it makes a vast difference to an investment market whether or not they predominate in their influence over the game players. . . . it is the long-term investor, he who most promotes the public interest, who will in practice come in for most criticism, . . . Speculators may do no harm as bubbles on a steady stream of enterprise. But the position is serious when enterprise becomes the bubble on a whirlpool of speculation. When the capital development of a country becomes a by-product of the activities of a casino, the job is likely to be ill-done. The measure of success attained by Wall Street, . . . cannot be claimed as one of the outstanding triumphs of laissez-faire capitalism—[1997 (1936), 155–159].

The fourth institutional innovation occurs as developed economies establish modern, activist central banks to finance state operations during national emergencies and to stabilize economic activity. For example, The Reserve System in the US is adopted only after continuous financial and economic problems compel action to reform. Periodic economic downturns, often precipitated by an inelastic currency supply, interest rate spikes, and bank runs, create hardships for business and agricultural interests. Price declines in farming and manufacturing, referred to as deflation, are often associated with business cycle downturns during this era. Deflation exacerbates debt burdens because lower prices usually mean lower revenues to pay fixed debt commitments to creditors. Prolonged difficulties in farming and the growing power of corporations prompt the Populist Party political challenge in the late 1800s in the U.S. A financial panic in 1907 leads to the National Monetary Commission's study of the banking industry. The Commission's report reviewed U.S. financial laws and banking history, and confirmed the destabilizing effects of the banking system. The report noted that insufficient regulation and supervision prevailed, and that significant concentration of financial resources had developed. Central banks come to exist to regulate financial sectors, and eventually conduct monetary policy to address recurring inflation and unemployment concerns. Most importantly, central banks act as lenders of last resort for the banking system, whereby currency can be injected into economies experiencing financial crises. Capitalist banking occasionally suffers from illiquidity and disruptions in money flows that central banks can correct. A more liquid banking system could supply illiquid firms and consumers with needed funds to make payments to creditors and forestall bankruptcy. Prior to activist monetary policy, economies had no public policy institution empowered to create an elastic currency or to determine interest rate levels.

Progress on creating more stable financial sectors is nonetheless inadequate as developed countries retain the gold standard that ties the quantity of money to gold reserves. While monetary authorities can affect bank liquidity, the gold standard, by design, continued to impose inflexibility to the currency supply. Financial crises and deflation periodically continue to plague economies. Secondly, money as an issue recedes as a central concern in national politics. While financial issues attract academic and professional economic interests, system design and reform fell from democratic debate. Monetary policy becomes the focus of attention, not private control and concentration of wealth. With money no longer politicized, private financial interests remain free to pursue their activities unmolested. The importance here is the decline in democratic input on money issues in democratic societies.

The first era of globalization is driven by the interplay of national identity and desire for economic expansion. Capitalist economies must grow to remain healthy, and domestic demand conditions often limit profit opportunities for business and banking interests. Nationalism creates feelings of pride and unified interests. These two factors work to compel largely European powers to colonize and seek economic domination of territories in Eurasia, Africa, and the Pacific. Japan and the U.S., two nations resulting from struggles against imperial control, join imperialist efforts to develop new economic opportunities and balance off the power of European empires [Bayly 2004, 228–233].

Globalization in this era is one of competitive imperialism. The advanced state of military and economic development of the European powers combines with political disunity and cultural diversity of Africa and the Middle East to permit European domination of these areas. Colonial powers compete over sea routes, over-land routes connecting regions of influence, and access to oil deposits. Foreign economic penetration by business, assisted by military force, opens up the world for resource extraction, new consumer markets, and additional labor supplies. Armed control of regions make conditions safe for property interests. Nationalist aspirations for independence and resentment over foreign control inspire revolts that make imperialism a costly undertaking in lives and treasure [Wallbank et al., 1985]. Ultimately the operating costs of far flung empires exceed the ability of mid-twentieth century European nations to marshal the resources and public will to sustain colonial control.

THE INTERWAR YEARS: 1914–1945

The strong drive towards globalization is halted and reversed by the onset of war and an inward looking nationalism. The devastation of the War is carried into the 1920s. Economic depression and hyperinflation afflict parts of Europe. War and economic conditions force an end to the gold standard. Unstable exchange rates, predatory devaluations and protectionism, and capital controls become more of the norm. Britain's effectiveness as a world leader diminishes and the U.S. refuses to assume responsibility for resurrecting and promoting globally interconnected economic relations.[6] Exports as a share of world income, and world economic growth rates, fall during this period (King and King 2005, 211).

Economic conditions in Europe can only be described as depressed and difficult. Falling raw material and other prices lower incomes to producers and raise fixed payment debt burdens. High unemployment and banking sector problems prompt bank runs. Most importantly, indebtedness among countries arising from WWI expenditures, exacerbated by economic conditions in the 1920s and inadequately addressed by post-war policies, create a fragile debt structure. The Versailles Treaty imposes ruinous reparation burdens on countries that cannot afford to repay, or to rebuild and invest in domestic economic recovery.[7] Private investors sell currencies for gold. Meanwhile, the American central bank assists London in attempting to reestablish the pound as the world currency. The Fed drives down interest rates in the U.S. to foster an interest rate advantage for Britain to attract capital and elevate the pound's value. This worsens Britain's domestic performance by making its manufacturers internationally uncompetitive [Brawley 1998, 243–245, 259].

The U.S. economy booms in the1920s, fueled by investment in the then-new science-based industries. Commercial advertising and consumer credit fuel consumption. An enlarging middle class, increasingly oriented toward spending and materialism, validate business capital spending. America emerges as the world's largest creditor nation, and private business increases FDI, much directed to Latin America and Europe. One effort to support European recovery from WWI is the Dawes Plan. While American tariffs make it difficult for Europeans to sell into the US to earn dollars, the Dawes Plan provides loans to Germany and reductions in reparations owed to the Allies. Despite some outward US private investment and lending, and the Dawes Plan, the nationalist interwar period is best exemplified by American isolationism [Henretta et al 1987 698, 712–715].

The Galbraith Thesis on the 1920s American boom argues that stock market speculation becomes central to the culture of the decade. Property and financial asset values rise with economic growth, but by the late 1920s, asset values exceed economic fundamentals. Every increase in asset values encourages more buying, and rising collateral of traders prompts more borrowing that accentuates capital gains on assets. An irrational exuberance sets in, as the markets appear to provide people with effortless riches. Galbraith attributes the stock market boom to an excessively positive psychological mood. This was a time where "as in all periods of speculation, when men sought not to be persuaded of the reality of things but to find excuses for escaping into the new world of fantasy" [Galbraith, 1997, 11–12].

Only a multivariate explanation suffices to comprehend the causes of the global great depression of the 1930s. Stock market crashes, public policy, a collapse in business profitability, the international debt structure, and banking crises play an interactive role in contributing to depression. Economic contraction in America intensifies poor European conditions and is crucial in spreading contractionary forces globally.

The 1929 American stock market crash is both a cause of the 1930s economic depression and a consequence of the business investment downturn in the late 1920s. The decade of the 1920s saw some increase in the number of people participating in the stock market and a substantial increase in debt to purchase shares. The increase in borrowings propelled stock indices higher, and bankers provide more credit as the net worth of their clients increase. People bought on margin, leveraging their cash infusions with broker-supplied credit.[8] Stock prices, or any asset's value, should be in some proportion to the underlying economic fundamentals that gave rise to that asset. That is, there should be some balance between the profits generated by companies and the stock market valuation of the equity shares sold by those companies. The late 1920s stock market action de-linked share values from economic fundamentals. The over-valued, over-bought market is eventually recognized as unsustainable, eventually prompting selling. Price declines lead ultimately to panic selling and a price collapse. Facilitating the price collapse are margin calls, efforts by creditors to require borrowers to put up more cash to back loans as borrowers' net worth falls. Borrowers acquire more cash by selling shares, putting more downward pressure on equity values.

Investor pools are an additional factor in creating an overvalued market. Speculators and traders formed groups to trade stock. Their efforts sought to parley their combined wealth to "market time," namely to buy low and sell high. Sometimes groups would manipulate prices to create more capital gains than what are feasible from the underlying economics of the companies owned. Group participants would buy and sell the stocks owned by the group to one another. The additional volume created is marketed as demonstrating increased general interest in these particular shares. Higher volume and prices encourage unsuspecting non-group traders to purchase these equities, driving the prices still higher. Group participants would sell out after a price run-up. Investor pools assisted in creating an overvalued stock market, one susceptible to panic selling and crashing.

The second factor creating the Great Depression is public policy. Fiscal policy helped to create the depression and monetary policy contributed to the downturn's severity. Fiscal policy refers to government tools of taxation and spending to affect aggregate demand. "New Era" 1920s policy combines tax cuts oriented to wealthier Americans with budget surpluses. Tax cuts fuel the stock market advance but reduce expenditures going for goods and services. Budget surpluses fund declines in public debt but simultaneously create a contractionary force on economic activity. The government in other words begins taking more money out of the private sector's income-spending stream than it was putting into that stream. This policy put upward pressure on stock prices while creating a drag on corporate profit growth, investment, and employment.

The Federal Reserve's monetary policy affects aggregate demand by altering bank reserve levels and interest rates. The nation's central bank took a hands-off approach to the late 1920s speculation, and later, after the decline in loan demand reduces interest rates, misinterprets the low rates as an indication of easy monetary policy.[9] The Fed therefore took no action in 1929 and 1930. Then in 1931, as U.S. trade deficits cause gold to flow out of the country and to reduce the money supply, the Fed increased interest rates modestly. Little borrowing is taking place because of the economic collapse, and now the higher rates further discourage borrowing and spending. Fed policy is hampered by the gold standard.

The third factor creating depression is likely the most important. Two occurrences conspire to push down profit rates to levels that could not sustain economic advance. Decade long investment produces too much capacity and yet too little demand to buy what the economy is producing. Expectations for profit drive investment, and investment drives profit for firms making capital goods. Anything that undermines expectations or investment causes profits to fall, inducing economic contraction. The 1920s boom fosters ebullient expectations and investment commensurate with those expectations. But eventually private sector demand fails to sustain increases sufficient to buy what industry is producing and could potentially produce. Demand fails in part to grow fast enough because like all private sector booms, growing income inequalities lead to rising savings propensities, especially among more well off Americans. This meant that too little money is reentering the income-spending stream of the economy, evidenced by the fall in corporate profitability. And once the downturn is underway, the liquidity preference of the population increases, due to anxiety stirred by bank closings and unemployment [Keynes 1997, chap. 24]. Higher liquidity preference drains money from circulation, causing profits to fall. Compounding these difficulties is that rising productivity is inadequately shared with workers. Greater productivity accrues to profits mostly, and profits exceed business investment [Galbraith 1997, 174–178]. Rising interest rates in the late 1920s increase borrowing costs. In sum, downward pressure on revenues and upward pressure on costs in the late 1920s eventually undermine profitability. Business responds by cutting investment, production, and employment.

A fragile international debt structure presents a fourth contributing factor in creating depression. As described above, the European combatants of WWI suffer economic devastation and accumulate substantial debts during the war. Loan defaults and bankruptcies create losses for creditors. High inflation and unemployment discourage private investment. Countries raise tariff barriers to protect domestic industry but this action promotes more economic contraction instead. Currency traders worry about national commitments to the gold standard, and therefore sell currencies and buy gold. Competitive devaluations in currency values prompts more trade restrictions. Economic conditions and policies prevent debtor nations from repaying loans.

The contradictory public policy of the 1920s and early 1930s detrimentally affecting international trade is summed up by a passage from a Franklin Delano Roosevelt campaign speech in 1932:

A puzzled, somewhat skeptical Alice asked the Republican leadership some simple questions: Will not the printing and selling of more stocks and bonds, the building of new plants and the increase of efficiency produce more goods than we can buy? No, shouted Humpty Dumpty. The more we produce the more we can buy. What if we produce a surplus? Oh, we can sell it to the foreign consumers. How can the foreigners pay for it? Why, we will lend them the money. I see, said little Alice, they will buy our surplus with our money. Of course, these foreigners will pay us back by selling us their goods? Oh, not at all, said Humpty Dumpty. We set up a high wall called the tariff. And said Alice at last, how will the foreigners pay off these loans? That is easy, said Humpty Dumpty, did you ever hear of a moratorium? And so at last, my friends, we have reached the heart of the magic formula of 1928 [Lissakers 1991, 217].

Keynes attributes the competitive struggle for foreign markets in the 1930s as one cause for global economic difficulties, and the failure of such actions leading to fascist military ambitions. Keynes writes:

> . . . under the system of domestic laissez-faire . . . there was no means open to a government whereby to mitigate economic distress at home except through the competitive struggle for markets . . . But if nations can learn to provide themselves with full employment by their domestic policy . . . there need be no important economic forces calculated to set the interest of one country against that of its neighbours. . . . there would no longer be a pressing motive why one country need force its wares on another or repulse the offerings of its neighbour, . . . International trade would cease to be what it is, namely, a desperate expedient to maintain employment at home by forcing sales on foreign markets and restricting purchases, which, if successful, will merely shift the problem of unemployment to the neighbour which is worsted in the struggle, . . . [1997, 381–383].

Banking is a fifth problem area. Banking industry difficulties pose both a cause and effect of economic decline. The causal mechanism took two routes. Banks' profit margins are squeezed as banks compete for borrowers and depositors. Competition places downward pressure on loan rates and upward pressure on the cost of funds, reducing profit margins. Squeezed margins prompt cut-offs in credit. A second causal route stems from the conflict of interest inherent in banks of the 1920s that engage in both commercial lending and investment banking. Traditional banking is a conservative enterprise where loan officers took great care in extending credit to protect the bank and its depositors from defaults. Investment banking is riskier. It entails taking large positions in bonds and stocks and selling them off to the general public in small blocks. Banks get caught up in the stock market advance, and contribute to that advance by extending credit to their investment-banking affiliates and to the public to buy stock. Some banks dump bad loans off to dummy corporations whose stock is held by their investment-banking affiliates. Stock market declines endanger the viability of affiliates who could not repay loans to their banks. Some affiliates purchase shares of their parent banks, and the banks provide loans to the affiliates to make such purchases. The underlying conflict of interest results in a fragile financial structure susceptible to economic downturn.

Banking problems are an effect of general economic distress as well. As loan demand falls and defaults increase from recession, bank profits fall leading to bank failures and less lending. Fewer loans restrict the ability of people to buy and invest, worsening the downturn.

It's instructive to lay out the cause and effect chain reaction initiated by WWI. War and its aftermath prompt countries to focus attention on domestic affairs and thus end the first era of globalization. Ensuing and persistent economic difficulties create hardships in Europe and the relative decline of British hegemony. The U.S. and Japan rise in importance but neither offer leadership that fosters peaceful global economic prosperity. The fall of the American economy in the late 1920s leads the world into depression and a collapse in world trade. Extreme socioeconomic conditions world-wide bring about radical political solutions as expressed in fascism. Military aggression, in part to relieve domestic stress, ensues and embroils the world in a second world war.

GLOBALIZATION'S SECOND ERA: 1945–1980

The economic collapse and social disruptions engendered by depression and war force policymakers to construct a post-war world founded on new macro-economic policies, welfare states, and a more stable, growth-promoting international economic system. The following overview of reform efforts demonstrates the comprehensiveness of institutional restructuring.

Post-war policymakers understand that the previous period of "Finance Capitalism" destabilized economic life. They therefore made a serious effort to rebalance economic power by elevating the political-economic importance of business and labor. Policy concurrently equalizes unionized labor's position to the power of employers, both through legislation and through success of unions themselves in contract negotiations. Labor law establishes minimum wages and maximum hours, requires employer acceptance of unions and collective bargaining, and outlaws child labor. Unions succeed in getting employers to not hire replacement workers during strikes, negotiating for benefits to complement wage payments, and most importantly, in getting firms to share productivity and profit improvements with employees. This "Labor Accord" creates more peaceful industrial relations and aligns labor's interest to the employers' interest. Corporations retain control over investment and production decisions and over corporate governance in general.

Various legislative and regulatory reforms are passed as well to stabilize the banking system. In America, reform efforts through the 1940s are known as the "New Deal" program. Deposit insurance and bank exams are established to prevent bank runs. Interest rate regulation is instituted, and branching restrictions are maintained, to limit competition and stabilize bank profit. The finance industry is compartmentalized where specific kinds of institutions provided specific kinds of finance and services. This limits competition. The Glass-Steagall provision separates commercial banking from investment banking. A "community need" test is applied by regulators in deciding on mergers and new bank charters.

The central bank authority in America becomes centralized in the Federal Reserve Board. A uniform discount rate would now be set by the Board, and over time as the government bond market deepens, the main monetary policy tool becomes open market operations.[10] The Board could also now vary bank reserve requirements and stock market margin requirements. Such tools are directed at stabilizing finance. To promote long term business investment and limit public sector finance charges, the Federal Reserve took on the responsibility of supporting bond prices. The central bank would use its money-creating powers to buy government bonds. This kept upward pressure on bond prices, and hence downward pressure on interest rates.

The Employment Act of 1946 commits the American government to maintain an economy with high employment, growth, and price stability. With this act, there becomes an implicit acceptance of budget deficits as a means to stabilize profits and spending in the private sector. Counter-cyclical budget deficits and commitments to middle class social welfare entitlements bolster aggregate demand. Wage-price controls, sometimes called "incomes policies," are implemented, during periods where war strains resource supplies, to contain inflation without harming employment levels.

The second era of globalization is marked by the dominance of the management controlled corporation whose governing independence is founded on the separation of ownership from control. Stockholders in this era tend to be diversified, numerous, and unorganized, and thus lack a capacity to influence corporate strategy and investment. Owners are usually insufficiently informed to effect change within the firm, and direct their interest toward earning income, and lowering portfolio risk through liquidity and diversification. Firms are more independent of external funding needs, as they rely heavily on internal cash flow to finance investment, and the influence of financiers wanes as the ownership of enterprise becomes more dispersed. Growth and stability are prominent goals of corporate executives. Corporate planning and politicking are employed to significantly influence markets and drive globalization.

Despite an historical reluctance, the American government drops its laissez-faire orientation for a much more activist/interventionist approach to societal problems. The Reconstruction Finance Corporation makes loans to private business and banks. New security laws set forth rules to stabilize the stock exchange, reduce speculation, and increase information to shareowners. Various social and public works programs are started and expanded. Social spending increases as a percentage of government spending. Federal income taxes become more progressive, requiring higher income people to pay a relatively larger share of government expenses. And the New Deal backed the labor movement, evidenced in law, regulation, and practice. All of these efforts facilitate the growth in the middle class, increase aggregate demand, and encourage a large share of Americans to "buy into" the economic system. By augmenting opportunities and prosperity across a wider portion of the public, the New Deal successfully builds a community of people committed to capitalist values.

Capitalist economies of Europe and Japan create "communitarian capitalism" following the war. Welfare states are established to fund social programs and regulate industrial relations. Commercial banks are owners of and play the key role in providing business groups with funding to catch up with the global competitiveness of the U.S. Governments employ indicative planning[11] and develop industrial strategies to modernize their economies. Some industries are nationalized. A social responsibility ethic prevails in business and government. The Japanese strive for market share while promoting labor productivity through bonuses, team work, and life time employment. Europe supports labor through legal protections for strong unions and employer granted long term employment contracts [Thurow 2003, chapters 2,4]

Capitalist countries give up on a domestic gold standard. Domestic transactions had been governed by a gold standard where the quantity of money was tied to gold reserve levels, and since gold supplies were limited, so was the money supply. This institution limited money creation, not just by the private sector but the public sector as well. The commodity standard curtailed inflation and promoted limited government, but was detrimental to agrarian and commercial credit needs and subjected economies to financial panics. Post WWII reforms de-link domestic transactions from gold, freeing central banks to maintain higher amounts of liquidity and lower interest rates.

The international trade and monetary system undergo a major overhaul beginning in the late 1940s. This reform has as its purpose avoidance of the precarious debt structures of the 1920s and to promote greater world trade. The Marshall Plan rebuilds Europe and Japan. The International Monetary Fund (IMF), World Bank (WB), and fixed exchange rates, collectively called the Bretton Woods institutions, accomplish three goals. The IMF provides liquidity to countries, the WB provides development funds, and fixed exchange rates stabilize world trade by reducing FDI risk. Bretton Woods creates a dollar-based, gold exchange monetary system. Fixed exchange rates keep speculators from treating currencies as tradable commodities, and reduce the uncertainty of business investment abroad since relative currency values are known in advance. In cases of fundamental disequilibrium, where countries experience large current account imbalances, countries can seek IMF approval to adjust exchange rates. These policies are followed by the General Agreement on Tariffs and Trade (GATT), periodic rounds of negotiations among nations, to gradually reduce tariffs and quotas to promote global commerce.

Trade patterns develop that place capitalist MDCs in competition with one another. U.S. policy is directed at reviving and then molding European economies and Japan along capitalist, democratic lines. WWII pushes America into a world leadership position, evidenced in U.S. post-war domination of the Bretton Woods system, New York as the world's financial center, and the dollar as the world's currency. The U.S. opens its market to countries willing to operate within its sphere of influence. Barriers to LDC integration remain. Cold War blocks divide the world into two camps that don't compete in economics, but compete for military and political alliances. The capitalist camp is initially short of dollars to adequately promote global commerce and liquidity. In time, from the American Marshall Plan, to country specific economic development assistance and hot wars, U.S. dollars increase in circulation. Though capital moves freely, countries employ capital controls to regulate cross-border money movements and most money flows finance trade efforts of business, not speculation.

Post WWII reforms in capitalist countries establish an activist welfare state and mixed economy domestically, and the Bretton Woods international economic order. These changes promote decades of economic growth and relative stability. The post-depression institutional changes create higher average growth rates, higher average productivity advances, lower unemployment, modest inflation, and shorter recessions. Such accomplishments are the outcome of institutions more effective in fostering prosperity than the previous international economic structure and policy, and did so in a context of relatively high taxation, government intervention, faster money growth, and greater income equality.

Not all events and policies are perfectly consistent with the new paradigm. A noteworthy exception in America is the Treasury-Fed Accord of 1951. By the late 1940s, contention develops over whether the central bank should pursue a largely high employment or largely a price stability objective. Or put differently, should the Fed's objective be to provide for an elastic currency or should it stabilize the purchasing power of money? Classical economists and the Fed saw an opportunity to redirect the central bank's main objective of supporting government bond prices. By 1950, a sizable government bond market develops that facilitates Fed open market operations to affect bank reserves. WWII and the Korean War, along with the post 1945 economic boom, put upward pressure on prices, thereby shifting some focus to inflation and away from employment concerns. Fed officials initiate a new operating objective and after some contention, manage to make an agreement with the Truman Treasury.[12]

The Accord reaffirms central bank independence from government influence. This affirmation releases the Fed from pegging government bond prices to keep interest rates low and releases them from monetizing government deficit spending. This agreement permits Fed influence over the monetary base. The importance of the Accord cannot be overstated, in effect establishing the following outcomes:

1. The Fed would now conduct a counter-cyclical policy aimed at price stability.
2. The Fed would give up influencing long-term interest rates; the bond market would takeover this function.
3. The policymaking arm of the Fed would shift from the Federal Reserve Board to the Federal Open Market Committee (FMOC), giving greater banker influence on determining monetary policy.
4. The theoretical basis for monetary policy would shift from the Real Bills Doctrine to the Quantity Theory of Money.[13]

THE 1970s TRANSITION PERIOD

The Second Era of Globalization undergoes some change for reasons unrelated to its overall effectiveness. "Managerial Capitalism" of the mid twentieth century is largely a successful institutional arrangement that promotes widespread domestic and global prosperity. Flawed, yet accepted, economic diagnosis of complex events during the 1970s works to undermine the basic Keynesian philosophical consensus that supported active government in economic policy.[14] A shifting intellectual position provides the philosophical foundation for elite financial and employer interests to pursue a more deregulated, more mobile capital economic climate allowing investment to reach world wide. The 1970s set the stage for a new kind of globalization. While important institutional detail live on from mid twentieth century globalization, new institutions and policy reshape the international economic system into International Money Manager Capitalism or "The New Finance" of the third wave in globalization. Three important developments are crucial to bringing about economic evolution.[15]

The New Domestic Macro Policy

By the 1960s, many economists believed that budget deficit spending and state intervention could routinely stabilize economic activity. And economists discovered what appeared to be a fairly stable inverse relationship between inflation and unemployment called the Phillips Curve (PC).[16] Keynesian style activism could lower unemployment by stimulating spending, but as unemployment fell beyond some point, inflation would rise modestly. Policymakers could pick a point on the Phillips curve where the resulting inflation-unemployment tradeoff was socially acceptable, and drive the system to that point. The economy could be fine-tuned through manipulation of the government's budget. An optimal tradeoff is a point such as "A" in the graph below where unemployment is low and inflation is modest.

The very low inflation rates of the early 1960s give way to somewhat higher rates by the end of the decade as social program[17] and Vietnam War spending accelerate. Inflation moderates in the first three years of the 1970s, but then moves up to higher levels in the mid and late 1970s. And the unemployment situation simultaneously worsens, where higher rates exist along side higher inflation in the 1970s.[18] This worse tradeoff is reflected in a rightward shift in the PC to PC2 as noted in Figure 2.1.

Classical economists develop the natural rate of unemployment (Unr) theory to explain what happened. The Unr is the unemployment rate that main-

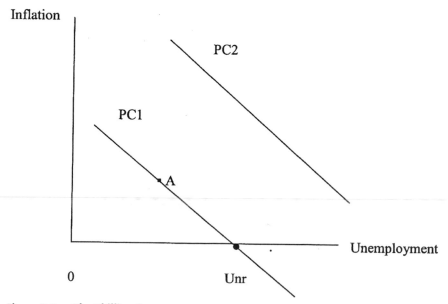

Figure 2.1.   The Phillips Curve

tains price stability; it's the non-inflationary unemployment rate (see above). If activist public policy tries to exploit the Phillips Curve tradeoff to drive unemployment below the Unr, the lower rate obtained is unsustainable they argue because it necessarily generates accelerating inflation. An optimal policy would control money growth to align aggregate demand to the natural rate of unemployment. Such a policy would create price stability and therefore economic conditions more suitable for growth. Non-inflationary economic growth, induced by improved technology and productivity, can then occur, lowering the level of the Unr by shifting inward the PC.

The combination of repetition in argument and the events of the 1970s allow for the gradual replacement of the Keynesian macroeconomic consensus that underscores mid twentieth century globalization with new but modernized Classical thinking. A reinvigorated free market economic logic excites the economics profession and imbues public policy. Economists employ the quantity theory of money to argue that money growth can and must be controlled by the central bank (see chapter 4). Growth in money determines growth in aggregate demand, and by consequence, the price level. This "Monetarism" emphasizes the necessity of creating no or very low inflation as a prerequisite for economic stability and prosperity. "Supply-side economics" emphasizing the importance of creating entrepreneurial incentives, justifies upper-class tax cuts and streamlining government regulation and intervention. Growth arises from expanding the productive potential of the economy, not by having policy-induced demand increases.[19]

The New Employment Policy and Anti-Unionism

Up until the mid 1970s, labor's economic position remains relatively strong vis-a-vi employers where workers are unionized and employed within stable oligopolistic industries subject largely to domestic competition. This is true in Britain and the U.S. But the 1970s mark a turning point for Anglo-American firms because globally competitive pressures grow, manifested in declining profit and market shares. Some American firms initiate shifts in production and investment to overseas locations while others react to intensifying competitive pressures in the 1980s by seeking tariff protection. Increasingly, American and British companies become globally structured that weakens their affinity or loyalty to any single nation. Globalizing operations offers gradual independence from union demands and the opportunity to access much less expensive inputs. A corporate strategy of global positioning allows firms to elevate profit and sales growth, but at the expense of unionized labor and to the benefit of property interests and some classes of specialized workers. That is, lower host-country labor costs recreate a competitive economics for firms, rewarded by financial markets in terms of higher stock prices and much bigger executive payouts.[20]

The Reagan and Thatcher administrations move public policy more in favor of employers. Pressures build in the late 1990s for Europe and Japan to pursue similar labor policies. It is essential not to understate the importance of policy in undermining First World unions. The deliberate policy move to open up trade and capital flows with Second and Third World countries, the hallmark of globalization Three, pits high income, high living standard people against workers in dramatically inferior economic status. Under Second Wave policy, high income nations largely competed against themselves, where firms differentiate themselves not on huge cost differences but on price, product quality, and service. New policy sets a new trend. And amplifying that trend are technological innovations more easily permitting global commerce and finance, and the end of the Cold War which greatly increases consumer and input markets for globally positioned firms to exploit. So it is clear that it is not high First World wages or low productivity per se that compels a new wave in globalization but a combination of public and corporate policy, technology, and geopolitical events that redesign the global employment landscape.

The End of the Bretton Woods International Financial System

Up until the early 1970s, countries follow the Bretton Woods system which made the dollar the international reserve, pegged world currencies to the dollar, and fixed the dollar's value to gold. Bretton Woods was about expanding and stabilizing world commerce and finance. The IMF and World Bank were set up to provide liquidity and fund investment projects throughout the system. International transactions were controlled some through capital controls, tariffs, and quotas but gradual tariff reduction among leading nations facilitated international trade.

By the 1960s, U.S. economic competitiveness wanes, given its success in rebuilding Europe and Japan after WWII and the heavy investment of those countries in developing their own economies. Combining with the high value of the dollar, the U.S. trade surplus transforms into a persistent deficit. Increasing U.S. imports and FDI, fueled in part from American domestic economic expansion, increase the amount of dollars abroad. Vietnam War and Cold War spending add further to the dollar supply. The growing world dollar supply threatens the dollar-gold relationship established under Bretton Woods. The dollar over-supply meant that foreigners could drain U.S. gold reserves by requiring payment for debts and goods in gold. Gold reserves do decline, prompting the "Nixon Shock" which de-links the U.S. dollar from gold and took the U.S. out of the Bretton Woods system. The U.S. dollar subsequently depreciates.

Inflation rates increase and real interest rates[21] fall in the 1970s, attributed by some to high government spending that continues in the decade. Government budget deficits are specifically blamed for inflation. The dollar continues to depreciate on world markets. Oil producers earn dollars from selling oil and see their dollars lose purchasing power. In part, this decline in the "terms of trade" for oil producers perpetrates two oil price shocks that create more inflation throughout the globe.[22] Central banks are blamed for accommodating the inflation by allowing money to grow too quickly. These events have three important effects: The American dollar continues to depreciate; inflation rates remain higher than historic norms; and real returns on financial assets are depressed.

The domestic and international events described above create deleterious economic results for financial asset holders and more difficult domestic profit conditions for commerce. Substantial deterioration in economic fortune prompts a political response by economic elites to reinstate favorable upper class-based macroeconomic policy and ideas. The convergence then of Classicism, deregulated global commerce, and deregulated global finance produce four noteworthy political economic consequences that characterize the modern age of globalization.

1. Classical School Dominance: Classical economic theory reemerges during the transition period as the defining intellectual thought. Not only does this philosophy reestablish itself firmly within the economics profession and the financial class, but affects how legal decisions are made, encourages the development of "rational choice" theory in political science, and influences how historians conduct research and interpret American history. Free markets are seen as an optimal means to allocate resources and market outcomes are seen as efficient. State intervention is eschewed because of an argued inefficiency and ineptness. Markets replace government as the regulating mechanism.[23] Supply-side economics is promoted whereby emphasis is placed on work and production, and success or failure is seen residing largely within the individual. Public policy's role in fostering production and individual enterprise is to incentivize people via deregulation and tax cuts; deregulation liberates business activity, and tax cuts enhance the reward for being productive.[24]

   How is it that Classical economics has again become the eminent doctrine of our time? Keynes' insights [1997 (1936), 32–33] of Classical theory dominance of the early twentieth century are forever applicable. With some adaptation and modification, Keynes' insights suggest that

Classicism contains appealing principles to Anglo-American capitalist culture. It advocates freedom, a cherished principle of the American founding. It sanctifies wealth creation, a principle conducive to material self interest. Through the first two principles, and its encouragement of competition, Classicism supports a dynamic society of novel goods and technology. Its propounding from leading universities, think tanks, governments, and international institutions grants it authority, and therefore public respect. But perhaps most significantly, Classicism's longevity derives from its "virtue" and the wealth and power that back its implementation into policy? Keynes says it best:

"That its teaching, translated into practice, was austere and often unpalatable, lent it virtue. . . . That it afforded a measure of justification to the free activities of the individual capitalist, attracted to it the support of the dominant social force behind authority."

2. Monetary Policy is favored over Fiscal Policy: Given the new negative view of government, power to manage and guide the economy shifts to central banks. Monetarism and the natural rate concept inform policymaking. Central bankers place top priority on achieving price stability, arguing that sustainable growth is best assured from such a policy. Central banks are given complete independence over regulating bank reserves and short-term interest rates, and bond markets set all other rates. Some Anglo-American central banks officially adopt policy of inflation targeting.[25]

3. Money Manager Capitalism: Given the increased importance placed on free markets and finance, the stock market is re-energized with more cash and new kinds of institutions. "Supply-side" tax cuts and globalization fuel the profits of multinational firms and financiers. This money flows into the stock market frequently through professionally managed pension and mutual funds, and increasingly by unregulated hedge funds. Corporate takeovers, corporate stock repurchases, and dividend hikes create Anglo-American bull markets. Equity ownership concentrates and institutional owners gain increased clout on corporate boards. New financial strategies develop employing complex derivative assets.

4. A Neo-liberal Political Order: Economic policy is characterized by major political party agreements to implement a so-called Neo-liberal (elite) economic agenda. This agenda fosters a multi-part program of globalization based on cost competition throughout the world. These policies are designed to extend the specific ideas of free markets, deregulation, and privatization throughout the world, which become known as the Washington Consensus. The purpose is to enhance not just trade but capital flows. To accomplish this, economic barriers to trade and capital flows are reduced or eliminated, moving economies toward an integrated world system. The

corporation and capital markets become the dominant economic institutions. Country governments are supposed to implement policies to foster the profit and growth of corporations and capital markets.

The Executive Board of the IMF publishes Public Information Notices (PINs) that provide IMF assessments of countries' economic and financial conditions, and recommendations on reforming their economies and policies. The quote below is an example of Washington Consensus thinking in Executive Board PINs directed at affecting the member countries of the Central African Economic and Monetary Community.

> To improve monetary policy implementation and help deepen financial markets, Directors recommended dismantling restrictions on interest rates, and lowering the excessively high-required reserves. . . . Directors emphasized that medium-term financial sustainability in the region will require prudent macroeconomic policies and broad improvements in competitiveness. Given that oil reserves are limited, greater urgency should be accorded to addressing the structural impediments that constrain the competitiveness of the non-oil sectors. This will require strong efforts to overcome regional structural rigidities, including through more flexible labor markets, trade facilitation and liberalization, and a business and legal environment that is more conducive to private sector growth. Directors also noted that inflation must be kept low and fiscal spending constrained to avoid the risk of an exchange rate overvaluation [IMF PIN # 06/90, 8/7/06].

These four important consequences of the transition period, Classicism, the central bank, money manager capitalism, and Neo-liberalism, characterize the New Finance of the third wave of globalization of 1980s, 1990s, and the twenty-first century. While modern globalization is built on top of government activism and welfare states, policy and philosophy favorably shift towards global financial and commercial interests. This era marks a novel institutional system spreading across the globe capable of effecting change in global economic performance and national socio-economic institutions.

GLOBALIZATION'S THIRD ERA: 1980—PRESENT

Rapid change and development mark the modern era. No one policy or event however has such great influence alone to define an era. Typically, a series of events and policy changes occur, which build momentum over time that send a society off into a different direction. Eventually, institutional change revolutionizes economic life. Critical trends in the economics of globalization are redirecting modern America and will continue to do well into the 21st century.

The current course is integrating parts of South America, Mexico, India and China, Southeast Asia, and Eastern Europe into the larger capitalist system.

What is driving the modern age of globalization? The wholesale structural transformation of economic life, embodied in the current era called Globalization Three, is unfolding because of opportunity, capacity, and the profit motive. Public policy has created opportunity. Countries in the past twenty years have passed free trade bills and made efforts to integrate national economies into regional trading zones. The North American Free Trade Agreement, Central American Free Trade Agreement, Murcorsur, The Central African Economic and Monetary Community, and the European Union are examples.[26] Countries have deregulated transportation and banking industries, and have reduced tariffs, opening up incumbent firms to global competition. Emerging market economies are adopting capitalist institutions that allow cross-border commerce due to growing standardization in laws, institutions, and regulations.

Technology has created the capacity for major structural change. Improvements in telecommunications, information technology, and the expansion of the internet all facilitate commerce and finance. Cost-based competition creates a profit push for business to go global. Falling and low communication and transportation costs compel market extension. Relatively high middle class living standards in the MDCs push firms to seek lower labor costs elsewhere. Taxes and social program financing burdens in MDCs prompt business to seek production platforms in places where such responsibilities don't exist, or are less costly. The creation and integration of emerging market countries create new profitable frontiers of expansion. The growth in world trade is demonstrated by a strong upward trend in exports relative to country domestic production since the nineteenth century.

And there is an interactive dependency among policy, technology, and profit. Governments that intend to join the globalization trend or are already caught up in it, promote technological development trough tax breaks and subsidies to industry, and industry constantly strives to boost labor productivity, partly with new technology, to increase cost competitiveness and profit. U.S. government policy takes on the historical role of hegemon. Policy pushes globalization by funding military and economic development efforts in foreign lands, an imperial role analogous to its own hegemonic policy of mid 20th century and the policy of the colonial powers in the 19th and early 20th centuries.[27] Military and foreign policy efforts are directed at increasing economic connections and protecting commercial traffic. This new imperial purpose creates a clash between civilizations, between those societies immersed in cultural and economic tradition and those embracing and fostering more liberal, open, modern, and commercial orders.[28]

Current trends and developments define today's globalization. First, globalization is integrating national economies through cross-border flows of capital, technology, firms, people, and resources. Growth in trade and financial interdependence tie together countries' economic performances and pressure governments to standardize policy and law.[29] Governments are limited in regulating activities which can easily shift location across borders. Globalization allows commercial interests to seek lower production costs worldwide, thereby intensifying competition among people and governments for capital. Property income is boosted as well when these same firms can now sell anywhere in the world, choosing to do so at the highest prices possible. Competition is increasing, simultaneously with rising demand, for the world's professional and educated workers for employment, affecting income distribution and job security. Competition is encouraging capital investment, organizational innovation, and product development further affecting material well-being. Foreign sources of income for American firms are growing, rising from around $40 billion in the mid 1990s and approaching $160 billion in 2004 [WSJ 12/19/05, pA2], and foreign stocks make up a greater percentage of the typical American stock portfolio.

The IMF has identified five important trends of the current age in terms of world integration [Lanc 2006]. Examining 140 countries, IMF economists measure country net external financial positions to determine whether the countries are net creditors or debtors. They look at portfolio investment, FDI, and international reserve positions.

Trend one: International financial integration has increased markedly particularly among advanced countries. This trend is attributed to the increase in trade linkages, the reduction in capital controls, domestic financial deepening, advances in telecommunications, and the increased availability of information. Integration is measured as upward trends in external assets and debts relative to country GDPs.

Trend two: Current account imbalances have widened sharply, with emerging Asia and the oil exporters increasingly becoming net creditors, the United States experiencing a worsening in its net external position, and Europe maintaining a stable net debtor position.

Trend three: Because foreign assets and liabilities now often exceed 100% of GDP, differences in rates of return between external assets and liabilities lead to significant shifts in capital flows across countries.

Trend four: U.S. investors earn more on their external assets than foreigners earn on their investments in the U.S. The positive earnings differential for U.S. investors arises due to much American investments placed in stocks and productive capital while American liabilities are largely in debt instruments.

U.S. liabilities are largely denominated in U.S. currency but U.S. owned foreign assets are significantly denominated in foreign currency.

Trend five: The vulnerability of emerging market economies to financial crises has waned as these countries increasingly rely on cross-border equity and FDI, and less on debt. Some emerging market countries have become net creditors by running large current account surpluses and accumulating reserves.

Other important developments are the restructuring of employment markets and education reform. An increasing amount of output and particularly jobs derive from the service and information technology sectors. Greater demands exist for a skill- and knowledge- based labor force, which must constantly train and retrain. Bureaucratic streamlining, horizontal management, and work-teams characterize some of the more creative firms. Self-employment and entrepreneurial upstarts are more common. Difference in opportunities and income, and premiums paid for education, are separating developed-country workers along economic class and education lines. Professionalization and corporatization characterize trends in higher education. Unions have declined in importance and more work is done on a temporary or contract basis. Organized labor is seen as disruptive to the efficient allocation of people through labor markets. In sum, corporate restructuring and investment, in response to competitive pressures, are causing changes in work-life that are in turn pressuring education reform.[30]

Globalization is reducing middle class blue collar manufacturing jobs in developed countries. Empirical evidence demonstrates that U.S. manufacturing employment tends to shrink during economic expansion, as in the late 1990s and 2003–2005, and during recession [Wachovia]. Production gains arise from productivity improvements, as companies face pressures to cut costs and off-shore production.

Figures 2.2 and 2.3, both from Wachovia Bank, show a restructuring American economy as job growth is overwhelmingly distributed in non-manufacturing industries, and that service spending is rising relative to spending on tangible goods.

The firm operating during Globalization Three is transformed. The Reich-Thurow thesis[31] argues that corporations must restructure into new business models, one kind for industry domination, the other as successful niche player. The confluence of forces driving globalization necessitates radical change in business structure for companies to survive and prosper. If global industry domination is sought, the model is to disaggregate the corporation into networks of decentralized, diffuse knowledge workers. The firm must be more agile and flexible to meet global demands and apply new technologies.

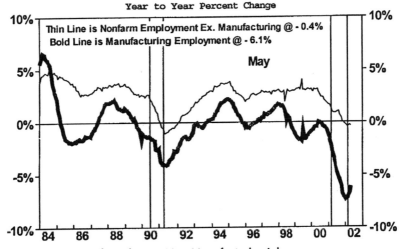

Figure 2.2.   Manufacturing vs. Non-Manufacturing Jobs

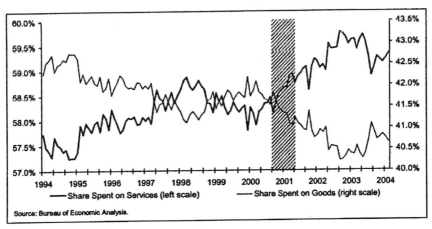

Figure 2.3.   Goods vs. Services Spending

Partnerships are created within or connected to the firm. More work is globally contracted, outsourced, and off-shored, as corporations seek lower costs and greater efficiencies [BW 1/30/06, 50–64]. Competitive advantages are harnessed by pushing productivity through IT investment, accessing low cost labor and resources globally, and by enhancing labor force skills and knowledge.

Niche oriented companies sell off divisions and focus on producing high in demand, specialized products and services sold at premium prices. Off-shoring is to save labor costs, but is especially sought to boost efficiency and customer service. Globally distributed firms must assess and react to changes in global stock prices, interest rates, and exchange rates, all of which are impacted by mobile financial capital flows. Smaller global firms, who are not well known and have complex financing needs, rely on globally sourced private placements. Whatever the firm's market orientation, prevailing pressures make firms seek employees, inputs, customers, and financing world-wide. And the modern enterprise is more noted for its intangibles than its capital investment. More attention and money is devoted to product design, employee training, R&D, and organizational change. The firm is about creativity and innovation [BW 2/13/06, 63–68].

The heightened competitive pressures that exist have prompted a phased restructuring of operations. While competitive pressures are partly manifested in cost reduction, other pressures are exerted to improve product quality. Initially firms in this period sought quality enhancement through better time management and emphasizing simplicity over complexity. Some companies sought to instill corporate values in employees and reinforce values through coaching. Total Quality Management (TQM) is the second evolution in building quality. TQM combines active management, work teams, and commitment to continuous quality improvement to improve competitiveness. Firms applying TQM plan long term to build quality through innovation and giving workers a sense of purpose in the company. Profit sharing and variable pay schemes come into effect. The latest adaptation to quality improvement combines focus on quality enhancement and cost reduction through a process of outcomes assessment. Companies measure their efforts at meeting these twin goals and use the results of their findings to improve processes. Six Sigma, as this scheme is known, measures production defects in order to develop a universal measurement of quality to which all company production outcomes are compared [Underwood 2006].

One additional noteworthy trend is the refashioning of the role and scope of government. National government operations are now seen to be more limited, yet active in some designated areas. Overall, public policy is more fiscally conservative, oriented toward enhancing economic incentives through tax cuts and regulation streamlining. State activism is directed at improving education and infrastructure, and instituting the "Washington Consensus"[32] model of privatization and complete cross-border integration throughout the world. Business cycle management is turned over to central banks and fiscal policy is pressured to promote balanced budgets[33] to increase savings to the private sector and to contain inflation. While nation-states continue to direct domestic policies and diplomacy, business enterprises reconfigure themselves into global production, distribution, and marketing machines with no commitment to national loyalty or nationally based operations. Corporations are not simply multinational but transnational in that numerous business functions that make up firms' operations are positioned globally and lie beyond the regulatory scope of national governments.[34]

Government and international institutions supported by governments reactively intervene in global economics to limit the negative fall out of myriad financial crises. The international debt crisis of the 1980s is the first of many destabilizing events necessitating public action. The genesis of this crisis lay in the huge income redistribution from oil consuming nations to oil producers in the 1970s. These dollars work their way into international banks that loan developing countries money to build their economies. High interest rates, an oil embargo, and world recession interact over the late 1970s and early 1980s to inhibit the ability of indebted nations to repay bank loans thereby deleteriously affecting bank profitability. Two Mexican financial crises, the Asian financial crisis, the Russian default, and economic difficulties in South America and Turkey follow chronologically. Emerging market financial instability characterizes the first part of the third era in globalization.[35] BCA Research confirms the correlation between the Federal Reserve's policy rate with periods of financial crises and currency depreciation. A rising rate presages crisis and a falling rate is essential in overcoming the crisis [BCA Research 2006, p19].

The General Agreement on Tariffs and Trade (GATT) is replaced by a 150 member country body known as the World Trade Organization (WTO). Headquartered in Geneva and operational in 1995, the WTO adopts GATT principles of fostering an open and expansive international trading order, and fulfills the Bretton Woods era desire for an international trade organization. The WTO seeks country reduction of tariffs and quotas, reduction or avoidance of non-tariff trade barriers, and openness to capital flows. The WTO tries to generate consensus among its members in creating policy, though Anglo-American and other large economy nations have substantial influence in policymaking. In principle, a free, competitive, and non-discriminatory trading system is promoted. The WTO budget is funded by member countries whose proportionate share is determined by each country's share of the combined trade of members.

The General Council is the highest decision-making body with representatives from all member countries. It hosts negotiations on multilateral trade rules. The WTO has a dispute settlement mechanism to address cases of alleged WTO rule violations and is given enforcement power by sanctioning governments who fail to comply with its decisions. Trade policy reviews are conducted of member country national trade laws to evaluate whether they conform to WTO agreements and principles. Some sixty agreements have been reached by the WTO. Agreements cover agriculture, goods and services, intellectual property, and export subsidies, among others. No agreements exist on labor or environmental standards. In order to more effectively influence WTO agreements, countries form alliances to negotiate common economic interests; the European Union, the Association of South East Asian Nations, and the common market known as MERCOSUR have formed alliances.[36]

Paralleling change in commerce and government is evolution in finance, critical in defining the contemporary era. Global financial markets and capital flows have grown in relative importance to domestic activity. This is perhaps best evidenced by the dual role now taken on by the American dollar. Of course it remains the currency of national transactions and payments. But the dollar is a world currency as well, and it is this vital function that maintains high demand for its use, and hence high value. Much of world commerce and lending takes place in dollars. Some countries have implemented dollarization or have opted for currency boards. Dollarization entails the replacement of local currency with the American dollar, relinquishing monetary policy control to the U.S. central bank. A currency board entails linking the supply of domestic currency to the supply of dollars earned through foreign trade or direct investment from U.S. companies. Both policies represent efforts by countries to limit domestic inflation and government spending by integrating the world's dominant country means of payment into their financial system. While dollarization and currency boards remain the exception, emerging market countries are reducing trade and capital barriers, and are adopting central bank independence, as accompanying measures to the use of the dollar as a world currency. In fact, central banks are now the dominant public policy institution, eclipsing the state, and are thought capable of fine-tuning economic activity to moderate business cycles.

In terms of domestic economics, financial assets are growing faster than total production and the diversity and complexity of these assets exceeds that of the prior era.[37] So far during this new finance era there is a dramatic expansion of the supply of and demand for finance, an increase without precedent. Examples abound. Credit card debt is at record levels, and multiple cards with balances are maintained. Traditional mortgage financing has expanded to sub-prime lending, no interest mortgages, and cash-out/re-financing where debt levels rise. Business is taking advantage of increased finance. High yield bonds and venture capital provide funding to relatively small and up-start firms normally locked out of needed funding. Loan securitization, where banks package loans and issue securities whose payment flows come from the loans, provides diversification to the financier and more reserves to banks to initiate additional lending. Growth of limited liability partnerships has provided entrepreneurs with funds as well.

Global financial interdependence is demonstrated by the increasing importance of foreign ownership of U.S. debt instruments. From 1990 to 2001, foreign ownership went from $800 million to $3.5 trillion, a doubling in percentage terms from 6% to 12% of outstanding domestic debt. A shift in ownership of U.S. debt has also occurred where private foreign interests have increased their holdings relative to foreign central bank holdings, and now hold far more corporate and public sector bonds than in 1990 [Bryson 2002]. Domestic financial sector importance is evidenced by a 224% increase in sector stock prices from 1995 through mid 2002 [BW 7/15/02, 40]. There is an increasing importance of exports in total production and the increasing importance of foreign capital investment in emerging market countries.

International Money Manager Capitalism (IMMC) is the product of global economic evolution. IMMC has the potential to modify the business cycle and impact income distribution. In this development stage, financial firms such as pension and mutual funds, hold separately and in conjunction with one another, large blocks of individual company stocks and bonds, making these enterprises the principal owners of major corporations and financiers of business investment. These institutions have acquired effective voting rights, influence over directors, and the ability to significantly alter a firm's financing costs and market value. These institutional asset holders challenge executive compensation plans, corporate board make-ups, and corporate bylaws that protect management from takeovers. Large volumes of capital are placed in capital markets providing clients with savings vehicles for retirement and portfolio diversification. This drives the demand for equities and long term bonds. Financial institutions are also more aware of their potential power and more aware of their responsibility to large numbers of clients. In-house research and close contact with companies they back make these institutions more informed and willing to act to affect corporate governance. Major corporations make considerable efforts to attract institutional support and maintain investor relations departments [Van Lear 2002; Hawley and Williams 2000].

Financial and non-financial firms are increasingly intertwined. Their portfolios consist of a mixture of capital and financial assets. Non-financial firms are more dependent on interest income and deal extensively in currency trading and financial derivatives. Some companies run pension funds, and despite the separation of commerce from banking in the U.S., some companies own Industrial Loan Corporations, state chartered, FDIC insured quasi banks [WSJ 1/26/06, pA3]. Banking and commerce are closely linked in Germany and Japan. Financial firms are responsible for a larger percentage of investment. Financial and non-financial firms are now major financiers of venture capital companies that fund start-ups and private equity firms that buy into established companies to foster reorganization. These equity holders take active positions in management and tie management interests to stockholder interests. This closer association between finance and commerce is evidenced by increased stock buybacks, dividend payments, and mergers that push funds into financial markets and financial institutions, who in turn allocate the funds back into stock and bond markets or into new stock offerings. Some firms issue debt capital to fund stock repurchases. This symbiosis enhances fund flows between the sectors and limits the supply of stock to maintain asset values. And the larger fraction of Americans participating in retirement plans creates a broader base of interest in and consistent support for stock buying and building portfolios.

Banking is fully global and stands in sharp contrast to post-war domestic banking. Most noteworthy is the ongoing decline in the importance of the banking industry as a financial intermediary relative to mutual and pension funds, and hedge funds. Source of business debt financing is increasingly savings capital raised from financial markets, not new money created from loans which are in turn based on the banking systems' creation of deposits. In defense of market share, banks have responded in two ways. Bank restructuring, predicated on developing new income sources and a new behavior, was initiated by the industry in the 1980s. Fee income and other forms of non-interest income are relatively more important while loan income is less important. And banking is a more aggressive, risk-taking venture than in the past. Loan officers market loans harder. Executives take on more risk by funding corporate takeovers, making emerging market loans, and dealing in complex financial assets known as derivatives.

A second response was to launch on-going political efforts to push for deregulation of banking and "modernization" of finance. Lobbying for deregulation led to interstate banking in the U.S., permitting banks to branch and own operations nationwide.[38] Freedom from branching restrictions precipitated bank asset concentration and a decline both in the number of banks and the number of small banks. Canada, Germany, and Japan have concentrated banking industries. Lobbying success culminated in the rescinding of the Glass-Steagall Act in America that separated investment from commercial banking and New Deal legislation that compartmentalized finance into separate industries. Now financial institutions of all types can commingle, and are doing so, into financial conglomerates, as allowed for by the Gramm-Leach-Bliley Act of 1999. An even closer banking-commercial linkage is evidenced in the European and Japanese systems.

Economic power has shifted to money management. Financial institutions increasingly devote their efforts to accumulating and allocating funds globally based on risk-return criteria, operations known as asset and liability management. Funds are shifted among currencies, commodities, bonds, and stocks, risks are assessed, and leverage is applied to enhance potential returns. Pension funds, mutual funds, investment banks, and hedge funds are in a global competition over finding the most profitable commercial ventures to support. Control over global financial capital, decisions to invest or not, and the era's renewed focus on shareholder return, makes these fund companies instrumental players in financing and speculating on world economic development. Though some transnational non-financial corporations depend highly on outside finance, many enjoy unusually high profits, and therefore business earnings create an economic independence from external finance. What is happening then is that corporate earnings and other institutional savings become part of a global pool of money that in part seeks new investment outlets but largely flows to financial markets boosting asset values.

Interesting and sometimes complex financial strategies are employed by money managers. The following is a representative sample:

1. Arbitrage. In this strategy, a trader takes advantage of an existing price differential in an asset by purchasing the asset where it is the cheapest and selling it in the market where the price is higher. To be profitable, the price difference must exceed the transaction cost.

2. Carry Trade. In this strategy, a speculator borrows at low short term interest rates and lends the funds long term at higher rates. Alternatively, a currency trader may borrow in one currency at a relatively low rate and lend in another currency at a higher rate. The risk here is that short rates may rise or that the currency that the loan was made in depreciates.

3. Stock-Bond Nexus. In this strategy, a trader recognizes that a company's stocks and bonds, and a country's stock and bond markets, are in fact related. Asset values can move in the same or opposite direction depending on the expectation of some event or new policy. The bonds of a company targeted for an expected buyout may depreciate if the acquiring firm employs much debt in the transaction, even though the company's stock may rise in value. A trader expecting this outcome can take a short position on the bonds and a long position on the stock.[39]

4. Securitization. In this strategy, a bank or broker will commingle mortgage loans or country debt into marketable securities. The securities represent a tranch or portion of the overall portfolio, and these portions can have varying associated risks of default on principal or depreciated market value. The sale of the securities brings in new funds to the bank or investment bank that originated the loans, and disperses risk across a potentially broad class of investors.

5. Derivatives. Derivatives are contracts which can be bought and sold and whose value is derived from or depends on the value of some underlying asset.[40] A typical strategy is whereby a lender sells the obligation to cover a borrower's default to a third party for a fee paid to the third party. This fee is the derivative's price. Another derivative is the option contract where a speculator purchases the right, but not the obligation, to buy or sell an asset at a certain price by a certain time. The premium is the price paid to have the option, and the trader can speculate on the premium varying or on the value of the underlying asset varying. Complex derivative products and derivatives sold in illiquid markets carry potentially high risk if defaults occur and parties responsible for covering such defaults cannot meet their financial obligations.

6. Forward contracting. In this strategy, a trader contracts today to buy or sell foreign exchange, stocks, or other assets in the future. If the trader is a hedger, their intention is to lock in the future price to avoid the risk of a price change. If the trader is speculating, they believe they can profit from the difference between the price of the asset on the futures market and what they think the actual price will be in the future. For example, if the speculator believes the actual forward price will be higher than the prevailing futures' market price, they will purchase a forward contract to buy the asset at the futures price, and then hopefully sell the asset for more money at some date in the future.

7. Long-short hedge. This strategy is typically employed by hedge funds. The money manager classifies assets into those that are expected to rise in value and those expected to fall in value. The manager buys group-one assets and sells-short assets from group two. Short sales require the manager to borrow an asset, sell it, and then buy it back, hopefully at a depressed price, to make a capital gain. Hedge funds attempt to gain from both bull and bear markets in certain assets, and enhance their holdings and potential returns through leverage.[41]

8. Junk Bonds and leveraged Loans. These liabilities are speculative grade debt instruments. Banks, investment banks, pension funds, and hedge funds supply capital to riskier and/or small, less known companies through these instruments. Creditors have claims on corporate assets in case of default and receive higher returns for taking on risk. IMMC has increased the available savings to borrowers and these liabilities offer outlets for funds.

9. Historical Patterns. Traders analyze data to determine whether particular variables display historical patterns or associations. Where such historical patterns are discerned, traders can exploit minor and temporary divergences for financial gain. For example, values of emerging market bonds can display a link to MDC bond values, the former offering higher returns

due to associated higher risk. If the rate spread narrows, suggesting a possible historical anomaly, speculators would sell short the emerging market bonds and buy the MDC bonds. Hedge funds engage in this financial strategy and assets under hedge fund management have grown from $50b in 1990 to $1.1t in 2005 [WSJ 3/9/06, pA1].

The IMMC era is about reconfiguring the economic structure and public policy to elevate financial sector income and political power. Much more attention is now paid to finance. More financial services avail themselves to borrowers, savers, and traders, and concurrently, higher debt levels among borrowers are presently more acceptable. While business promotes household sector deficit spending (sharp drop from surplus to deficit in personal or household financial budgets), the financial industry supplies the money to fund sustained efforts to deficit-spend.[42] General economic prosperity is thought to occur only when finance is healthy. Financial statistics, sometimes exclusive of other economic or social data, are used to judge societal welfare. The main public policy tool is monetary policy conducted under the auspices of financial elites. Desires to open more markets and permit unrestrained financial investment and speculation are effectively pushed through the political process regardless of the party in power.

Finance-induced household deficit budgets produce business sector surplus budgets. The typical small surpluses in corporate budgets in the past can now range higher as household budgets have shifted from modest surpluses to modest deficits. Elevating world stock markets propel household consumption through a wealth effect. The strong general trend in the U.S. stock market since the early 1980s exemplifies the marked upward movements in many world markets. The strong move upward begins as globalization three commences [see WSJ 1/12/06, pA12].

Global output growth has averaged 3.8% per year since the early 1970s [Wachovia]. While respectable, this is down from the Second Era growth rate of about 5.7%. Per capita figures across the two eras show the same fall off in performance.[43]

Table 2.1 identifies the main differentiating traits of the three eras of modern globalization. The last two rows require some elucidation as this part of the summary characteristics allude to justification for hegemonic expansion and consequence of such expansion. All three eras have economic gain in some form as a driving force, the extension of power abroad, and the globalization of capital as an effect.

What is interesting is the political justification for globalization. Era 1 nationalism implied a superiority of a nation state and a calling to export modernization and civilization abroad through colonization. Era 2 saw socialism

Table 2.1.   Distinguishing Characteristics of the Three Eras of Globalization

	Era 1	Era 2	Era 3
Hegemon	Britain	United States	United States
Financial Center	London	New York	New York
Technological Innovation	Shipping	Air Transport	Internet
Key Currency	Pound	Dollar	Dollar
Exchange Rate System	Gold Standard	Bretton Woods	Flexible but Managed Exchange Rates
Capital Flow	Free	Regulated	Free
Financial Practice	Oligopolization Of Industry	Bank Loans and Internal Finance	Money Management
Financial Institution	Investment Banking	Commercial Banking	Hedge Funds, Financial Conglomerates
Business Firm	Largely Domestic But Growing International Portfolio	Multinational	Transnational
Driver	Colonization	Cold War	Internationalization Of Capitalism

as a threat to free democratic capitalist countries and thus the cold war was born. The current era justifies expansion or intervention to extend American or Western ideals and culture to promote and protect freedom from terrorists and dictators, and therefore westernized, modern nations confront diametrically different societies that result in a "clash of civilizations." Terrorism and regional conflicts are seen as threats to a superior way of life, thereby justifying hegemonic expansion and with it a particular economic system.

NOTES

1. Application of institutional analysis of American economic performance is well done by Gordon [1994] and Hart [1994].

2. This section draws on Brawley's "Turning Points," chapter 13.

3. Bubbles occur when valuation exceeds what the underlying economic fundamentals justify.

4. Each era of globalization is marked by capital flowing to "new frontier" investments offering higher return rates and lower production costs.

5. This is the essence of the Keynesian critique of finance during the 1920s.

6. The U.S. refuses to assume leadership during a period of national isolation and reaction.

7. The Allies prevent Germany from running a current account surplus to payoff war debts but neither do they cancel war debts, yet require large war reparations from

a prostrate nation. Read Keynes' examination of the Treaty of Versailles [1920 (1971)].

8. The American margin requirement at the time was 10%, allowing investors to borrow up to 90% of the value of stock purchased.

9. An easy monetary policy is one where policy tries to induce growth by adding to bank reserves.

10. Open market operations (OMO) refer to central bank security purchases from and sales to banks and bond dealers.

11. This is a form of government planning that induces and leads private investment to direct economic development along a particular path.

12. See the series of articles on the Accord in the Economic Quarterly, volume 87, 2001, put out by the Federal Reserve Bank of Richmond.

13. Real Bills calls for central banks to accommodate business financing needs while the quantity theory argues for central bank restraint in supporting bank lending.

14. The Keynesian consensus refers to the economic profession's general acceptance of active demand management and regulation of finance.

15. Cornwall and Cornwall [2001] extensively address this period.

16. The PC tradeoff arises for two reasons, one due to cost and the other due to demand. Increasing demand means more spending, and to meet higher consumer demand, firms increase hiring. As unemployment falls, fewer workers remain in the unemployed pool. Increased bargaining strength of labor to get higher wages and increased pricing power of firms because of rising sales, create a relationship of rising prices with falling joblessness.

17. Social spending in America during the 1960s and 1970s embodied the government's Great Society agenda.

18. Economists call the simultaneous occurrence of inflation and weak economic activity "stagflation."

19. Note how the lessons of economic history can be forgotten in just a generation. Past depressions were consequences of over-production and restricted money. And supply-side economics is just a modern restatement of classical economics.

20. The following sources discuss and document the new employment policy: Gordon [1994], Bluestone and Harrison [1982], and Thurow [1996] chapters 2 and 8.

21. Real interest rates equal nominal rates minus inflation rates; real rates measure the purchasing power of returns to bankers and creditors.

22. Turmoil in the Middle East and Arab anger over U.S. support for Israel prompt the embargoes as well.

23. But the "market regulation" concept is never fully embraced in policy as governments at all levels continue commitments to income supports and heavily invest in business incentive programs to lure private capital. See BW [8/21/06, 108–111] for example.

24. Canterbery [2000] argues that these tax cuts heavily favor upper income people, and tax savings are channeled into financial markets benefiting financial asset holders.

25. For a review of inflation targeting policy performance, see Dotsey [2006, 10–20].

26. Since 1990, nations have signed more than 180 regional free-trade agreements [Kumar 2006].

27. See Fischer [1996, 117–234] for a historical review of the economic and military policy of world powers.

28. See Huntington [1996]. His thesis is that the current world order is a multipolar, multi-civilization world of conflict based on distinct cultural identities. Also see Friedman [2000].

29. Cross-border mergers and acquisitions have grown substantially since the mid 1980s. The number of deals has increased from 1000 per year to over 7500 per year after the mid 1990s. Value of deals has grown from under $2 billion to typically over $6 billion during the same time period [WSJ 3/11/06 p.A6].

30. These trends are well discussed by Reich [1992] and Thurow [1996].

31. This argument is laid out in Reich [1992] and Thurow [1996, 2003].

32. See the JPKE symposium [2004–2005] on the international financial system and the Washington Consensus.

33. Many MDC governments continue to resort to deficit spending as experience teaches that this budget stance is expansionary to domestic business conditions.

34. The point that firms have no national identity and what counts is whether or not global corporations invest in any given economy is central to Reich's argument in his 1992 book "The Work of Nations." Agnew [2005] addresses the dilemma of governance in the modern age.

35. For a recount of the international debt crisis see Lissakers [1991] and for more recent crises read Blustein [2003], Krugman [2000], and Stiglitz [2003]. Also see chapters four through six in this text.

36. See the WTO's web site: http://www.wto.org/index.htm. Because developing countries are playing a greater role in world trade, they are playing a greater role in the WTO. See http://www.wto.org/english/news_e/news06_e/annual_report_15dec06_e.htm.

37. Technology stocks dominated the S&P 500 index by market value in the 1990s and financial stocks are doing so in the first decade of the 21st century [WSJ 2/27/06, pC1].

38. The Riegle-Neal Interstate Banking and Branching Efficiency Act was passed in 1994 in the U.S. To curb excessive concentration, the law caps any one bank's deposit control to 10% of the nation's total deposits if acquired through acquisition.

39. A short position is taken upon the expectation of a price decline, the long position for a price rise.

40. The underlying asset is the asset to which the contract is written.

41. Speculators can take long-short positions in not only single assets like commodities and currencies, but entire national stock markets, based on changing national economic policies and global political economic events.

42. Undoubtedly, the renewed and intensified competition within society to succeed, and materialistic values, along with greater access to money, help explain unprecedented private sector budget deficits.

43. See Davidson [1996, 180–181] and BCA Research [2006, 13–14].

Chapter Three

The Political Economy
of Contemporary Globalization

Some economists such as Whalen [1997] and Bivens [2006] have made the case that international money manager capitalism (IMMC) has created negative social and economic implications by narrowing the focus of corporate governance to enhancement of shareholder value. Major financial institutions are pushing firms into mergers and acquisitions, restructurings, and disinvestment in domestic operations, to raise earnings per share at the expense of workers and communities. Concern exists that corporations are now focused on shorter-term financial performance criteria and not long-term investment, resulting in damage to U.S. firms' ability to globally compete and meet social needs. Stockhammer [2005/2006] examines the shareholder revolution affecting the power relations within the firm, influencing modern firms to reduce investment, retain more profit, and pay high salaries to executive to favor shareholder interests. Increased shareholder power imparts slower growth to the economy. These are important microeconomic issues.

This chapter addresses the global-economic and political economic ramifications of IMMC. That is, what are the particular consequences arising from the historical evolution of global economics as described in the previous chapter? For instance, what affect will the new finance have on global economic stability, employment, and income, and what kind of policy derivatives should be contemplated? The last section addresses how public support for world commercial integration may be undermined.

How is it that the world arrived where it is now? This is addressed fully in chapter two but a summary review provides a good lead into analysis of the political economic effects of modern globalization. The economic problems of the 1970s, and policy failures of that time, resuscitate Classical economic thinking about economic policy and employment. The 1980s reflect a policy shift toward unencumbered free trade, and the rise in importance of finance and trading in the economy. The fixed exchange rate portion of the Bretton Woods system collapses under pressure from the dollar overhang. Capital flows and finance are deregulated. Oil and currencies become commodities open for speculation. More free trade agreements are signed in the 1990s, followed by the EMU at the end of the decade. The end of the Cold War in 1989 opens up additional countries to economic restructuring, and offers more labor and product markets to international business.

DRIVING MECHANISMS BEHIND GLOBALIZATION

America is the driving force of modern globalization. To drive such a worldwide restructuring requires a willingness to promote capitalist economic development abroad while maintaining economic prosperity at home. Promoting world economic development is accomplished in three ways. First, the U.S. government drives capitalist development by encouraging American capital investment abroad by insuring corporate property from expropriation and offering certain tax breaks. Government officials assist corporations in accessing markets and in getting business deals. The global American military presence provides business with government contracts to service a variety of military and nonmilitary needs. This pattern of encouraging and subsidizing transnational investment is copied in other leading capitalist nations like Britain and Japan.

Second, the U.S. and the IMF push the Washington Consensus as an underpinning to national public policies. Emerging market countries adopt free market, limited government systems as they shed less efficient or out-dated institutions. And third, the U.S. runs rising current account deficits to flood the world economy with dollars. The consequence is to reaffirm the dollar's central role in cross-border transactions and as the primary reserve asset [D'Arista 2004],[1] and to facilitate economic growth in emerging markets built on export booms.

Relentless U.S. driven globalization requires an understanding of the two kinds of capital mobility. Financial capital mobility is hyper activated in the current age. Internet technology and the ending of capital controls has created a trillion dollar a day foreign exchange market and innumerable speculative opportunities on financial and commodity markets. These money flows are activated by global opportunities to seek higher rates of return and to profit from capital gains.

The second kind of capital mobility is physical capital mobility. Globalization Three opens up commercial competition based on production cost differences. In that there is a growing interconnection among all nations, cost differences are magnified, prompting capital to move wherever advantage can be had. Relentless pursuit for competitive cost advantage makes such capital move with abandon. And in part, these pressures arise from the fact that financial capital is so very mobile and from financial institutions playing a greater role in affecting business structure and strategy.

This enhanced capital mobility is manifested in trend increases in foreign direct investment (FDI), portfolio investment (PI), and international trade.

The U.S. trade deficit became negative in the mid 1980s, and became increasingly negative throughout the 1990s into the 21st century. Growing deficits arise from American capitalists' redeployment of capital abroad to minimize production costs, and from American based companies' desire to import low cost foreign inputs and goods; both efforts are to gain competitive advantage and raise profits. U.S. trade deficits bolster foreign countries' economies, reflected in trade surpluses and high domestic growth rates.[2] These positive economic outcomes from selling to an ever increasing U.S. demand drive these countries to open markets and deregulate, thus integrating themselves further into globalization. That is, as foreign countries' economic welfare improves from globalizing, they are enticed to create more momentum towards integration and copy most developed country (MDC) capitalist systems. Hence it is the U.S. that is driving globalization by creating a symbiotic relationship with any and all nations willing to adopt modern capitalist institutions reflective of the Anglo-American experience.

The U.S. engine for global expansion has its own momentum. The opening up of and access to burgeoning labor, goods, and commodity markets create a continuous on-going search to lower production costs and to find more consumers. With virtually the entire world open to integration, and much of the emerging markets yet to be integrated, the process of integration will likely proceed for decades. This powerful American engine is reflected in its own transition to global openness. In 1985, US imports represented 20% of America's domestic purchases; in 2005 the figure climbed to 37% [The Economist 3/18/06, 69]. Combined US exports and imports in the mid 1970s represented only 6% of GDP, but by 2005 the figure grew to 30% [Wachovia].

Growing trade deficits in the U.S. help other countries sustain an export oriented economic strategy. Trade surpluses finance internal investment and add to FDI and PI flows back to U.S. and other MDC markets. These flows allow for lower borrowing costs and asset price appreciation in the U.S. Since this era of globalization is built on rising asset values fueling consumption, the American economy benefits. And capital inflows, by augmenting domestic demand, permit MDC countries to pursue more Classical macro policies.[3]

Financial capital mobility has its consequences as well. Cross-border flows and shifts in flow direction affect financial, currency, and commodity markets throughout the world. Differentials in return, liquidity, and risk determine where, and in what volume, these flows go. These money flows add to domestic savings and bank reserves. Positive trends of net inflows provide additional funding for investment and easy financing conditions. As argued by Tom Friedman [2000, chapters 7–9], market penetration by capital pressures governments to adopt common world standards in governance and economic institutions. Resistance to liberalization limits further development and access to capital.

U.S. economic prosperity is a pre-condition for rapid globalization, and during this era, prosperity is accomplished partly through an income distribution shift creating a larger proportion of upper middle class spenders and partly from collateralized deficit spending by households. A larger population share of well-off upper middle class consumers sustains spending growth. In America, the top twenty percent of income earners account for forty percent of consumption [WSJ 3/12/07, A2]. These consumers are materialistic and upwardly mobile. Prolonged and substantial increases in net worth, coming about from rising financial asset values and rising home prices, fuel spending beyond income and generate economic prosperity. U.S. household indebtedness as a percentage of disposable income has risen from 52% in 1960 to over 90% in the early 2000s; the savings rate has declined from 7% in the late 1980s to slightly negative in 2006 [Wachovia]. It's not just that higher wealth makes people spend more because they feel wealthier or that people now consider carrying higher amounts of debt acceptable.[4] The substantial hike in indebtedness is underpinned by asset values that trend higher and are perceived to resist marked, permanent declines, for reasons explained below. These forces combine to create an influential "wealth effect" as reflected in a rise in real household net worth from $30 trillion in 1990 to $50 trillion in 2005 [WSJ 12/30/05, pA16].

The expansionary tendencies of wealth driven spending appear to have a structural basis due to changes invoked from globalization and the "new finance." Take financial markets. The bulk of MDC populations are now mini capitalists. Their portfolios, and what is happening on the broad financial markets, have greater importance in their economic thinking and planning. Stock price enhancement positively affects psychology and actual spending much more so than decades ago. Institutional features in modern finance are unique in that they enhance consumer access to credit and foster spending.

While national stock indices can go down, and do so suddenly, modern MDC stock markets seem to have somewhat of a floor underneath them and the capacity to retrace lost ground. Supply and demand conditions of stock markets are responsible. In some countries such as the U.S. few companies issue stock to finance investment, relying mainly on debt and internal funds. Dividend payouts are largely funneled back into the market and stock buy-backs by companies promote equity demand. Financial markets pressure firms to merge in an effort to raise stock prices through enhancing competitiveness or concentrating assets. Because globalization presents an inviting climate for entrepreneurialism, small company innovators prompt acquisitions by large companies, raising market valuations. Bond markets are supported as aging and retirement focused populations add fixed income assets to their portfolios.

Take housing markets as another important economic stimulus. Structural changes in this sector assist overall demand. Demand is promoted, as addressed above, by lower interest rates and increased access to credit and refinancing. Housing is viewed as an investment asset that complements retirement accounts and public pensions. More people in capitalist MDCs have bought into the "ownership society" mentality, and owning a home reflects their advent into the property ownership class. In terms of the supply side of the housing market, strict limits exist to the supply of dwellings. Restrictions arise in some areas due to environmental or suburban sprawl concerns. Developers and builders now consciously control inventory by building only when a contract is in hand or financing is approved. Supply is carefully managed. The demand and supply underpinnings are structural, and together, the forces of demand and supply put upward pressure on real estate values. The Dallas Federal Reserve Bank documents strong trend increases in U.K. and U.S. housing prices since 1980.

GLOBAL STABILITY AND INSTABILITY EFFECTS

On the favorable side, it is likely that the current era of IMMC is producing a more stable global macroeconomic environment. In general, three important attributes of our new economic era tend to promote stability: First, disinflation and low inflation characterize the U.S. economy and the international system since 1990. Second, major financial institutions have diversified holdings of corporate financial assets, and a merger wave in the financial sector is occurring. And third, money manager capitalism promotes a new relationship between corporate investors and their financiers. Let's look at these in some detail.

Lester Thurow [1996, chapter 9] argues that inflation is an "extinct volcano." The war against inflation of the 1970s and 1980s was won not by tight monetary policy but when the factors that created inflation went away. Oil

prices collapsed with the weakening of OPEC and the rise of many oil producing countries.[5] Governments around the world are working to temper
health care inflation, and national health care systems employed in some
countries restrain costs. World unemployment and excess capacity limit inflation by moderating wage growth and business pricing power. Many firms
outsource and invest in new technology to cut costs and prices. Downward
pressures exist on U.S. and world real wages as large new additions to labor
supply arise from more countries joining the global trading system. Elec-
tronic commerce has increased competition, and by reducing inventory and
real estate costs, E-commerce allows firms to reduce prices. And this era's
capital mobility in the context of free markets and deregulation will create
bouts of economic distress and contraction, undermining demand and the
ability to increase prices. These trends suggest that prolonged inflation periods will be less frequent and less likely to occur. Central banks will have less
justification to raise interest rates to curb inflation and will by matter of practical importance be more concerned with developing country financial crises
and slow growth in developed countries than with inflation.

Pension and mutual funds routinely own dozens to hundreds of companies'
bonds and stocks to diversify portfolios. Hedging strategies are commonly
used to offset swings in financial asset values, and better risk management
strategies exist. An increasing portion of money is held in broadly-based index funds. Multinational banks are merging and are creating full-service financial conglomerates. Global banking allows for diversified loan portfolios
and industry concentration. These developments suggest that MDC financial
sectors should experience fewer financial difficulties due to diversified financial portfolios, risk spreading, and market power. This implies less frequent need for lender of last resort operations by monetary authorities to stop
financial crises.

But most importantly, financial sectors should be a major contributor to
stability because of the important economic relations established in international money manager capitalism. What has evolved is that larger and larger
amounts of money are allocated by large financial conglomerates that have
increasingly closer ties to top management who plan business investment.
Uniformity in attitude and recognition of common financial interests by firms
and their financiers have produced financial institutions who are committed
long-run backers of large businesses which account for much of the global
economy's investment. Corporate strategic management favors stockholders'
interests above other stakeholders. "Excess funds" are expended in higher
dividend pay-outs and share buybacks. And this institutional commitment is
strengthened as the clients of pension and mutual funds increasingly provide
their money with long-term capital appreciation objectives.

Moreover, since financial institutions now have more power in corporate governance and more committed money from clients, the ownership and control functions of enterprise are becoming more integrated. Commitment of funds and functional integration should bolster entrepreneurial risk taking and optimism by preventing sharp fluctuations in perceived business investment returns. In other words, the above noted developments should stabilize the flow of funds to, and the stock prices of, the business sector, which in turn will promote and stabilize investment, even in the face of falling business profitability or higher interest rates. Furthermore, sustained upward movements in asset prices will generate wealth effects that bolster private sector spending.

An additional stabilizing factor emanates from service, and especially financial, industry employment trends. MDC economies are evolving into post-industrial age economies built on health care, education, and business and financial services. These industries are labor intensive, and therefore demand increases generate large employment gains. Very skill-based, higher education based jobs pay handsome wages. The finance industry in particular is growing in proportion to the overall economy. This development makes anachronistic the conventional Keynesian critique of money leakage away from commerce and into finance. Instead of this leakage simply depressing demand for goods, money now flows into the financial industry creating jobs and private sector spending. The proliferation of financial products and services offers employment outlets for the growing white collar workforces of the modern era.

There are however dimensions to international money manager capitalism that could be problematic. For many years there has been an ongoing decline in the importance of the banking industry as a financial intermediary relative to mutual and pension funds and financial conglomerates. The significance of the growing importance of non-bank intermediation of funds to finance investment is that these institutions do not create money, as traditional bank lending does, but simply allocate what has been saved. Yet investment that is financed entirely by current savings cannot produce growth. Only aggregate net deficit spending produces growth by augmenting incomes and balance sheets, and this requires money creation [Wray 1991]. Money growth depends on private sector credit demand, which in turn depends on business profitability and aggregate demand. Yet, the source of business debt financing will increasingly be savings capital raised from the financial markets, not new money created from loans which are in turn based on the banking systems' creation of deposits. The relative decline of bank money creation suggests that money growth rates will be somewhat low and the money that does exist will move faster through the economy during expansions. To the extent that interest rates are kept high, country macroeconomic performance could exhibit low growth rates generally and at times stagnation or recession due to the restraint on the demand for borrowed money.[6]

And the evidence suggests that in the U.S. traditional commercial banking is in a relative decline. Non-financial borrowing from banks and thrifts has fallen since the mid 1970s to a modern-day low of 22% and 9% respectively. Commercial bank share of total financial assets has fallen from 41% to 29% over the 1970 to 1994 period [Edwards 1996, 12–13, 15]. Mutual fund assets are now greater than total bank assets [Federal Reserve Bulletin].

Another tendency toward stagnation could arise from the growing income and wealth inequality to which international money manager capitalism contributes. Many studies in the 1980s and 1990s demonstrate that national income dispersion has increased and in general, roughly the top twenty percent of the population has received the significant majority of higher real incomes and wealth. Money manager capitalism assisted wealth concentration by encouraging corporate restructurings and global investment, and by distributing money management services and savings vehicles principally to those individuals who have seen the biggest income gains. Much of the MDC economy output growth and asset price increases in the last two decades are driven by the spending and risk-taking of higher income earners. Thus what has developed are economies overly dependent on a relatively small group whose spending inclinations may be dampened by lower profits and/or asset values. Spending reductions would lead to a general fall in aggregate demands and lead to national economic downturns. People will prefer to hold their wealth in cash and not spend, making a revival in economic activity, spurred by the private sector, unlikely.

What makes growing socioeconomic stratification in the current age so insidious is its concealment. While well documented empirically, inequality appears to have no discernable negative affect. In fact, structural economic change, creating shifts in commercial and employment opportunities across the globe, have actually spurred risk taking and stupendous material rewards. Churning in the success-failure pool of companies, workers, technologies, and investors creates a kind of excitement for economic life, and an acceptance or embracement of dynamic globalization.

Yet Globalization Three puts in place a long run trend toward inequality that might eventually stall growth prospects and undermine acceptance of unfettered world integration. First and foremost are income squeezes on MDC middle classes. Trends in job security, due to employment churning and globalizing labor markets, and trends in middle class entitlements and social protections, presage the undercutting of mass consumption driven growth. Because global competition is significantly based on accessing or creating falling cost structures, existing pressures compel transnational corporations to match cost cutting efforts of rivals. Companies are hence slowly withdrawing from worker benefit commitments other than those most directly related to productivity, such as education funding. Employee pension [see WSJ 1/12/06 p.C1 and D1] and health care benefits are being trimmed to boost profits for investment or income to pay financiers and owners. Moreover, public social programs and income supports are threatened. MDC demographic trends combine with prevailing Washington Consensus thinking to encourage governments to rescind social obligations.

But the story does not end here. Growing MDC consumer indebtedness must have some limit, probably realized over the long run. Increased tax inequalities, arising in developed countries and already in place in less developed countries (LDCs), should assist all of the above mentioned factors in slowly limiting consumer demand growth. All in all, wage dispersion, job insecurity, tax regressivity, benefit reductions, less generous state income supports, and debt saturation will contribute to liquidity preference and spending aversion among the world's middle classes.

Moreover, there is interdependence between most workers on the one hand and affluent people on the other. Growing inequality in this stage of capitalism has prompted the bottom two-thirds of Americans to spend more, by borrowing more and saving less in order to maintain living standards, thereby driving the profits and stock prices of the affluent. Wealthier Americans are spending but also saving much and reaping the rewards of asset price appreciation, yet the continued spending of most Americans depends on continued good profit and stock price performance of the affluent. Any disruption in the spending of much of the public or any curtailment in business investment and job creation by the affluent would negatively affect aggregate economic performance. The American economy will remain vulnerable to this interdependency between the income classes and between the financial and business sectors.

Two other long run problems await IMMC. Complete world economic integration will be the consequence of a decades-long process of trade, capital flows, economic unions, and regulatory standardization. Therefore, one must expect the synchronization of national business cycles into a world business cycle. A process of national economic integration implies interdependency, subjecting once independent economies to economic synchronization. The fluctuations in profits and investment responsible for national business cycles will simply play out on a global level. The challenge here is whether nation states will work in unison to coordinate global economic demand management policies, or whether some supranational institution is given such a charge. And furthermore, complete world integration will bring to an end the easy ability of capital to augment profits through market extension. By the latter part of the 21st century, or soon thereafter, international business will have tapped into all new and disconnected regions of consumers, workers, and resources. Where can capital go afterwards to get the marked growth surge it needs for its vitality? Capitalism must extend itself and expand to remain healthy. Capitalism always needs a frontier.

INCOME AND EMPLOYMENT EFFECTS

There is no doubt that globalization imparts a dynamism to economic life. Economic activity and trade flows increase. New opportunities abound. The competitive and technological landscapes are reconfigured. Investment, business creation, and employment are stimulated.

But there is tension between stability and change. While progress and prosperity can be associated with change, too much of the latter is socially disruptive. Unfettered globalization pushes society towards rapid change, negatively affecting community life for some.

What are trade liberalization's affects on incomes? Contemporary globalization sets in motion world-wide competition in "old economy" manufacturing industries due to nation-state commercial integration. New economy industries, along with finance and real estate, grow rapidly and add to modern socioeconomic dynamism. The old economy rate of decline, measured in domestic plant capacity and employment, may exceed or fall short of the growth rate in new economy industries. As manufacturing investment increases in LDCs, new economy industries flourish in some emerging market and MDC countries. Therefore, world income inequality falls while in-nation inequality may rise if new economy employment and income fail to keep pace with the decline in old economy industries.[7] Those industries that set new trends or quickly adapt to global opportunities reap the most in income, while those producing domestically for the older economy see their incomes lag or decline. National incomes tend to increase, but economic churning caused by globalization alters gains and losses. Capitalist class income typically benefits because the owners and controllers of restructured and relocated enterprises are often the same people. While there are wholesale turnovers in workforces, and cuts in pay and benefits of retained employees in the advanced countries, property owners gain from manufacturing investment targeted to LDCs and investment in new economy endeavors.

How about globalization's affects on employment? Here again the effect is not simple. Growing interconnectedness stimulates old and new businesses to develop or adopt new technologies and products. New jobs and skills are built around the new industries. Employment is put into more flux as business services, finance, and high technology jobs expand in number while MDC manufacturing jobs decrease. The skill mix is changing and job location is changing. Along with shifting wage prospects, more uncertain employment prospects impact human welfare and the ability to make and plan family commitments. Less labor market stability shifts the balance of power to capitalists.[8] Productivity advances justify reduced employment but higher pay for some remaining employees.[9]

Consider a typical scenario as pictured in figure 3.1 where a multinational firm operating largely in a MDC reacts to growing global demand by contemplating the location of additional investment to meet the demand. Should the firm invest in the MDC, thereby adding employment in that country, or should the investment go off-shore? The labor market conditions are such that workers in the MDC earn far more than in a LDC or emerging market country. In the model below, the firm currently employs E1 MDC workers who earn W1 while employing e1 LDC workers who earn w1 in wages and benefits. The firm faces a steep labor demand curve signifying that wage changes have much less effect on employment levels than does the level of demand or spending on the firm's output. That is, sales and profits influence employment levels more than labor costs.

There are three basic decisions that could be made:

Case 1: Invest in the MDC. In order for the prices and profits to compete with the economics of LDC investment, this decision leads to an increase in employment of MDC workers to E2 but a sizable cut in W for MDC workers to W2. LDC employment remains at e1.

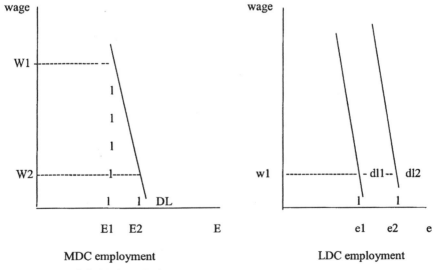

Figure 3.1.   Global Labor Markets

Case 2: Invest Off-shore. This decision leads to a rightward shift in LDC de-
         mand increasing employment to e2 but at the same wage of w1. Lit-
         tle pressure exists in many LDCs to raise wages much or at all due
         to high unemployment and no organized bargaining power. No jobs
         are added in the MDC and the currently employed labor continues to
         receive W1. The LDC investment is likely to create insecurity in the
         firm's MDC workforce since the new investment led to a capital out-
         flow.

Case 3: Shift some current production abroad and increase investment in the
         LDC. A third possibility is that the lower LDC employment costs are
         so enticing that the firm cuts some MDC employment and produc-
         tion, shifting operations and newly investing into the LDC. Both la-
         bor demand curves shift, MDC demand to the left and LDC demand
         to the right. Option three contributes to "factor price equalization"
         where prevailing pressures exist for MDC labor to offer wage con-
         cessions to stem further job erosion while the large increase in LDC
         labor demand lifts wages above w1.

Two noteworthy conclusions arise from this analysis. First, global cost differentials largely determine job location, not volume.[10] Second, it is important to understand the causality at work. In reality, it is not MDC consumers
who demand that domestic firms increase imports of foreign products, but
that companies redirect investment and employment offshore to reap more
profits from large cost savings. As these imports increase, more foreign products are offered to MDC consumers to buy. Or similarly, more free trade bills
are passed in the MDCs that open up home markets to foreign companies to
sell into.[11]

Power is shifting to globally positioned firms that create huge logistical demands upon manufactures and shipping companies and sell vast quantities
and varieties of consumer goods. This power is expressed through backward
linkages to producers and forward linkages to labor markets. These firms
force manufacturers to seek low cost production platforms world-wide, and
can do so because of their control over marketing vast volumes of goods. To
keep their own expenses minimized and efficiency high, these firms are creating increasingly flexible labor markets. Some full time hiring is done, but
companies also purposely hire part-time workers or hire from companies that
"rent" workers. Total benefit payments are therefore reduced and actual employment of part-time labor occurs to perfectly flex with daily changes in demand. More people are hired onto the payroll than can be fully used in order
to give maximum flexibility to management's use of "labor resources" and to
create insecurity, dependency, and desperation in the company's workforce.

Wherever this form of business practice is employed, a country's unemployment numbers are biased low as any hours worked by an individual gets them classified as employed.

Problematically, raising labor market volatility is not the only adverse effect of capitalist globalization. Unfettered globalization is incapable of producing global full employment. The crux of the problem is that profit maximization is the top priority of business, particularly business dominated by money managers. IMMC imposes a strict limit to job creation somewhere moderately to well below full employment.

Entrepreneurial activity is motivated by profit. Profit (P) equals revenues (R) minus cost (C). That is, $P = R - C$. R can be increased by increasing price or by selling more. C can be cut by lowering wages and benefits. Price and wage changes have rather immediate positive effects on P for individual companies, but over time price hikes and wage cuts tend to reduce demand in the global economy.[12] The profit drive also prompts firms to constantly seek productivity improvements which reduce labor per unit of output. Productivity enhancing technology puts downward pressure on production expense, but has the simultaneous result of undercutting demand.[13] Therefore, the profit drive tends to prevent the global economic system from ever reaching full employment.

But worse still are the systemic cyclical changes in overall demand. IMMC economies will continue to experience ebb and flow in commercial activity due to booms and busts in private sector spending. Upturns in spending, employment, and production are routinely followed by downturns. Fluctuations in business spending arise from shifts in profit expectations and changes in consumption arise from changes in the public's liquidity preference. More people confront greater uncertainty in these times, making future events more difficult to anticipate. This creates a kind of anxiety about economic life that can now be affected by global factors, anxiety manifesting itself in risk aversion, caution, and savings.[14] So the system is prone to producing some unemployment, even during periods of relative prosperity.

The age of the money manager has been transformative to nation-state income distributions. Piketty and Saez [2006] produce an across-country study comparing trends in the income share of high income earners and the composition of earnings of high income recipients over the course of the twentieth century. The income share of high income earners falls over the inter-war years and remains relatively low during globalization two in both communitarian capitalist countries and Anglo-American economies. This income share rises to its early twentieth century high in America and Canada, and nearly so in England, during globalization three, but no change occurs in communitarian countries. Moreover, as the high income share rises in Anglo-American economies, the composition of income changes from primarily interest and dividend income to salary income. In the U.S. the high income share fluctuates between 14% and 19% in the early twentieth century, falls from the late 1930s to the late 1970s reaching a low of 7%, and then rises sharply to the middle teens by 2000 [WSJ 11/21/06, pA1].

Stock market declines and progressive taxation explain the income share fall. Reversal in the high income share comes about just as the third era of globalization begins. Steep cuts in progressive taxation and more defense oriented federal government budget expenditures in the U.S. partially explain the new trend. But importantly, corporate restructurings arising from deregulation policy and globalization forces account for rising income concentration as well. What is interesting is that though money managers and finance capitalists have an elevated position of power and importance in economic life today, they and the corporate boards they influence are willing to pay enormous sums to executives to reconfigure and redeploy corporate assets. Deregulation has allowed financiers to reshuffle corporate assets into new enterprises. Globalization has allowed for global repositioning of assets. This capital mobility allows the controllers to exit from reliance on unionized labor and to exit from high tax, high regulation areas. In effect, these moves shift income distribution to favor corporate controllers and their agents over other economic interest groups.[15]

A broader historical context for the above point adds to its importance. In Anglo-American and western capitalist societies in the previous two centuries, economies withstood major restructurings as they evolved from agrarian-based to manufacturing economies, from local to national markets, and more recently from manufacturing to heavily service oriented systems. And when certain economy-dominating industries restructured into profitable and stable national oligopolies, organized labor came into being, facilitated by large numbers of people working in one place and motivated to act as a countervailing force to big business. What the current era of globalization offers to business and banking is another period of dramatic restructuring, not dissimilar to past times, where economies are completely remade through new patterns of investment. Globally directed investments overthrow any kind of stable employment relations and reconfigure power within business relations. Eventually global restructurings will lead to global oligopolies, but oligopolies without unions, as the motives of competition, power, and profit foster the concentration of commercial ownership world-wide.

PUBLIC POLICY CONCERNS

Public policy could come to hamper global growth if policymakers succumb to their Classical philosophical predilections. Policymakers and their consultants are typically Classical in orientation due to their education and class, but also because of the structural growth tendencies of the current age. Because there is a systemic penchant toward growth, as reflected in globalization's driving mechanisms described above, policymakers believe they can safely pursue deflationary demand policies. During booms it is possible to contract budget deficits and restrict credit supplies, but not under less-than-boom economic conditions. Policymakers cannot for long undermine asset driven private sector deficit spending without paying the severe consequences of depression.

As documented by Wachovia's economic department [2005], since the mid 1960s almost every time the American central bank drives up its policy rate, the economy slips into recession and the unemployment rate spikes every time recession occurs. Interest rate management over this period has contributed to an average unemployment rate of 6%.

Central bankers also mistake the low or falling inflation rates during globalization as evidence of their success in pursuing Classical monetary policy. Economic change precipitated by globalization is responsible for low inflation, not restrictive credit policy (see the details of this argument above). But central bankers give modern monetary policy, directed at building inflation-fighting credentials in the minds of the public, credit for lower inflation across the world since the early 1980s. Excerpts from a Federal Reserve official speech are instructive:

Let me be clear, however. Understanding the economic logic of the evolution of monetary policy over the last several decades should take nothing away from the significant achievements of Alan Greenspan. He served as Fed chairman for more than 18-and-a-half years and his record during that time was exemplary. Under his leadership, the Federal Reserve brought inflation down to historically low levels, which contributed to a period of extended economic expansion interrupted by only two brief and mild recessions. Indeed, the term "The Great Moderation" has been given to the phenomenal improvement in macroeconomic performance during the period following the mid-1980s, just before Greenspan took over. In essence, he successfully completed the task begun by his predecessor, Paul Volcker, of re-establishing the expectation of price stability that had been lost in the inflationary period of the 1970s.

In the 1960s and 1970s monetary policy typically allowed inflation to rise noticeably during economic expansions. As the economy recovered from a recession and growth picked up, the Fed kept interest rates from rising as much as they should. So inflation was essentially ratcheting upward throughout the period before 1980. The story of the Volcker-Greenspan era, then, is the story of how expectational stability was restored—the story of how the Fed regained the public's confidence that it would and could keep inflation low and stable.

Over time, however, inflation has stabilized at a low level and inflation scares have become much less frequent as the public has learned that the Fed would respond systematically in a way designed to keep inflation low and steady.

The conduct of monetary policy in the last two decades has brought us to a very favorable place. Inflation is low and stable, and the public appears to be fairly confident that inflation will remain persistently low and stable. This is the Greenspan legacy, and it is now our responsibility, under the leadership of the new chairman, to preserve that credibility [Lacker 2/14/06].

Despite the above statement, factors unrelated to central bank policy have reduced average national inflation rates. As argued earlier in this chapter, globalization creates multiple downward influences on inflation. Moreover, the world has largely not suffered in the current era from prolonged, major world conflagration, food shortages, or oil crises associated with sustained spikes in resource costs and high government spending. Income distribution struggles that lie at the heart of inflationary income demands do not have the necessary economic circumstances to underpin competition over income shares.

These combined influences are consequential for the Phillips Curve (PC). The PC curve is now flatter, shallower in slope, as shown below in the pivot from PC1 to PC2. Business pricing power weakness and labor inability to contract higher wages creates less inflationary potential at any unemployment rate. The non-inflationary unemployment rate is lower. If recognized by central bankers, monetary policy can remain more stimulative. While labor's ability to extract more income for itself is undermined by globalization, higher average levels of employment can conceivably prevail.[16]

In actuality, central banks are more successful in creating downturns or weak economic environments than in controlling inflation. High interest rate policies of G-5 nations[17] in the 1970s induced two world economic slumps, the second lasting from 1979 through 1983, by adding to the negative effects on demand arising from major oil price hikes. The consequence of these policies was the early to mid 1980s international debt crisis. High rates in the late 1980s helped to bring down world stock markets, and to create the early 1990s recession in the U.S. and a 15 year prolonged slump in Japan.

Higher values for rates and the dollar contributed to the late 1990s emerging market financial crises, and European Central Bank interest rate hikes contributed to double digit unemployment in the EU. The run-up in rates in the U.S. in 2000 contributed to recession and the stock market collapse. The American central bank is so keen on preventing inflation that they begin to raise rates in June 2004, and do so for 17 straight times, well in advance of

Inflation

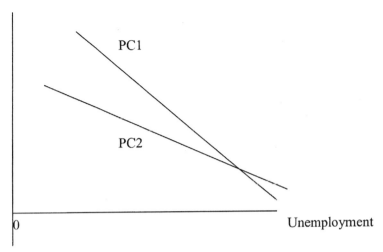

Figure 3.2.   The Phillips Curve Pivot

the economy reaching its 30 year average and quite modest capacity utilization rate of 81% [Wachovia]. The housing and construction slowdown, and GDP growth fall off, in the U.S. in the 2006–2007 period is largely due to Fed actions.

All of these policy induced problems necessitated rapid reversal of restrictive policy.[18]

Central bank policy should be much more directed at promoting entrepreneurial incentives. Easy credit, low interest rate policies create positive incentives to expand business by fostering rising revenues and pricing power. As borrowing and spending increase, businesses face rising sales revenues and a pricing environment conducive to investment and prosperity. A surer way to promote new additional investment comes from rising revenues and cash flow, not by efforts to put a drag on economic activity and eliminate any pricing power.

If public policy becomes too counter-cyclical during robust economic times, the U.S., U.K., and Australia could reproduce stagnant Japanese-style economic performance domestically, despite globalization's asset driven, structural growth inclinations.

The needs of globalization pose a balancing act for policymakers. Governments must balance their responsibilities of sufficiently promoting economic

Table 3.1.   Public Policy's Balance of Responsibilities

Promotion of Incentives	versus	Promotion of Stability
private profit		employment
property agglomeration		income equality
trading and speculation		economic security

incentives while maintaining economic and financial stability. Too much focus on inciting incentives can lead to economic instability yet too much attention to stability can engender stagnation. Table 3.1 shows the tradeoffs.

The free market advocates and the frenetic globalizers of the current age are pushing strongly for public policy promotion of economic incentives as embodied in unencumbered free trade legislation and the Washington Consensus. Critics of fast paced globalization and its effects advocate and lobby for government attention to financial stability and economic protections. Institutional arrangements exemplified in welfare states, Bretton Woods, and public investment are sought to achieve stability. The question is who will win out in applying political pressure on the state to run policy in their direction.

Similarly, there is a governance issue confronting the state. There is no serious contention over the size of the state or degree of federalism. An argument to substantially reduce the size and scope of the state or to recreate a 19th century American style highly decentralized government garners no support from the major parties actively involved in globalization. The contentions are over, on the one hand, how internationalist national government

	Corporate Governance	Democratic Governance
National Governance	Era One	
Supranational Governance	Era Three	Era Two

Figure 3.3.   Governance options

is in perspective and policy and, on the other hand, whether governance will largely come from the transnational corporations or from a democratic public sector. This second contention is a less visible one to the general public. The matrix above identifies four possible outcomes of these contentions.

Era one is best placed in the upper left box. This period is one of domestic national governance and an international order dominated by business and financial interests. Era two is located in the lower right-hand box because this period is exemplified by interventionist domestic and international economic policy heavily influenced by democratic governance. The current era is positioned in the lower left box. This characterization of governance arises partly from the carry over of Bretton Woods institutions combined with very modern efforts to regulate international economics via the European Union, the World Trade Organization, and multilateral trade agreements. Yet there is substantial corporate influence in pushing for and the writing of trade agreements, there is no longer a regulated international financial system, and nation states have difficulty at times in cooperating on intervention during crises and in forging collaborative expansionary policy. The contemporary World Bank and IMF largely promote international business and finance, not regulate and govern these interests. The Bank for International Settlements is not currently a governing body nor is the U.N. Thus there is a real subservience of the public interest and publicly-directed governance to commercial interests at this juncture.[19]

FOSTERING PUBLIC SUPPORT

But it is not only public policymakers who must be sagacious and socially conscious. Global capitalists must be as well. Globalization is raising inequality within nations, subjecting millions to increased economic insecurity. If the income and wealth distribution system of globalization creates an ever-growing world lower class by gutting the purchasing power of the middle class, and continues to shrink public safety nets such as pensions, system-wide stagnation could set in. The percentage of the world's population benefiting from increasing net worth will be more than off-set by the population percentage living off of too little income and too little asset ownership to drive the global economic system. Social and political discontent can result. There are genuine limits to how far inequality can be pushed before negative consequences arise.

Globalization greatly enhances new and lucrative opportunities, and the freedom to pursue opportunities. If some people disproportionately benefit from globalization, if the distribution of gains from globalization is seen as unfair, public support for the current system of rules, opportunities, and power distribution will wane. The threat is not so much an opposition to world integration as it could be opposition to the reward system. Consider the following worrisome developments thus far from globalization:

1. Large increases in incomes of those running multinational firms. It is not uncommon for directors to receive over $100,000 per year for 30 days worth of work on a board. Executive pay differentials with workers have increased 100 times over the 1970s. Hedge fund managers can take 40% of the profits for themselves [WSJ 4/5/06 pA2]. Median CEO income at the largest companies rose 10% in 2005 to $8.4 million [BW 5/01/06, 36].[20] Globally based businesses are earning record profits and running sector-wide budget surpluses while households, especially in the US, are running record debt levels and budget deficits. US non-financial companies hold record cash levels, valued at $1500b in early 2006, the consequence of an average 18% yearly growth in cash since 1990 [BW 4/17/06, 70–71]. Executives can gain substantial price appreciation of stock on public companies taken private and later resold to the general public as restructured firms; had the same restructuring taken place without the alteration in ownership that concentrated stock holdings, the public shareholders would have reaped the rewards.[21]

2. Stock option grants. The granting of stock options is concentrated in executive hands, and options may be re-priced or replaced as old ones are exercised [WSJ 12/27/06, A1]. The grant or strike price may be at or below the current market price. Some companies have been found to back date options to a time when the market price was lower than the current price when price trends run against executives [WSJ 3/18/06 pA1, 6/10/06 pA3; 10/12/06 pA1]. Top executives set up "stock trading plans" permitting trades of company owned stock at fixed dates to protect them from perceived illegal insider trading. Yet large capital gains from trades suggest that executives nevertheless exploit inside knowledge for personal advantage [BW 11/13/06, 40].

3. Pension and severance packages. Executives reap multimillion dollar packages that are part of total compensation schemes when they are hired. The trend in MDCs is to reduce pension coverage of employees, to shift risk to employees by eliminating defined benefit plans, and to shift pension management and financial responsibilities to government.[22] Because most laborers make much more modest pay than elites, most have accumulated inadequate private retirement accounts that range from tens of thousands to a few hundred thousand dollars [Market Watch 4/4/06].

Typical severance packages are measured in weeks or months worth of pay not years or in millions of dollars.[23]

4. Growing wealth inequalities. The Federal Reserve completes a triennial consumer survey of assets and liabilities held by Americans to compute the distribution of net worth. Figures covering the period of globalization three show a marked increase in wealth held by the top 1% of Americans. In 1989, the top 1% held 30.1% of the net worth, in 1995, 34.6%, in 2001, 32.7%, and in 2004, 33.4%. The minimum net worth for the group in 2004 was $6 million. The bottom half of the population holds 2.5% of the net worth [WSJ 4/5/06, pA4]. Two-thirds of the estimated $41 trillion to be inherited in the next five decades will go to the wealthiest 7% of estates [WSJ 12/11/06, pR4].

5. Growing income inequalities. The 1990s boom and the economic rebound of the 2000s in the U.S. have shifted income towards business from labor to a rather dramatic extent. Widening profit margins and subdued labor income growth have shifted economic rewards and incentives to ownership at the expense of work. It's not that wages aren't growing, but relative income growth favors property interests. For example, yearly profit growth has ranged between 10% and 30% well above low single digit growth in wages; profits were up 29% in early 2006 over 2005 while take-home pay was up 4%. Though inflation is tame, price growth exceeds unit labor cost growth, the latter measure sometimes recording negative growth rates. The U.S. national minimum wage measured in terms of buying power stands at a 50 year low.[24] Dramatic increases in executive income have driven the ratio of CEO pay relative to average income from around 30 in the 1970s to 500 in the late 1990s, and in 2005 the figure stood at 369 [WSJ 10/12/06, pA1].

6. Exploitation of productive enterprises. Private investments in public equities (PIPEs) are deals where shares are sold to hedge funds or other well connected financial institutions, sometimes at discounts to the public share price. Receivers of PIPEs get an instant paper gain in wealth, and may get a voice in management if enough shares are purchased.[25] Similarly, well connected institutions get first access to so called IPOs, initial public offerings, or receive privileged information about hedge fund holdings or special redemption terms [BW 7/17/06, 34]. Private equity firms act as cash extractors from companies taken over. Equity firms use their ownership control rights to make their companies issue more debt to the public, or to allow access to company savings, in order to receive income flows, ostensibly to pay for advisory and management fees [BW 10/30.06, 58–66]. Financial control can lead to increased returns by

shutting down higher costs plants, cutting worker benefits, or off-shoring assets in distressed but operatively viable companies.[26]

7. Mergers and acquisitions (M&A). Advanced capitalist nations allow for energetic M&A activity. Firms of all sizes buy each other or blend operations into new firms. Because ownership in most companies is rather concentrated, combining one enterprise after another simply agglomerates productive wealth for the disproportionate benefit of a few. Globalization expedites such activity by providing cross-border opportunities to consolidate capital. Sometimes firms previously engaged in illegal activities are at some point allowed once again to grow more dominant, offering insiders more riches [Market Watch 4/4/06].

8. Tax fairness. Tax burdens are falling for unearned property income while rising on worker income. States and countries have shifted to more regressive tax postures [Mitrusi and Poterba 2000]. The US corporate tax rate has fallen from 40% of cash flow in 1950 to 15% in 2001 [Medlen 2005 572–573]. Unpaid taxes in the US are estimated to be $350b per year [BW 4/17/06, 34], much of which is owed by business whose incomes are not subject to withholding.

9. Bankruptcy and Off-shoring. Traditionally bankruptcy was about giving a company a fresh start after forces beyond the company's control endangered its operation. Firms could financially restructure while maintaining on-going operations and jobs. But in a global free market, firms can use bankruptcy to rid themselves of personnel responsibilities, and to shut down facilities in MDCs to outsource work abroad in low wage areas. And since firms are really webs of numerous profit centers, they can target those operations under the most financial pressures for closure and justify breaking of commitments to higher paid workers. And sometimes firms simply elect not to upgrade operations in MDCs, and hence save money by outsourcing or off-shoring [BW 4/24/06, 52, 55].

10. Employment Benefits and Deregulation. Growing cross-border competition based on costs is pressuring MDC companies to trim benefits to compete. Meanwhile, the deregulatory-free market theoretical principle underpinning globalization is echoed in national economic policy via a permissive policy of health care company consolidation. Health care deliverers and private insurers consolidate to gain market power against one another, contributing to rapid price advances in the industry, and directing more income their way [Market Watch 4/17/06]. These circumstances thus create reinforcing pressures to shift employer financial responsibilities for benefits to workers or the state. Communitarian economies that employ heavy public sector involvement in health care fair better longer due to regulatory and price control intervention, but

pressures are building there as well as their economies become increasingly exposed to the stresses of globalization.

11. Industries Exploiting National Crises. Rising global demand for oil, driven by economic growth and the admission of China and India into the global community of major country players, and civil unrest in a few oil producing nations, made energy into a serious issue in the first decade of the 21st century. Expected future limits in growth of fossil fuel supplies and foreign policy contentions over oil access contribute to making energy security a priority problem among nations. Despite the short run financial pinch and longer run concerns for economic and social stability, energy companies reap enormous financial gains from their strategically important positions as energy producers and distributors. Private leverage over public affairs is reflected in high consumer dependency on oil and in industry concentration. Global energy crises lift profit margins and sales above normal returns coming from world economic growth. Crises create huge shifts in money flows, a redistribution towards energy producers. These financial gains strain relations with the public as companies are seen profiteering on human hardship and the Iraq war, and use windfalls to pay exorbitant salaries, retirements, and dividends to insiders.[27]

12. Commodification of Businesses. Capitalists can raise popular angst when people see businesses treated as tradable commodities merely for short term capital gain or income extraction. Finance capitalists will sometimes take public companies private to avoid complying with accounting and financial openness regulations. Investments are financed by combinations of debt and cash, and once control is achieved, bonds are issued backed by corporate assets, the proceeds of which are paid out to the investors for a quick return.[28] Alternatively, some businesses employ trading divisions in-house to speculate on price changes of products produced and distributed by other divisions of the company. Knowledge of operations in one part of the business is exploited for trading gains by another part. Capitalists will also assemble large firms by combining together small companies and breaking apart the same firms into smaller more specialized companies reaping investment banking and brokerage fees in both transactions. When firms are used in these ways, the respected business focus of material provisioning for society is undermined as entire, or portions of, companies are directed towards personal gain through trading or manipulation of assets and finance.[29]

13. Military Sacrifice. Hegemons throughout history ran expansionary and aggressive foreign policies. The American experience continues this tradition. Regardless of whatever benefits accrue to foreigners from hegemonic intervention, domestic costs to the hegemon's population are high.

Foreign adventures require huge budgetary outlays often dispersed over many years. Large budgets tend to redirect policymaker attention away from domestic social programs and festering long run policy concerns. But most important is the human sacrifice imposed on the population from military engagements. Great disruption in family and community life, and personal physical sacrifices, arise from the "call to duty." While foreign civilian sacrifices exceed those shouldered by people living in the hegemon, and while war is conducted away from the borders of the hegemon, imperialistic governments exploit the limited economic opportunities of a portion of its population to fill the most difficult and sacrificing jobs in the military.[30] Domestic anti-war/anti-globalization political agitation can grow, along with resentment for sheltered elites and the privileged.

Globalization can stall not just from rising uneasiness over the distributional system within major MDCs but from contention over "excesses" which ostensibly cause no immediate harm to anyone. Trading on inside information or extending options to executives shortly prior to public disclosure of favorable information [BW 6/26/06, 40] are examples. Multinational corporate pressure on LDC manufacturing to persistently lower costs is another. The first two activities can lead to higher asset prices and the third action seems to compel efficiency and lower MDC consumer prices. Generally improving asset and employment markets tend to quell criticism of questionable activities when everyone appears to gain; higher net worth for some, more jobs for others. Whether certain business practices, corrupt or otherwise, are masked by overall good economic performance or are simply made more palatable to some, belies the truth that no system can exist for long when the leadership conducts itself reprehensibly.

NOTES

1. This means that U.S. investors can easily own assets abroad denominated in foreign currencies while taking on liabilities to fund those assets denominated in American currency.

2. The US generated 45% of global consumption growth from 1996 through 2005, yet the US only accounts for 20% of global production [Samuelson 3/6/06]. On specific country current account positions, see IMF World Economic Outlook, 4/06, p.28.

3. One should note here that while elitist and more austere fiscal and monetary policies are viable for a time, this is only sustainable under certain conditions; currently these policies *appear to do no harm*, and may actually be *misperceived as causing* domestic economic success.

4. The generalized pattern is for English speaking, MDC capitalist economies to run current account deficits internationally and deficit financed consumption domes-

tically. Those countries with the biggest external deficits have declining saving rates, rising consumption to GDP, and the largest run up in asset prices [White 1/06, 11–12].

5. The 21st century may be characterized by energy price increases and energy supply instability due to increasing global oil demand and peaks in daily production output. Energy security is impacted by foreign policy conflicts [Roberts 2004].

6. Into 2007, MDC central banks and governments have kept credit conditions expansive.

7. And if a nation fails to successfully integrate old economy workers into the new economy or into middle class retirement.

8. See Palley's [1998] discussion of these issues in chapters 5 and 6.

9. Productivity increases are used to reduce public sector employment as well. See Financial Markets Center's Reserve Bank Pay & Staffing Trends: July 18, 2006. The Center states "Over the past half-decade, the Fed has eliminated almost one-fifth of the jobs at its regional Reserve Banks. Meanwhile, average pay levels have risen for the remaining employees and soared for Reserve Bank presidents, some of whom received huge one-year raises as the result of a 2005 change in compensation policy. A new FMC report has the details." http://www.fmcenter.org/atf/cf/{DFBB2772–F5C5-4DFE-B310-D82A61944339}/RBpay_staffing_0706.pdf

10. The Bush Administration asserts its opposition to minimum wage hikes because such increases supposedly undercut American company competitiveness, yet the Administration doesn't apply the same argument when hyping free trade bills that really do put American companies in a severe cost-competitive disadvantage globally.

11. Autor et al [2006] document the polarization of the U.S. labor market during the current era of globalization: high income wage inequality has steadily risen, low income wage inequality stopped rising in the 1990s, and employment growth largely occurring in high and low wage jobs at the expense of mid-level wage jobs. The authors attribute labor-demand shifts driven by technology change and outsourcing as important explanations for the polarization.

12. Because of more globally competitive product markets in this early phase of globalization three, price inflation is very moderate.

13. Productivity improvements limit job creation, or may undermine demand if the bulk of the improvement goes to capitalist income. Policymakers can overcome the employment-lessening effect of productivity increases by pursuing expansionary public policies. The era's price pressures assist in keeping demand up.

14. On business cycle analysis, see Van Lear [1999], Goldstein [1999], Sherman [1991].

15. A historical comparison is evident here. During the industrial era of the 19th century, great fortunes were amassed by corporate entrepreneurs whose money created finance capitalists out of successive generations of family members. This money became the capital that funded the "finance capitalism" period in Britain and America. The great surge in executive salary income during the last twenty-five years is fueling the current money manager era. The difference is that in the earlier period fortunes were amassed from creating and amalgamating industrial capital where in the current period it often comes from the reshuffling and redeployment of industrial capital.

16. Supportive empirical evidence for PC flattening is provided by The Economist magazine in the issue dated September 30, 2006, page 88.

17. G-5 refers to the Group of 5 major industrial nations. The group expanded to the G-7 and at times, the G-20.

18. How is it that argument can run counter to experience for so long in monetary policy matters? The world is a dynamic, complex place where not much is constant for long. Policymakers can use public confusion and causal uncertainties to justify the continued practice of harmful measures.

19. See Rodrik [1997] for a 1990s assessment of the consequences and policy implications coming from globalization.

20. CNN reported on June 22, 2006 that average American CEO income in 2005 was about $11 million and average worker pay was $42,000.

21. Takeover groups called private equity firms work with executive insiders to buyout public companies, take them private, revamp operations, and then offer these companies back to the general public [NPR 11/22/06]. To the extent that price appreciation is really due to effective restructuring, executives benefit from price appreciation that just as well could have occurred with the company in its original public ownership form had the executives done the job they were hired to do.

22. Despite Exxon Mobil's record profits from high oil prices in the mid 2000s and $27b in cash holdings, the firm's pension fund is $11b under-funded according to generally accepted accounting principles [BW 5/29/06, 36].

23. On compensation disparities, and balancing stockholder demands for pay for performance versus instilling incentives in top administrators, see BW, 2/26/07, pages 44 to 45.

24. See the series of articles under "Business Outlook" in Business Week magazine: May 15th, 22nd, June 12 2006, and the Charlotte Observer newspaper 5/13/06, page 4A.

25. See BW 4/10/06, pages 51–52 and the WSJ 12/27/06, page C1.

26. See "Monied Investors . . . " WSJ 10/26/06, C1,C4.

27. For an example of public reaction to oil industry profits, see Market Watch 4/26/06 and 4/27/06.

28. Sometimes the acquiring company issues bonds in its own name to pay dividends to itself and the acquisition's top executives prior to any effort to improve the target company's performance and in order to offset any losses in share prices upon sale to the public. The loans are paid off later in the IPO. See WSJ 4/13/07, pC1.

29. Examples abound. See WSJ 6/30/06 page A1, 6/30/06 page C1, and "Ahead of the Tape" 7/5/06 page C1. Also see WSJ "Cash Machine" 7/25/06 pA1. IMF economists report on this development and how it affects bondholders and corporate balance sheets in the April 2006 "Global Financial Stability Report," pages 16–20. Other ill effects include companies saddled with debt and employee layoffs or benefit cuts to shift cash flow to paying off debt.

30. The military acts as an "employer of last resort," and given the disruptive transformation in labor markets brought on by modern globalization, ample numbers of people exist to fill military needs.

Chapter Four

Global Central Banking

Monetary theory and policy have produced contending arguments about the role and effect of money in the economy. Disputes exist over monetary policy formulation and desired economic outcomes. The central banking that dominates capitalist economies today is founded on Classical economic thinking. But while rhetorically Classical, in practice policy tends toward a more activist Keynesian approach employing interest rate adjustments. This chapter describes modern central bank theory and policy in the current age of globalization, and then compares the conventional view with its critics. Contention exists over the adoption of targets, the specific effects of real world central bank policy, and whether policy should focus on controlling domestic inflation rates or fostering systemic financial stability.

The chapter moves on to describe the European Central Bank (ECB) and proposals for reform. The merits and demerits of the European Union and central banking in that region are examined. The chapter continues with more discussion of necessary reforms prompted by concerns for democratic input, stemming financial crises, and preventing income concentration. Keynes' understanding of proper central banking and its ineffectiveness during recessions is reviewed. Two basic kinds of central banks exist and their distinctive traits are compared.

The chapter ends with an exploration on contemporary policy difficulties for central banks. Inflation control is not possible, and continued unemployment-inflation tradeoffs persist,[1] requiring government-instituted incomes policies to address. International capital flows alter interest rates, currency values, and asset prices, complicating central bank policy. The conclusion surveys the findings and thoughts of reformers who in part desire a central bank employment target, adequate recognition of policy induced income distribution effects, and the need for a financial policy to replace the currently employed monetary policy practiced by central banks.

CONTEMPORARY CENTRAL BANKING

A consensus exists among classical economists that a central bank's top priorities should be to promote price stability and to avoid political influence. But a division exists over whether policymakers should have discretion in the conduct of policy formulation. Some classical economists argue that discretionary monetary policy tends to generate economic instability and inflation. Those who oppose discretion favor a rules-based policy that determines the interest rate or money growth that the central bank must set. Rule advocates believe that central bankers with discretion change policy too often in light of economic performance or events, producing inconsistency and unpredictability in policy. Any central bank with discretion is insufficiently committed to low inflation [McCallum 1989, chapter 12]. Policy based on defined rules prevents monetary policy itself from creating economic instability. Additionally, a rule-driven monetary policy prohibits government from financing its spending by printing money, thereby keeping government finance honest. By limiting inflation, money maintains its purchasing power and resources are not misallocated to placate special interests [Cox 1990; Hetzel 1997; Goodfriend 1997; Cukierman 1992].

Classical economists have derived various rules to guide monetary policy in a way to avoid inflation bias and political pressure. They believe that the quantity theory of money is the only useful framework for explaining why prices rise. Rules proposed by Classical economists are derivative of the principle that money growth explains the existence of inflation. In the money equation $M = m \sum MB$, where M stands for the money supply and MB for the monetary base, central banks control MB to control M, and thereby the inflation rate in the economy.

Nevertheless, many economists and policymakers are opposed to the rigidity imposed by rules and favor a discretionary monetary policy, independent of government, led by conservative central bankers committed to low inflation [Barro 1996]. And in fact, this is how central banking works. The quantity theory of money and the natural rate of unemployment concepts inform central bank policymaking. The quantity theory argues that money growth must be controlled to contain inflation. Growth in money determines growth in aggregate demand, the amount of total spending in the economy. If monetary policy tries to exploit the Phillips Curve tradeoff to drive unemployment below the natural rate, the lower rate obtained is unsustainable because it necessarily generates accelerating inflation.[2] An optimal policy would control bank reserves to align aggregate demand to the natural rate of unemployment. Whenever actual unemployment falls below the natural rate, policy should reduce bank reserves and raise interest rates. The aggregate supply curve is vertical at the natural rate of output, implying that economic growth cannot be pushed by greater aggregate demand unless preceded by an increased capacity to produce.[3]

In Figure 4.1, a central bank sets the interest rate (i) by determining the money supply Sm. The price level (P) in turn arises from a money growth driven aggregate demand (AD) intersection with a vertical aggregate supply (AS) at the natural rate of output (Onr).

For some economists, central banks have too liberally used their lender of last resort power, and have actually increased the likelihood of financial crises [Goodfriend and Lacker 1999; Symposium 1997]. Ostensibly to avert crises, lending to countries and companies tends to simply delay the failure of insolvent enterprises, ultimately increasing the total costs of bailouts and bankruptcies. Government or IMF lending also encourages moral hazard. This is behavior where companies or countries learn to take unduly high risks as fear of failure is diminished from official commitments to provide bailouts. With government money available, some firms take excessive risks to compensate for past losses, thereby increasing risks to creditors. Critics charge that central bank discretion and the ability to print money lead to excessive lending, inflation, and more instability than otherwise. Private lines of credit on the contrary are more carefully and prudently extended as private lenders are incentivized by the profit motive. Incentives to limit lending are weak in central banks.

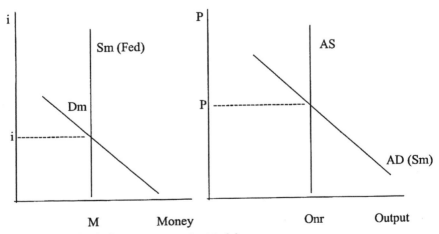

Figure 4.1. Classical Macroeconomics Model

Classical economists therefore advocate that central banks build a reputation of limited lending [Goodfriend 22–25]. Policymakers must take the position that liberal lending is counterproductive, and move to foster economic stability by encouraging less risk-taking within the private sector. A reputation of lending restraint would reduce financial crisis occurrences because the private sector could not count on central bank assistance in times of distress. A supplemental approach [Symposium 267–290, 294] is for central banks to rely on market discipline to limit excessive risk-taking. Specifically, competition creates failures, prompting more prudent behavior among remaining enterprises. An economic system open to failure produces fewer failures. Similarly, if banks had to fund some of their loans from uninsured capital, the providers of that capital would give oversight and discipline excessive risk-taking with higher interest rates.

ASSESSMENT OF CENTRAL BANKING

The classics favor banker financial interests as expressed in policies designed to control inflation to preserve the purchasing power of money and promote saving among the wealthy. Central bank independence from the government is seen as prudent and necessary. While classical central banking is typically described as policy constructed to address the broader public purpose, a real anti-government sentiment underlies the argument for a classically run monetary policy. Since most savings in capitalist countries is supplied by wealthy individuals and large corporations, not the general public, and given the staunch commitment to the ideas of a natural rate of unemployment, a high dollar value, and high interest rates, actual policy practice is very favorable to elite economic interests.[4]

Policy pronouncements coming from the U.S. central bank and empirical evidence demonstrate greater concern for and attention towards inflation minimization over job maximization. Despite low inflation, high consumer debt levels, a drop in growth, and availability of industrial capacity, the Fed's assessment of economic conditions justifying their policy is excerpted below from their public policy statement as reported by Market Watch [1/31/06] issued after the Fed made their 13th consecutive rate hike in January 2006:

The FOMC said inflation was low and inflation expectations remained contained. However, slack in the economy was disappearing, and could add to inflationary pressures, the committee said.

Since June 2004, the committee has been raising rates steadily in an effort to bring the federal funds rate to a more neutral level —that is, where rates are neither stimulating nor slowing growth.

The FOMC has been battling to keep core inflation within a comfort zone of about 1% to 2%. In the past year, core inflation has increased 1.9%, but the recent trend has seen inflation heat up to a 2.2% pace.

Meanwhile, growth dropped sharply in the fourth quarter to 1.1%, the slowest in three years. However, most economists believe the slowdown was a head-fake and that growth will return to a rate around 3.5%, close to the economy's potential.[5]

Looking ahead, the Bernanke Fed must deal with a slowing housing market, a large current account deficit and high household debt levels.

Empirical evidence demonstrates an inverse association existing between labor income growth and unemployment [Wachovia 2006]. Falling joblessness puts upward pressure on labor income as the unemployment pool of substitute workers contracts. Each time these variables move in labor's favor, recessions follow, partly driven by central bank policy. The Fed raised rates in the late 1980s, contributing to the 1990 downturn and slow recovery, and raised rates again in 2000, contributing to the 2001 recession and slow recovery. Both recessions reverse the favorable trends for labor. And despite no duplication of strong pro labor trends in jobs and income, and the Fed's own admission of low inflation, rate increases in 2005 and 2006 go into effect. In contrast, restrictive policy is not employed to moderate rapid increases in asset values or profits.

Wray's [2004] study of the Federal Reserve's decision-making process in the mid 1990s reveals that, while the Fed analyzes policy distribution effects, policy-makers avoid involving themselves in politically contentious debates concerning such issues. Minutes from meetings show that officials are aware that higher interest rates raise incomes of wealthy creditors at the expense of the indebted lower and middle classes. Policy positions show a bias toward profit income over wage income, and a more lenient stance on inflation driven by higher profit margins than inflation driven by rising employee compensation [21–24].

Two days after the Fed meeting in January 2006, business journalism [Market Watch 2/2/06] reported the following:

Unit labor costs—the cost of the labor used to make one "unit" of output—increased 3.5%, a stiff warning that inflationary pressures could be rising.

However, real hourly compensation (adjusted for inflation) fell 0.4% in the quarter. For 2005, real hourly compensation rose 1.8%, the fifth straight year below 2%.

Unit labor costs are up just 1% year-on-year, the slowest growth in six quarters.

The Fed is clearly concerned about rising unit labor costs because either profits will shrink or business will offset rising costs with price hikes. Lower profits hurt stock prices while inflation lowers the real value of payments made by business and consumers on financial liabilities to financial companies. Yet it is admitted that unit costs and the purchasing power of labor income are up little over the year. Data from Wachovia [2006] reveal that from 2001 through 2005, unit cost growth was often negative, and when positive, grew at less than 1% per year. Not only is core inflation low, but corporate price hikes exceed unit cost growth.

Class bias towards creditors is revealed in the following journalistic accounts of Federal Reserve policymaking:

> The boost in short-term rates will be reflected in higher costs for borrowers and greater returns for lenders and savers.

> Another factor given some weight by economists is that the new Fed chairman wouldn't mind pleasing the bond market. "There is a feeling that Ben Bernanke needs to show that he can be a tough guy and he needs to impress the bond markets by doing so," said Tannenbaum. A rate hike at the March meeting "would show he is going to focus on inflation and he could buy himself some credibility," Tannenbaum added.[6]

Despite how one may interpret Fed policy, intentions, and goals, central bank policies of credit restrictions and higher short term rates have little efficacy on inflation. Restrictive policy slows economic and employment growth, but offers little in the way of controlling inflation. Inflation arises from business price hikes. Price increases require firms to make decisions to do such. Only weak profit and sales conditions can compel business to change their pricing strategies. Central banks who desire price stability must necessarily curtail commercial vitality by raising borrowing costs. Prices are not likely to be raised in a dampened economic climate. There are contending economic interests, and central banks can choose a policy that creates a given balance of interests. Policymakers engaged in devising and critiquing the institutions of globalization must consider just what specific central bank functions and policy outcomes are desirable, and then design and implement the necessary institutions and policies.

Further insight to central bank policy under globalization is found from economic reports written by Classically-trained banking economists [The Bernanke Era Begins]. The following is one such excerpt:

> With resource constraints once again on the Fed's short list of concerns, one of the critical questions for Ben Bernanke to answer this week will be what measures of resource utilization will the Fed look to under his leadership to determine if the economy is bumping up against its long-term growth constraints? Specifically, will he focus on labor market indicators, such as the unemployment rate, pool of available workers and compensation costs or does he favor some sort of output gap measure? How he answers these questions will go a long way toward informing the financial markets what data to scrutinize in coming months.

> For many policymakers most labor market indicators are already at uncomfortably low levels. The unemployment rate has recently fallen to 4.7%, its lowest level since July 2001. By comparison, the average unemployment rate for the past 40 years has been 6%.Other measures of labor market strength are also flashing warning signs.

> The pressure on businesses to rein in benefit costs is a direct result of growing global competition, which has made it much more difficult for businesses to pass along their higher costs to their end-consumers. As a result, businesses have been striving to boost productivity and slash costs [Wachovia 2/13/06].

Consider the first paragraph above. First, economies have no real growth constraints; they can grow at double digits rates at times. Besides, investment in capital and infrastructure relax current capacity constraints. The modern U.S. average capacity utilization rate is 81%, and at the time of this writing, the current rate stood at 80.7%. Note that the inflation gauge is not inflation, but labor market conditions. The last sentence references that financial markets are monitoring monetary policy.

In the second paragraph, labor market conditions are expressed as worrisome. One might infer that unemployment at 6% is preferable to 4.7%. And the last paragraph remarks that globalization pressures companies to limit cost increases. Is Fed policy of credit restriction about making labor markets weak enough to prevent upward pressure on business expenses?

Central banks argue that capacity limits in economies require moderation in aggregate demand to prevent inflation. High interest rates are used to moderate demand. Yet production capacity is a function of business investment; there are not natural or predefined capacity limits to any economy.[7] The Federal Reserve Board's Federal Reserve Bulletin provides evidence that demand-driven production pulls up capacity [2006]. Firms react to higher profits and prices that occur concomitantly with rising production by investing in more capacity. The higher prices firms set help to finance plant expansion, yet central banks purposely try to prevent such an outcome.

Monetary policy thinking in Japan is revealing about the penchant to raise rates. Despite persistent mild deflation in the 2000s and low growth rates, the Bank of Japan is considering raising interest rates if "the economy's expansion is in place" and will do so "gradually regardless of price trends" [WSJ 4/30/07 A2].

One final point. Central bank policymakers tend to come from elite economic backgrounds, and are rather wealthy people. Their position, status, and wealth impact their thinking about the conduct of monetary policy. The Greenspan Fed consisted of several high income policymakers. Reports on the wealth of the new monetary chief Ben Bernanke confirm the tradition.

Ben Bernanke, President Bush's nominee to lead the Federal Reserve, is worth between $1.1 million and $5.6 million, according to his 2004 financial disclosure report. Most of the financial wealth he and his wife have accumulated are in a large retirement account and mutual funds, records show. The Bernankes own about 100 times as much as the typical American family. In 2000 (the most recent Census Bureau data), the median household net worth excluding home equity was $13,473 [MarketWatch 10/24/05]. Income disclosures by recent and new Fed members document multiple members with six figure incomes and assets in the multimillions [FMC 3/16/06]. Interestingly, people of prominence typically argue for minimal state interference in economic policy, unless that interference explicitly promotes elite interests. Central bank economic influence and political independence is well defended and conveniently divorced from the conventional wisdom that an activist state is invariably harmful.

And economic elites have various routes to affect policy outcomes at the American central bank. Five of the twelve voting members of the Fed's policymaking arm the FMOC are Federal Reserve Bank presidents. Reserve banks are privately owned by regional commercial banks that elect Reserve Bank boards who in turn elect Reserve Bank presidents. Moreover, the Federal Advisory Council (FAC) consists of banking CEOs who come from each of the Federal Reserve System's twelve districts and it meets four times a year with the Board of Governors who oversee central bank operations and monitor economic developments. The FAC-Board sessions are held in private and give the bankers an avenue to argue for particular banking and financial needs with the Fed's top leadership.[8]

Despite concerns in March 2006 of a housing market slowdown, consumer indebtedness, and manufacturing job losses, only moderately good employment and wage conditions provoke worry over inflation, as expressed in the following journalistic account of monetary policy and US economic performance:

> Despite unfavorable weather, U.S. nonfarm payrolls increased by a better-than-expected 243,000 in February, the Labor Department said Friday. The jobless rate ticked back up to 4.8% in February, from a five-year low of 4.7% in January. The number of unemployed people rose by 153,000 to 7.2 million. "The economy is still growing at an above trend pace and with slack in labor and product markets all but fully absorbed, inflation pressures will begin to gradually build this year," said Stephen Stanley, chief economist for RBS Greenwich Capital.

> Economists say the labor market is fundamentally sound. Payroll growth in December and January was revised lower by a total of 18,000. January's gain was cut from 193,000 to 170,000. Average hourly earnings increased by 5 cents, or 0.3%, in February to $16.47. Hourly earnings are up 3.5% in the past year, the fastest growth since 9/11. "With average hourly earnings suggesting that wage pressures are rising, this report will keep the Fed on the offensive against inflation pressures," said Drew Matus, an economist for Lehman Bros.

> The Federal Reserve is expected to raise its overnight interest-rate target to 4.75% on March 28. Fed officials are concerned that increased "resource utilization," especially in the labor market, could set off a spiral of wage and price increases. The Fed is expected to raise rates again in May, although officials are careful to not commit so far ahead, saying everything depends upon the incoming economic data [Market Watch 3/10/06].

Clearly, monetary economists are concerned about modest wage and employment growth, consider wage growth as inflationary (and are likely cognizant of income distribution implications of rapid wage growth), and are looking for excuses to slow economic activity prior to full employment. And what is not said is important: Profit growth[9] during the American economic recovery of 2002 through 2006 ranged from ten to thirty percent per year. The high rates of property income growth evoke no concern.

THE EUROPEAN CENTRAL BANK

The European Economic and Monetary Union (EMU) came into existence in 1999 and it represents a subset of nations of the larger European Union (EU). The Maastricht Treaty of 1991 establishes standards or criteria for EU nations to be admitted into the EMU. The Treaty requires that countries maintain price and exchange rate stability, limits on public debt and deficits, and long term interest rates reflective of price stability. National central banks (NCB) are to be independent of their respective governments. The Treaty centralizes a single monetary policy in the European Central Bank (ECB) while allowing individual nations to determine domestic fiscal policies. Once admitted, nations give up their currency for the EMU's single currency the Euro, and NCBs carry out ECB policy on interest rates.

The EU is a product of globalization. World economic integration is encouraging nations to create regional free trade zones where capital flows freely across borders. Europe has taken economic relations beyond regional zones to greater integration. The integration effort is also directed at promoting European economic prosperity and greater European world competitiveness by expanding markets for firms within Europe. The EU accomplishes several objectives. Exchange rate instability, currency speculation, and transactions costs among member countries are greatly reduced through the single currency in the EMU. Economic integration is encouraged with the elimination of tariffs and quotas, and restrictions on emigration. A national security objective is sought as well through the EU as increased integration and interdependency should greatly diminish incentives towards war among member nations. The European Commission promotes uniform regulatory standards across member EU countries.

Despite these apparent benefits from the Union, institutional defects avail themselves. First, national monetary and fiscal policies are divorced in that the ECB conducts Euro-wide monetary policy while the individual states set their own fiscal policies. No policy coordination is assured here. The implication is that member country governments no longer have central banks independent of the ECB, and therefore cannot count on their central banks to freely augment the money supply by buying country government bonds. A second problem arises from the "Stability and Growth Pact" (SGP), signed in 1997, which conforms to Maastricht Treaty economic criteria. This pact stipulates limitations to the size and hence stimulus of national budget deficits. Though economic conditions may warrant a public policy stimulus, exceeding the Pact's set limits subjects countries to fines or expulsion from the Union. These two problems create then a third issue. Given the existence of regional and country socio-economic divergences, owing to the fact that the EMU consists of countries with separate development and policy histories, no single monetary policy can possibly be right for all countries at the same time. The divorce of national monetary policy from fiscal policy, and Pact limits on national deficits, undermine policymakers' abilities to address both national economic conditions and national divergences effectively and in a timely way. The EU's goal of creating integration with prosperity is thus thwarted to some extent.

EMU public policy is consistent with pressures emanating from modern globalization to adopt Classical economic policies and beliefs. Free trade, privatization, and less and/or uniform regulation are now the established doctrine for any globalizing country. And as argued by Arestis and Sawyer [2002], the ECB, as well as the British central bank, set inflation targets and have price stability as the only official goal. Government budget deficits are eschewed and should not be funded with money creation. Monetary policy is believed to be powerless in affecting unemployment and must remain independent from political pressures, regardless of social conditions. Relatively high interest rates and restrictive credit conditions are maintained. This puts much of Europe under increasingly competitive and on-going deflationary influences,[10] reflected in growing inequality and stubbornly high unemployment rates [Palley 1998].

ECB policy in effect substitutes for a more public, democratically accountable incomes policy potentially arising from a coordinated European national government policy. The Bank's sole mandate is to achieve price stability, and the current theory used to explain the inflation process is a cost driven, that is wage driven, inflation explanation. The ECB therefore keeps interest rates sufficiently high to produce a less than full employment level of spending throughout the EMU zone. The resulting economic slack dampens wage pressures and keeps wage growth at or below productivity growth. Since labor needs a continuingly robust economy to accelerate wage growth, and high rates prevent such circumstances from being possible, monetary policy is affecting the distribution of income among earners of interest, wages, and profits.

REFORMING CENTRAL BANK POLICY

The third era of globalization is subject to financial crises stemming from rapid capital flow reversals and currency speculation. Altering central bank thinking and practice to fit the modern age is essential if policymakers desire globalization's economic advance to warrant continuance and wide support. Central banking can even promote democracy and relative equality, further solidifying popular support.

In The General Theory originally published in 1936, Keynes agrees with the Classics that the central bank can determine the supply of money and set interest rates, but differs from them on policy effectiveness. That is, circumstances can arise which reduce a central bank's ability to affect economic activity. For example, a dismal "state of credit" might lead banks to cut off credit, or desires to increase liquidity within the private sector would reduce borrowing and spending. These situations would undermine any central bank's ability to resuscitate an economy, no matter how low interest rates go. In fact, market rates may rise even as policymakers take actions to inject funds. As a matter of routine policy, Keynes wanted the central bank to pursue low rates because they are helpful in maintaining loan demand and spending; and in order to assist and complement monetary policy, Keynes made the case for the state to augment the supply of capital to put downward pressure on rates of interest [chapters 22, 24].

State intervention becomes necessary as a way to reduce the power of creditors who keep capital scarce. Keynesian economists argue that investment determines the level of savings and investment is enhanced from a low rate of interest.[11] There is no intrinsic reason for the scarcity of capital that keeps interest rates up to a level that prohibits full employment. Keynes says specifically that "it will still be possible for communal savings through the agency of the state to be maintained at a level which will allow the growth of capital up to a point where it ceases to be scarce." Keynes argues for the state to affect the propensity to spend through taxation and fixing the rate of interest in order to affect the aggregate amount of economic activity [375–378]. In this way, the state can increase the volume of investment and therefore affect employment levels, without directing the allocation of investment or owning enterprises.

From Keynes' perspective, central bankers should have discretion over what policy tools to use and when, but be constrained by government as to what goal or goals to meet. That is, technical policy decisions are to be left to central bank determination, but the larger socio-macroeconomic goals that the central bank is to achieve are decided by the democratically elected members of government. This reasoning is consistent with a general societal commitment to democracy.

Bibow [2001] describes the Keynsian vision:

As Keynes saw it, Parliament's role was to lay down the basic currency laws, whether gold or some price index should be the standard, for instance. The Government of the day's prerogative then was to determine the "main lines of policy," that is, the ultimate aims or goals of policy, to be pursued by the central bank. In addition, Keynes stressed the role of transparency, emphasizing that the central bank's conduct "should be deliberately exposed to outside criticism." Supposing that these various checks were in their proper place, the balancing principle in Keynes's envisaged form of democratic control reads: "The less direct the democratic control and the more remote the opportunities for parliamentary interference with banking policy the better it will be". Expressed in modern terminology, Keynes favoured instrument but not goal independence based on indirect democratic control and accountability. Legislated rules that hindered the operational powers of the central bank were undesirable, in his view. Instead, the technicians' overall scope for discretion would be constrained by goal dependence, stringent transparency requirements, and accountability. The central bank technicians would neither be elected by, nor directly accountable to, the public though. In this arrangement, the line of accountability for performance on the Government's remit would run from the central bank to the Government of the day, which in turn would be accountable to Parliament on overall economic policy performance, and thereby to the electorate. The government's "main lines of policy" would also provide the forum for policy coordination [5–7].

But policy goals of openness and full employment that lack efforts to stabilize global economic activity are inadequate. The Minskian thesis on central banking [1986, 313–338] exemplifies an approach to lessen a capitalist economy's proneness to financial instability by modifying the way a central bank operates. This thesis has its necessary extension to the globalization of capitalist economies. Current central bank practice to affect reserve levels to influence bank lending and deposit creation is open market operations. Banking subjects the economy to instability when the profit motive encourages banks to significantly increase loans relative to equity. Surges in bank lending can lead to inflationary and destabilizing increases in business and consumer spending. Moreover, during strong business cycle upturns fueled by bank credit, increasing numbers of banks are financing highly leveraged private sector borrowers. Leveraged operations dependent on short-tern debt are vulnerable to interest rate spikes. Financial fragility arises when rising interest expenses and falling cash flows conspire to deprive borrowers of the means to repay liabilities. International financial crises produce the same results from deflation and falling currency values.

Therefore, central banks around the world need new powers and a new operating procedure. Applying Minsky to international economics, central banks should take action to restrain bank lending during booms, booms brought about by globalization's third wave. Policymakers could essentially require banks to raise more investor funds relative to loans as expansions encourage deficit financing among borrowers. A new operating procedure that allows central banks to steer the evolution of their country's financial system by co-financing selected, low risk business debt would promote more stable expansions. Central banks should downplay the importance of traditional open market operations where activity is conducted in government debt. As an economic expansion wears on, government debt becomes less important on bank balance sheets and business loans become more important. In order to avoid a fragile financial structure from developing, central banks can lend reserves to sustain the expansion by "hedge-financing" private business, or in other words, financing firms not heavily in debt and whose cash flow can meet payment commitments.

The Minskian approach sees the money supply as largely endogenous. Private sector credit demands, not central banks, determine bank money creation. The demand for loans makes banking profitable, and banks supply deposits or money to borrowers who meet credit requirements. Therefore, new money is pulled into the economy by borrowers who are granted loans, and this "endogeneity of money" makes it *impossible for the central bank to control the money stock*. The Fed can only set interest rates by adjusting bank reserves; it cannot determine money growth. In the money equation $M = m \sum MB$, the direction of causation is now reversed, in that changes in M cause changes in MB; the monetary authority supplies reserves to accommodate loan demand at the policy rate set by the Authority.

In Figure 4.2, central banks supply reserves to banks along a flat supply of reserves curve (Sr), and they set the policy rate (pr) by equating banks' demand for reserves (Dr) with the reserve supply curve. Banks in turn set their lending rate (il) as a mark-up over the pr, and supply loans (new money) basically to all borrowers at that rate [Moore 1988]. As aggregate demand (AD) drives economic expansion, loan demand (Dl) rises. And as prices begin to rise and borrowers become increasingly debt dependent, risk rises. At this juncture, the bank loan supply curve turns upward and banks charge borrowers higher loan rates. Higher rates result as well from restrictive central bank policy that elevates the policy rate.

Table 4.1 identifies the main features that differentiate a Classically oriented central bank (CB) from a reformed Bank based on a Keynesian and Minskian design.

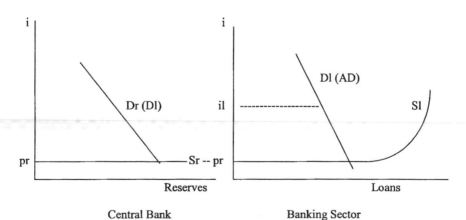

Figure 4.2.   The Endogenous Money Macro Model

Table 4.1.   Central Bank Model Comparisons

Criteria	Classical CB	Reformed CB
Inflation	High priority	Low priority
Unemployment	Pursue the natural rate of unemployment	Pursue a full employment level of jobs
Growth	Pursue non-inflationary growth	Achieve and maintain growth to create employment
Money supply (M)	Problems: Too much money growth & policy discretion	Problems: Too little M growth & private concentration of capital
Policy Procedure	Independent Quantity theory of M Limit bank reserves	A state function Endogenous money Liquefy banks
Interest rates	Set high	Set low
Dollar value	Set high	Set low
Class	Bias towards elite financial interests	Favors business and labor Interests
Government	Anti	Pro

CENTRAL BANK CONUNDRUMS

Globalization has made central bank policy more complicated. Policymakers cannot be focused solely on domestic conditions. Though exchange rates are flexible, obviating intervention to sustain fixed relations among currency values, globalization nonetheless creates a series of problems to confront.

Conundrum #1: Controlling Inflation in A Global Environment

With economic integration across nations, global conditions and pressures increasingly affect domestic finance. Global trade, investment, and finance influence national situations as nation state economies become more interdependent and open to global trends. While government mandates or Classical theory push central banks to control domestic inflation, the practice of monetary policy is one of adjusting domestic bank liquidity to affect short term interest rates. Moreover, global competition creates some volatility in prices, and through the effects of technology and productivity growth, competition often exerts downward pressure on prices. In fact, central banks must be vigilant with respect to offsetting deflation tendencies, as experienced in parts of depressed Europe and Japan.

In addition to global influences, domestic rate changes affect borrowing costs and spending, but allow for no direct influence on economy-wide prices and inflation. Central banks simply cannot perform the function granted them, namely to set the price level by controlling money growth. If we assume that policymakers can control the supply of money, such control does not afford control over inflation. For monetary control to affect inflation, the national economy and the global economic system would have to consist of millions of commodity or auction markets where prices are actually set by industry-independent demand and supply forces, not transnational corporate affected economic conditions. Producer and retail prices represent the outcomes of corporate planning and policy decisions, and marketing influences, not market forces. Thus to stem inflationary pressure, policymakers can only indirectly do so by reducing national economic activity by forcing up borrowing costs. Once profit and job growth are negatively affected and defaults increase for a sufficient time period, lackluster economic conditions can prompt firms to moderate price hikes.

Furthermore, in modern economies, inflation is largely structural. Most inflation occurs within the health care, education, and energy sectors. Health care and education systems are not subject to much productivity growth, and are very labor intensive. Competition tends to raise costs, not lower them. And these markets are rather unique in their supply and demand configurations, making them prone to inflation.[12] The energy industry remains subject to price-setting country producers and supply disruptions. There is then no way for any central bank to effectively address inflation that has structural causes, particularly cross-border structurally induced price pressures.

Moreover, no central bank can really control the domestic money supply let alone the world money supply. Most money is in the form of checking accounts or deposits denominated in domestic currency. Banks create money when granting loans by simply crediting a borrower's account, thereby providing a spendable deposit. Banks grant loans based on the economic viability of and demand for credit by consumers and business. In other words, world economic conditions drive lending; the more spending there is, the greater the money creation to fund the spending.[13] Policy resistance to capitalist finance demands would run counter to central banks historical mandate to foster commerce and would create a financial crisis if loan growth is heavily constrained. Policymakers are left with setting short-term market rates [Wray 1998] and therefore with substantial imprecision and time lag, attempt to control globally influenced domestic inflation by influencing domestic economic activity.

Conundrum #2: Managing Inflation and Unemployment Simultaneously

All central banks face a tradeoff between unemployment and inflation in their own countries. The Phillips Curve displays this tradeoff. Rising demand prompts more job creation, but as unemployment falls, costs of production and business pricing power rise. After some point, an improving business climate produces some increase in inflation. Avoidance of the dilemma is possible only with an incomes policy. Policies directed at affecting income distribution attempt to keep wage and profit growth in line with productivity improvements. That is, income payments are kept in line with the increase in production so that a conflict over income shares is avoided.[14]

Therefore, any efforts to employ monetary policy, which can only affect the level of economic activity, will result in moving the economy from one point to another along the tradeoff. Globalization has assisted, not hindered, central banks by putting downward pressure on inflation. Higher world competition, greater job insecurity and productivity, and increased numbers of oil producers, have pushed inflation lower for any level of national unemployment.[15] Nevertheless, world economic conditions and the degree of openness affect where any individual economy lies along its own national tradeoff curve.

Conundrum #3: Managing Economic Growth in the Face of Interest and Exchange Rate Changes

Central banks operate in a globally interconnected economic environment. Unencumbered capital flows, financial market deregulation, and market openings describe the current landscape. Fast changing and fast flowing money across borders undercuts policymakers' abilities to regulate domestic interest rates and set exchange rates.

America is a driving force in globalization. Its large current account deficits feed export oriented growth in Asia and elsewhere. Surpluses earned from trade are deposited around the globe, searching for the highest returns. These capital flows into country financial and real estate sectors supplement domestic saving flows. They often magnify trends in savings flows and asset prices. Incoming capital to bond markets elevates bond prices and lowers interest rates. Global capital flows alter domestic financial conditions, pressuring central banks to take offsetting policy measures. Efforts to control domestic variables and the value of currency can be frustrated, overwhelmed both by the magnitude and speed of foreign capital movements.

The so-called "Greenspan conundrum" is due to the above forces. Incoming capital to the American economy counters the affect of the Fed raising its policy rate. In the past, the American economy was less affected by capital flows, allowing for a rising federal funds rate and economic growth to raise short and long term domestic interest rates. But capital inflows hold down long rates, attracted by U.S. growth prospects and country diversification needs, despite tightening credit conditions for short term loans. The yield curve flattens instead of keeping its typical positive slope.[16]

Complicating policy is that there exists no definitive relationship between domestic interest rates and exchange rates. Take for example a net capital flow into a country. The inflow eases domestic financial conditions but may either increase or decrease the nation's currency value. Because of an economic upturn, the exchange rate may rise, offsetting the stimulus from lower interest rates. Alternatively, lower rates, rising debt levels, and inflation cause the exchange rate to fall, causing higher exports to amplify the domestic upturn in commercial activity. The proper policy course necessitates patience to see what happens to the exchange rate and judgment about the level of stimulus desired and prospects for economic stability.

The US Federal Reserve admits to globalization causing policy difficulty, though without suggesting that some alternative policy or institution supplant central bank policy preeminence.

China's policy of buying dollar assets to keep its currency tied to the dollar masks U.S. financial-market conditions and heightens the risk of inflation in the United States, said New York Fed President Timothy Geithner on Thursday. China's purchases of U.S. dollar assets could spur inflation by putting downward pressure on U.S. interest rates and producing more expansionary financial conditions than fundamentals warrant.

The Fed must respond to these inflationary forces, Geithner said.

Fed officials continue to be puzzled by the current market environment of low world interest rates, low risk premiums and large global imbalances, Geithner said. This economic picture was labeled a "conundrum" by former Fed chief Alan Greenspan. Most of the factors that created these conditions are outside the control of Fed policy, and Fed officials don't fully understand their implications, Geithner said.

In January, China released figures showing its foreign-exchange reserves hit a record $818.9 billion last year, an increase of 34% from a year earlier. About 70% of these reserves are thought to be invested in dollar-denominated assets. On the other hand, the U.S. current-account deficit for 2005 is expected to total more than $700 billion. China is not the only culprit. A steady inflow of dollars is also coming into the U.S. from oil-producing countries. Geithner said these flows are large enough to "distort the relationship between asset prices and the underlying fundamentals in our economies."

That makes the Fed's job tougher by increasing the difficulty of assessing whether current monetary policy is restrictive or accommodative, Geithner said [Market Watch 3/9/06].

Conundrum #4: Setting Policy During Asset Price Booms

Consumption and overall demand levels in countries throughout the world during the third era of globalization are driven by persistent upward trends in domestic asset prices in Anglo-American economies. In the 1990s the stock market boomed and in the early 21st century the housing market provided levitation to household spending. Central banks and commercial banks facilitated this climate by trending interest rates lower and easing financing conditions. High American spending drives trading partner exports and economies, and supplies increasing dollar reserves to the global system.

However, to avoid a US and a world recession, the Fed must continue to nurture the boom with low lending rates, fueling asset price appreciation. The more the asset values appreciate, the greater the advance in household net worth and hence in household spending. Yet asset markets are subject to excessive speculation and overvaluation that sets the stage for a collapse in values, negatively affecting the economy. All along household deficit spending raises debt commitments, making borrowers less sensitive to higher financing costs. But raising interest rates to avoid an asset bubble slows economic activity and risks recession from debt defaults. So how should the Fed proceed? Should interest rates be lowered or raised?

Countries that exploit globalization to rapidly develop must maintain "undervalued" exchange rates to foster current account surpluses, no matter how hot running are their domestic economies and asset markets. Emerging market central banks are reluctant to take any steps to moderate domestic conditions, even in the face of financial fragility and asset bubbles, where strong absorption of unemployed people into the modern economy is required. Central banks face this environment in China and India. Alternatively, the ECB and the BOJ face no such policy difficulty. Both Europe and Japan are burdened by intractable domestic aggregate demand weakness.[17] Their domestic and international situations do not create a contradictory policy environment. Given the Maastricht Treaty's mandated price stability objective, the ECB is limited in its ability to encourage asset price inflation to stimulate domestic spending. And in Japan, their asset price collapse is so substantial that zero interest rates are unable in any timely fashion to reinvigorate economic growth or produce a reversal in their stock market.

Conundrum #5: Managing Domestic Inflation in Divergent Environments of Global Economic Risk

Though modern monetary policy is fixated on inflation, policymakers must take into account the prevailing economic conditions of risk. Whether inflation is high or low, risk conditions can vary. High risk implies weak cash flows and balance sheets of agents or economy-wide vulnerability to capital outflows, while low risk implies the opposite. The matrix in Table 4.2 identifies four possible situations.

Table 4.2.   Inflation—Risk Policy Options for Central Banks

	Low Inflation	High Inflation
Low Risk	Anglo-America, EU	Large Oil Consuming Nations, 1970s
High Risk	Emerging Markets	Russia 1990s, Germany 1920s

Emerging markets often have low or relatively low inflation but are subject to the vicissitudes of capital flows, and therefore represent high risk economies. Russia in the 1990s suffered from high inflation, indebted firms and government, and depression, and therefore presented high risk to investors. But what should central bankers do in cases of low risk economic environments but where inflation is higher than target or within the targeted range? If the first case exists, bankers raise rates to force inflation to recede but often create sluggish or recessionary economies and must then reverse policy. Policy reduces growth to get inflation lower but necessarily raises economic risk to achieve the inflation objective. An MDC economy is made to resemble the risk (at least temporarily) of an emerging market economy. If case two exists, policymakers face a benign economy for awhile, but eventually, in seeking higher returns, the financial industry induces economic risk. Low risk-low inflation environments often offer low bond yields, and exhibit strong cash flows and balance sheets. Investors play this situation by taking on what is traditionally thought to be more risky assets and strategies to grasp for higher returns that appear in that environment to be safer than normal. Hence the policy intention of maintaining low risk is subverted by the profit motive and again a developed economy can be made to mimic the risk of an emerging market system.

What are central bankers to do? The next part of this chapter supplies a solution.

CONCLUSION

Actual central bank practice during globalization runs counter to the underlying theory that is supposed to inform policy. Despite Classical principles, policy has been rather active and Keynesian at a number of central banks. There are good reasons to practice active monetary policy. First, the experience of many dozens of international financial crises, banking problems, and commercial recessions since 1980 demonstrate an inherent instability in a globalization that is unmanaged. No intervention means allowing these negative experiences to be more severe and longer in duration. Second, to some extent, policymakers are held responsible for and their reputations depend on effective policy. That means they must conduct policy successfully to prevent or minimize economic distress. Failure to do so is professional failure. The BoJ has committed itself to maintaining a liquid financial sector and assisting the removal of nonperforming loans from bank balance sheets. Despite an inflation target and operational independence at the BoE, the Bank has effectively and flexibly applied rather Keynesian activism during UK economic slumps [Mihailov 2006]. The US central bank since the late 1980s has implemented expansionary policies to ward off negative effects of stock market declines, global economic instability, and domestic job growth weakness. While rhetorically making inflation fighting a high priority, the Fed practices a flexible policy driven by circumstances. Evolving monetary policy doctrines provide guidance to Fed policymaking, and policy "appears to be governed largely . . . by the main imperatives of the post-inflation era" [Galbraith 2006, 432].

Should a central bank raise interest rates to fight energy-price inflation? Absolutely not; in fact, rates should be lowered. Because economies are built around oil, energy buyers are highly dependent on the continued access to oil's derivative products. Demand is inelastic in that price hikes largely direct more consumer expenditures to energy and away from other industries and products. Aggregate profits and sales decline and higher income flows to energy companies. Oil price hikes slow economic activity overall, and therefore, interest rates need to fall to offset the drag on demand. Furthermore, if rates are increased during debt driven investment booms, the higher energy and financing costs feed through to more generalized inflation. When central banks fight energy price inflation by raising rates, policymakers create a greater slowdown, and may even cause stagflation as energy prices force retail prices higher as output declines.[18]

A symposium on central banking, employing empirical evidence from numerous countries, offers breadth of critique [JPKE summer 2006]. The symposium produces evidence and argument against modern efforts to impose rules on policymakers and on how inflation concerns dominate policy discussion and action. A summary of their findings is instructive. World inflation rates show a downward trend prior to the imposition of inflation targeting, so Classical policy should not be credited much for inflation control. Causes of inflation are rooted in cost pressures and an income distribution struggle among people, making reliance on interest rate management ineffective on inflation and damaging to employment and business sales growth. Inflation can arise as well from higher corporate markups and from currency depreciation that raises import prices. Modest inflation is associated with gains in output and efforts to maintain very low inflation harm growth. Central bank inflation-focused policy lowers income shares to labor and entrepreneurs, and monetary policy ought to have an employment target replace their inflation target. Instead of employing policies to create insufficient effective demand to fully employ everyone, governments must takeover inflation control. This can be done by maintaining buffer stocks or inventories of key inputs whose supply can be increased by public policy when private market conditions create shortage-induced inflation. An approach to contain cost-push/income distribution struggle inflation is an incomes policy that encourages the private sector to match income increases with productivity improvements.

A complementary paper arguing for a complete overhaul in global central banking is from Tymoigne [2006]. Central banks should drop traditional monetary policy aimed at price stability and adopt a financial policy directed at maintaining international financial stability. Traditional policy is completely misdirected. Inflation largely does not have a monetary cause and short term interest rate adjustments have no direct effect on business pricing. Frequent rate changes create volatile expectations and trading in financial markets. Given central bank ineffectiveness in fighting inflation, policy should be aimed at creating stable financial markets to induce stable commerce. Central banks should employ "systemic risk analysis" to evaluate global financial conditions, watching for conditions that could disrupt stable and growing economies. In sum, Tymoigne argues that central banks must:

1. Continue lender of last resort operations.
2. Continue supervision and regulation of financial institutions and markets.
3. Anchor private financial decisions buy guiding portfolio strategies and lending practices.
4. Cooperate with financial institutions to achieve a financial policy that stabilizes markets.

BIS economist William White [4/06] argues for essentially the same kind of reform where central banks become more concerned about financial imbalances and construct longer policy time horizons. The current policy focus on inflation is myopic and aggressively easing policy after economic downturns or asset price declines begin creates conditions for financial imbalances. He criticizes policymakers for not distinguishing between benign deflations brought on by productivity improvements and those from demand deficiencies. Policy is tightened only when overt inflations signs appear, not asset price booms or high leverage. For White, inflation-based policy has a destabilizing effect on the financial system. White wants central banks to examine financial stability indicators to avoid the build up of systemic instability over time.

NOTES

1. The tradeoff is not rigid but exists nonetheless.

2. The Phillips Curve relates inflation to unemployment. Keynesian theory holds that as spending drives economic activity, unemployment falls as jobs are created to meet consumer demands for goods. But as the system nears full employment, firms raise prices because demand is so buoyant and costs are rising. Therefore, unemployment and inflation are indirectly related.

3. The economy's AS curve is the production in the economy. In Classical theory, an economy grows by increasing production, generating an accommodating level of total spending (AD) to buy the products made.

4. The maintenance of a high dollar value and a natural rate of unemployment create some employment insecurity and intensify competition among workers for a shortage of jobs.

5. Policy efforts to hold back capital investment actually reduce the economy's total productive capacity or potential that officials seem to fear is rather limited.

6. For the first account, see Market Watch "FOMC Raises Rates . . ." 3/28/06, and the second account see Market Watch "Fed Likely to Tap on Brakes" 3/25/06.

7. Both Russian and Chinese economic experience supports this notion. Since the economic difficulties of the 1990s and the 1998 financial troubles, Russia has achieved substantial economic growth coming from strong export earnings and an investment boom. Chinese rapid growth is fueled by high domestic investment, money growth, and burgeoning trade surpluses. Despite 5% to 8% growth rates, Russia is experiencing declining inflation and Chinese inflation is usually ranging below 4% since the 1990s. See WSJ 3/13/07, pages A1 and A21, and Wachovia's "Russian Chart-book" March 26, 2007 on Russia, and Wachovia's Economic Group research report "Weekly Economic and Financial Commentary," March 16, 2007, and BCA Research, "Feature Stories," March 19, 2007 for data and discussion about Chinese performance. BCA also confirms that as a group, emerging market economies have generally experienced strong private demand growth with a strong secular decline in core price inflation from the late 1990s through to early 2007 [5/4/07].

8. The Financial Markets Center's website contains summaries of FAC meetings which are released to the public on request after a three-year time lag. See http://www.fmcenter.org/site/pp.asp?c=8fLGJTOyHpE&b=224876.

9. Profit data comes from the Wachovia Economics Group's "Economic Outlook: A New York State of Mind," January 18, 2007.

10. High interest rates and very low inflation keep the Euro's value high and hence make European exports less competitive on world markets.

11. Low rates foster more borrowing which augments investment that raises income and in turn savings.

12. Demands in these sectors are insensitive to higher prices and expansion of supply is expensive.

13. This makes money growth endogenously driven, and not exogenously controllable.

14. Classical theory rejects explicit government incomes policies but implicitly accepts central bank monetary policy affects on income distribution.

15. On this matter, see Thurow [1996, chapter 9].

16. The yield curve shows interest rate levels compared to the time duration of debt securities. The greater the term of the bond, the higher the rate in order to compensate security holders for rising risk and time commitment of money.

17. Central banks operating in countries where large current account imbalances exist confront a policy challenge. The U.S. case is instructive [Palley blog 10/23/05]. For Palley, the historically low interest rates foster US commercial activity while the unprecedented trade deficit and debt magnitudes tend to push the value of the U.S. dollar down. But the required monetary policy must be to keep rates up to incentivize foreigners to continue their purchases and holdings of American assets. And a strong dollar encourages continued American foreign investment and purchases of foreign goods.

18. Empirical evidence does not show any consistent correlation of energy price inflation to economic growth rates. See the work on the U.S. economy's resiliency to energy price spikes in Dhawan and Jeske [2006].

Chapter Five

The International Financial System

Since the end of WWII, globalization has continued apace. But the current era differs from the Bretton Woods period in that exchange rates among most countries are flexible and that capital moves across borders with little impediment. The U.S. driven globalization of the Second Era has expanded into whole new areas of the world with the ending of communism, enticing newly freed nations to integrate into the global financial system and become emerging markets. The dollar, euro, pound, and yen are the major currencies for transactions and reserves, and countries acquire these currencies by opening their economic systems to MDC FDI and orienting their commercial sector for export-driven growth.

The growing volume of global activity is handled through the globalization of money markets, the expansion of financial institutions and technology, and the development of new financial products and services. The foreign exchange market is a twenty-four hour, liquid, integrated, largely unregulated, market where the dollar is the most widely traded currency. Banks are major players in currency markets, and exchange rates among countries are not just affected by relative economic performance but capital flows driven by sentiment and expectations concerning economic fundamentals and public policy [King and King 2005, 243–264]. The current financial system works effectively in promoting international commerce, lending, and speculation. Nevertheless, the current system can be afflicted with excessive speculation, volatile exchange rates, and financial crises. Financial system difficulties cause disruptions in business activity and employment, and affect income inequalities and social conditions.

FINANCIAL AND ECONOMIC STRESSES

Competing explanations prevail that encompass economists' concerns, insights, and observations about how the international financial system causes, and is affected by, global political economic forces.

Deflationary Forces

This argument stresses the importance of the interplay between excess global production capacity and restrictive public policies followed at times by policymakers in large economies [White 2006, 5–6]. The 1990s decade began with recessions occurring in major economies, and declines in investment spending in Japan and Germany. Financial crises reduce demand in East Asia and fiscal austerity policies in the EMU reduce demand there as well. This demand deficiency coincides with increasing economic development in and output from India and China searching for markets. Productivity advances, driven by corporate management and technology, increase output. Large increases in labor supply arising from emerging market economies and a weakened labor negotiating position throughout the world cut business costs but demand too. The confluence of these forces creates excess production capacity, pressuring prices and profits downward. With demand unable to meet output capabilities, transnational firms merge and shrink capacity in line with market share. Layoffs and streamlined operations amplify deflationary pressures. Modern finance counters deflationary forces to some extent by expanding credit extension and raising financial asset values supportive of consumption.

Financial Market Liberalization

This argument focuses on how a deregulated global financial system contributes to heighten risk taking [White 2006, 7–8, Symposium 1997]. Liberalization refers to the deregulation and privatization of financial markets, where investors have more freedom to pursue profitable trading and funding activities. As freedom of activity grows, competition increases among participants for better yield and profit. If occurring during a period of change and evolution in economic life, greater freedom and competition take place in unfamiliar circumstances. New regulation, unimpeded capital flows, new financial vehicles and institutions alter the landscape for finance. The financial system is more complex and dynamic, and risk is often shifted and shared, making policy assessment of overall global risk more difficult. Together these developments enhance risk and encourage riskier, more speculative behavior among investors.

Global internal and External Imbalances

This theory argues that there is an unsustainable and unstable economic pattern developing between domestic budget balances and trade balances [White 2006, 11–12; Thurow 2003, 229–236]. Government budget deficits and consumer deficit spending in Anglo-American capitalist economies are generating domestic economic growth and resultantly trade deficits as private sector purchases of imports exceed exports. Emerging market (EM) economies in many cases benefit as reflected in growing current account surpluses; their surpluses mirror MDC deficits. Developing nations lure MDC FDI seeking low cost production, pumping more money into countries in surplus. Net cash inflows in EM economies are often invested back into trade deficit nations, lowering borrowing costs and fueling spending. The argument continues that these growing imbalances threaten world economic activity. Either lenders will reallocate asset holdings to reduce risk through diversification or simply stop lending because of perceived risk. Alternatively or simultaneously, MDC debtors will end their borrowing and deficit spending as indebtedness rises above perceived safety thresholds. The consequence of all of this is world recession due to the cessation of increasing symbiotic money flows among the world's key trading partners.

Pro-cyclical Finance

This theory argues that booms in financial markets facilitate strong upturns in business activity which then positively feed back onto financial markets. While movements in financial capital depend on concrete, factual differences in risk and return across asset classes, psychology and emotion too affect these flows [Kindleberger 1978]. Strong upward trends in asset values are typically mutually affected by expectations and facts, creating a reinforcing effect on the current trend. More money is attracted into financial markets in the wake of repeated capital gains and easy credit conditions, furthering the levitation in asset values. Consumer and business investment spending are helped from supportive financial conditions. Commercial sales and profit performance, and mergers and acquisitions, spill back onto the financial sector, encouraging further run-ups in asset valuations. Invariably, asset prices overshoot the underlying economic fundamentals that justified the initial increase in stock and bond markets. A psychology of optimism becomes euphoria that generates financial asset valuations that are not sustainable.[1] These market bubbles burst as investors increasingly realize they own assets in an over-bought, hyped market, so they begin to sell. White [2006, 8] aptly describes the reversion to the norm:

> The danger then becomes that disappointed expectations revert too far in a pes-simistic direction, and that balance sheet exposures slow spending further. On the one hand, this could reflect a simultaneous drawing-back by an overex-tended household or corporate sector. On the other hand, an exaggerated un-willingness on the part of the financial sector to provide credit could also be the problem.

Profit Squeeze

This theory's contention is that capitalist cyclical forces, after a period of re-covery and boom, put downward pressure on business profit rates that com-pel firms to cut investment. Financial markets contribute to the downturn by raising borrowing costs and restricting credit, and through downdrafts in as-set valuations [Kindleberger 1978; Minsky 1986; Wolfson 1994; Sherman 1991]. Figure 5.1 shows the profit margin cycle in the U.S. where margin peaks are followed by downturns roughly two years later (recessions are dis-played as gray vertical bars).

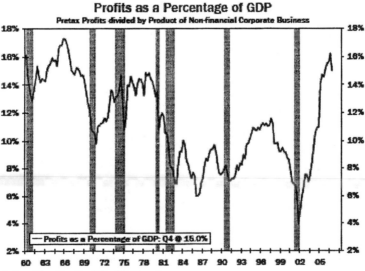

Figure 5.1.   The Cyclical Profit Margin
Source: Wachovia

In early expansion, investment is financed largely from internal funds, and as profit expectations rise, debt and equity financing are employed. Also early in expansion, many firms are in a hedge financing position where cash flows exceed financing costs, and are therefore in a relatively low risk position. But a recovery becomes a boom because more public and private spenders shift towards more speculative finance by taking on higher debt burdens. The pace of investment quickens as deficit spending drives profitability, improving an economy's overall fortunes. As the typical cycle proceeds, aggregate demand fails to keep pace with production and capacity, resulting in downward pressure on profitability which curtails cash flows. Rising interest rates, elevated by private creditors and central bank policy, add to the carrying cost of bank loans and new bond financing. Equity prices continue to rise well into late expansion but eventually turn down, raising external financing costs further. Collateral values decline, depressing investment and lending. This changing financial fortune for businesses and households afflicts the financial sector, as more lenders possess greater leverage and depressed stock prices. Financial distress or worry prompts bank lending cut-backs and encourages firms to cut investment to free up cash flow for debt payments.

Capital Flight and Exchange Rates

In this argument, economists emphasize the importance of rapid capital mobility across the globe creating volatility in currency exchange rates [Palley 1998, Chapter 10; Blustein 2003]. Financial capital enters economies based often on short term profit expectations. Rapid inflows bolster investment and economic development, asset prices rise, and growth generates jobs. Excellent economic performance entices more money inflows. These flows are subject to fast exits when negative economic outcomes, perceived or actual, cause reappraisal of profit prospects. Emerging market economies are particularly vulnerable given their recent emergence onto the global scene and less experience in domestic public policy management. As capital exits, downward pressure is placed on that country's exchange rate, causing additional selling of the foreign currency or foreign currency denominated assets. Because emerging market economies are dependent on outside financial capital, and U.S. hegemony means that the American dollar substitutes as a world currency, LDCs must often borrow in dollars, frequently borrowing short term to invest in long term projects. This creates a maturity and currency mismatch. Host country currency depreciation thus produces rising debt burdens denominated in more expensive dollars, and pressure by financiers to repay debts before earnings on investments payoff. Increased earnings in the home currency, something that cannot be done given worsening domestic economic conditions, create EM currency crises that precipitate banking problems as loan defaults rise [Symposium 1997].

Export-Led Growth Reliance

This theory is critical of international trade policy that places export-led growth strategies over a balanced approach of domestic demand and export oriented policy [Davidson 2002; Palley Blog 10/10/05, 11/13/06]. Many emerging market economies, and some MDCs such as Germany and Japan, rely heavily on exports to generate growth. A two-fold problem arises here. In that some nations run current account surpluses, other countries must sustain current account deficits. Countries running trade deficits create export surplus conditions elsewhere in the world. Secondly, inattention by public authorities to domestic demand vitality, as practiced in Europe and in some LDCs, creates a high dependency on sustaining export surpluses. This dependency pushes these nations to maintain "under-valued" exchange rates or low valuations relative to currencies of trade deficit nations. While export surplus nations enjoy growth and acquire ample reserves to invest throughout the world, countries in deficit rack up debt and can suffer deflationary domestic conditions. In turn, these countries may set off a competition for markets through competitive devaluations or depreciations, as they try to shift foreign consumer demand to their products, or through trade protection, in order to shift domestic consumption to domestically produced goods.[2]

A De-linkage of Finance from Funding:[3]

Financial markets play a supportive role for business investment by matching the savings of the public with the spending needs of commerce. Banks provide working capital loans to firms whose internal funds fall short of expansion needs. The loans create an expansion in the money supply, fostering growth in incomes. Investment banks underwrite the security issuances of firms who need long term funding. Central banks regulate liquidity conditions of the banking industry, promoting expansionary credit conditions when they make open market purchases of short term securities. Risk-taking enterprises often require financial capital to bring to fruition their investment plans. In the delinkage hypothesis, global finance is an undertaking unto itself. Finance is an economic activity with a life of its own in that profit and employment in this sector can be conditioned only on trading activity not connected in any direct way to the funding needs of the business sector. A distinction can be made between the overall market activity in financial assets, commodities, and currencies, and the underlying financial trading activity of institutions responsible for

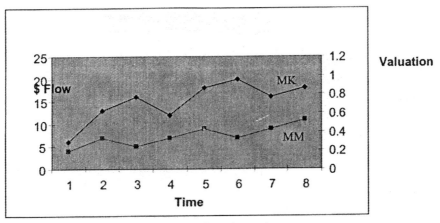

Figure 5.2. Stock Market Valuation and Market Makers

making financial markets. While everyone contributes to the volume and pricing in the overall markets, there is the separate market activity associated with banks, investment banks, and brokerage houses that create the markets. Consider the graphical model shown in Figure 5.2.

The dollar flow into a market is displayed on the left vertical axis and market valuation on the right vertical axis. Both variables are shown versus time on the horizontal axis. The overall market (MK) valuation takes on the usual cyclical pattern, displaying more volatility however than the more mildly cyclical underlying financial trading activity (MM curve). Market peaks occur at time periods T3 and T6. The difference between the curves represents trading by the general public (GP) whereas the MM curve represents trading only by the market makers. As the dollar flow into financial markets rises and falls, valuations are driven up or down accordingly. But the MM curve heads down prior to the peak in MK and moves up in advance of MK. The model is in equation form below:

(1) Total MK activity = GP + MM
(2) MK = f (BC, MM)
(3) MM = f (P, MK)

The overall market is a function of the business cycle (BC), that is, the underlying economic fundamentals of business, and a function of the underlying market making trading activity. In turn, MM is driven by the profit cycle P, not the BC,[4] and the overall market MK. The deal making institutions are very close to the business people they fund and the business conditions that entrepreneurs face. They therefore are more in tune with the profit cycle than the general public, including knowledgeable pension and hedge fund managers. Market making trading activity is mildly cyclical relative to MK, following the profit cycle which peaks (at t2 and t5) well before the business cycle peak and hence the peak in MK. The money inflow from MM lifts the market and then eventually excites the GP to raise its investment stake, taking the MK far higher than otherwise possible. However, MM selling starts with the decline in P not BC, and because the overall market valuation is quite high. Market makers sell as the GP is enthusiastically buying. The opposite occurs once the GP sells off, responding to the BC downturn, providing opportunity for MM to buy less expensive assets.[5] This relationship between general public market trading and market maker trading creates the "diamond shape" valuation form around market peaks in the above graph, of which only the top half is actually publicly visible.

As stock and other markets become increasingly global, huge sums of capital can be redirected across regions as the investing global public follows leads as to where to invest from market making institutions. The market makers have less volatile sentiments given their strategic position in funding business but their trading activity enlivens or dampens the public's interest in financial markets. To the extent that market makers induce positive or negative exuberance in public expectations for capital gains or losses, these importantly positioned financial institutions contribute to the vitality of business investment, and hence the growth and development of an economy.

DISCUSSION

Each of the financial system theories expresses concern for how the financial system may negatively affect financial conditions and the business sector in one country, or more than one country when contagion occurs.[6] Explanations of profit squeezes and deflationary forces, and critiques of export-led growth policies, place a comparative emphasis on the importance of real economy effects feeding onto financial flows. Financial market liberalization and capital flight theories heavily blame the financial system as root causes of problems, while the concept of pro-cyclical finance equally credits the real and financial sectors for excesses and business downturns. Insider institutional stock trading moderates overall market swings bringing an underlying financial stability to commercial investment yet insiders oriented towards making profit merely from trading activity, suggesting a less that full focus on fulfilling business capital needs for economic development, bring into question the ethics and utility of much of the financial sector.

Global financial panics and recessions often have multiple causes. Excess capacity and demand deficiencies may prompt some countries to pursue export-led growth strategies to relieve their unemployment at home. Financial market deregulation can encourage finance to become strongly pro-cyclical, or lead to capital flight and exchange rate volatility in emerging market economies. Domestic profit squeeze conditions may prompt nations to free up business and financial activity from regulation and pursue current account surpluses, upsetting trading partners' external balances and domestic employment conditions. On balance, negative economic events for the world have a number of causes or result from a chain reaction of effects. And it is not necessarily the case that individual countries fully understand or appreciate the extent to which the global system and policy are responsible for domestic bliss or domestic distress.

Basil Moore [2004] argues that a global economy needs a global currency. Conceivably, the world could literally employ one currency, or there could be three major currency unions, an American, a European, and either a Chinese or Japanese one. If three trading zones exist using major country money, these currencies would have relatively stable values and easily exchange one for another. Transaction costs and exchange rate volatility disappears. Inequality of income would no longer be disguised behind exchange rates [635]. But most importantly according to Moore, concerns over trade imbalances, and possible negative effects of sharp reversals, lose their policy significance as most countries end their reliance on using their own currencies in foreign exchange transactions. Moreover, central banks would not be constrained to keep interest rates up to maintain a "high" international value for the currency and to keep import demand limited by creating domestic demand sluggishness. In Moore's terminology, "the external balance constraint vanishes completely" [636–637, 641–642].

Moore opposes the creation of a global central bank or international currency union (ICU)[7] due to the inherent political difficulties of a broad-based treaty agreement. Moore's policy proposal is for countries to take unilateral action to adopt one of the major country currencies, most likely the one with whom most trade is conducted and that has geographical proximity. Once some countries pursue this policy direction, others will follow, and benefit by no longer being policy constrained in pursuing full employment domestically [644–652].

While not impossible, establishing a whole new international financial system via a treaty will be exceedingly difficult given an age of free capital flows and trade, and where the current system appears to be working. Bretton Woods, which called for official intervention and regulation, came out of a context where the previous financial system proved to be unstable and depressionary. While a global currency can potentially arise from decentralized initiative and eliminate national concerns over relative balance of payment conditions, a global currency cannot eliminate investor concerns of individual country economic performance and financial fragility. Currency traders and financiers will shift focus from exchange rate and reserve levels to domestic capital markets, banking systems, business profitability, and indebtedness.

An alternative approach to structuring a financial system is to base it on the free play of demand and supply forces for currency and on flexible exchange rates. The 20th century advocation of free trade and laissez-faire policy is best exemplified by Freidman [1953; 1980]. This argument is updated and given a broader context by Williamson's doctrine known as the Washington Consensus (WC) [1990; 2004–2005]. The WC argues for fiscal discipline, freeing of trade and capital flows from restrictions, privatization, and the promotion of growth through openness to FDI and through exports. Flexible exchange rates provide an automatic adjustment mechanism to balance trade and financial flows among nations. Exchange rate instability is seen as a result of unstable domestic conditions and any speculation engendered by flexibility tends to be stabilizing. Flexible exchange rates promote unrestricted multilateral trade and economic integration, and do not necessitate coordinated domestic policies among trading nations to keep trade balanced.

The weakness with the Friedman/WC thesis stems from two sources. First, flexible exchange rates cannot perform the balancing functioning desired, and second, placing international economics on a purely laissez-faire foundation provides neither stability nor growth.

Exchange rates represent relative currency values. These values are affected by economic fundamentals but psychology as well. Currencies are objects of speculation, and capital flows are motivated in part by speculation as currency traders try to exploit fluctuations in currency values for capital gains.[8] Once an asset such as currency becomes a focus of speculation, the speculation itself can accentuate changes in valuations. Unless world demand conditions are strongly promoted by coordinated public policy action, competition for profit and markets will invariably produce some losers. Relatively poor economic outcomes in some countries or regions beget alterations in capital flows that alter exchange rates. Balanced trade is unlikely, and experience during Globalization Three bears this out. Furthermore, any attempt to base export oriented growth in a WC domestic policy context creates too little effective demand globally.[9] An underappreciation for strong domestic demand conditions to complement international trade forces countries to find ways to shift price competitiveness from rivals to themselves, either through currency depreciation or domestic wage and employment reductions [Davidson 2004–2005; 1996; 1994].

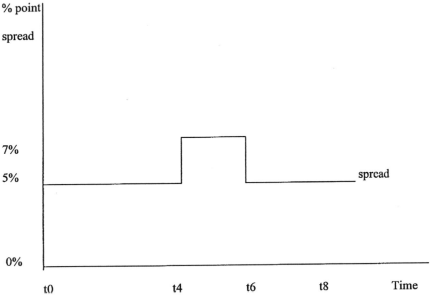

Figure 5.3. Bond Interest Rate Spreads

Financial freedoms are partly reflected in increasing speculative activity around a growing list of assets traded for capital gain potential. As a basic hypothetical example, consider that traders discover a rough normal rate spread between LDC bonds and MDC bonds of 5%.[10] Begin the analysis at time t0 as shown above, and assume that the conventional 5% spread is maintained until t4, diverges for two periods to 7%, and then reverts to norm. Due to fundamental uncertainty, no trader could know this spread pattern in advance. Nevertheless, traders who follow emerging market and MDC bonds, have two options. Option one is to speculate as to when a spread divergence may occur and option two is to take a position following the divergence believing that spread normality will return.

When speculators guess right, either option not only produces capital gain but creates stabilizing forces that tend to move the spread back towards normal. The typical buy low-sell high strategy is stabilizing. But if traders guess wrong, either option can create destabilizing forces on asset prices and hence on the rate spread. In option one, divergence may not occur at t4 causing traders to unwind, that is reverse their positions, actually squeezing the spread. In option two, divergence may last longer than expected, or may increase, causing an unwinding of positions that exaggerate the spread. As explained by Kambhu [2006], destabilizing unwinding can occur when traders are heavily leveraged and hold capital losses. Their risk assessment rises while the market becomes less liquid, creating a situation where prices can markedly change. Moreover, there is potential for destabilizing trading to spill over to other asset classes and to cross country borders affecting commercial and banking interests.

Are the growing current account surpluses and deficits necessarily a sign of international economic imbalance or financial fragility? No. National economies grow when one or more domestic sectors run budget deficits financed by borrowing and credit creation, producing corresponding budget surpluses elsewhere in the economy.[11] Global economic expansion requires "net deficit spending" as well, and these money flows are recorded in each country's balance of payments (BOP). The economic conditions producing growth within a country are merely being replicated internationally as nations move toward ever greater financial integration. And since cross-border money payments require currency exchanges, economists follow and record evolving BOP conditions among nations. Such attention to who is accruing net inflows and outflows of money creates an appearance of dangerous imbalances, but if all transactions were done in one currency, and policymakers understood the rudiments of the growth process, priority attention would shift away from the BOP.

Rising nation-state indebtedness, particularly by the hegemon or a group of developed nations who are driving growth, is not necessarily an indication of financial fragility.[12] An economy closed to international trade creates domestic deficit spending to grow. Domestic indebtedness rises as domestic lenders finance deficit spenders. As an economy opens itself to trade relations, its domestic deficit spenders can arise from FDI and deficit budgets can be financed from foreign financiers. Such a country's international indebtedness grows reflecting a shift away from domestic debt dependence to greater diversification of credit sources. Debt burdens per se are not necessarily any higher overall but simply consist of domestic and foreign sources of debt. And given the central role played by the U.S. dollar, and other major MDC currencies, MDCs can run persistent trade deficits. World growth and economic integration occur concomitantly; American capital outflows measured by current account deficits come back in similar dollar magnitudes measured by capital account surpluses [WSJ 12/21/06, pA16].

A creative but ambitious proposal to address potential depressionary forces arising from export-led, current account imbalance dependency strategies comes from Davidson [2004]. Davidson argues that current account surpluses and currency reserve accumulations represent over-saving by nations earning net money inflows. This is analogous to over-saving tendencies within domestic economies. The crux of the problem is the inability of the current international financial system to promote continuous growth in the global system as surplus reserves depress global aggregate demand. Financial crises and growing indebtedness are attending problems visited on deficit-ridden nations. Davidson's proposal, building on Keynes' ideas from the 1940s, is to establish an International Clearing Union (ICU) to clear transactions between countries based on fixed exchange rates. The ICU would monitor international balances among nations and require current account surplus nations to expend their reserve accumulations into deficit countries. These expenditures would bolster global demand by enhancing global money flows directed at purchases from or FDI into deficit nations. World output and employment would rise.

An ICU system necessitates agreement among countries to set up and comply with certain rules. International agreements are not without precedent, as evidenced by the Bretton Woods agreement in 1944, successive agreements that led to the EU and EMU, the founding of the World Trade Organization, and numerous regional free trade blocks. Nevertheless, adoption of a rather complex ICU system with fixed exchange rates [597–604] would be a real challenge. Overhauling a system that is apparently working to foster international transactions and investment, and to do so with no crisis or emergency compelling change, is a tall order.

Forcing surplus nations to expend their reserves, while promoting demand, is subject to criticism. For example, Mahn's [2005] concern is that surpluses may arise from a country's comparative competitiveness and productivity. Surpluses then represent reward for achieving a superior trading status. Deficit prone countries in contrast may reflect public policy failure or failure to compete, and therefore deficit countries should not per se be "bailed out" of their problems. Davidson's system would be "an open-handed system of welfare" discouraging a country to upgrade its competitiveness. And surplus countries are not necessarily predatory towards trading rivals, but if they are found to be so by purposely undervaluing their currency, then a tax on their surplus is warranted [39–41].

The Davidson plan does create an institution to counteract a laissez-faire, flexible exchange rate, free capital flow international system prone to demand deficiency and competitive devaluations. The perpetuation of global unemployment and poverty suggests existence of an on-going demand problem. Repetitive financial crises attest to problems of illiquidity and low demand. The international financial system works in that it is efficient but is at the same time defective in that it contributes to scattered world economic impoverishment.

Financial system efficiency goes a long way in creating contentment with the current architecture. But the system is hierarchical in the sense that the dollar is the key currency and all MDC currencies have a high status as

reserve and transaction currencies. Emerging market countries need to acquire these currencies to minimize global currency traders' and financiers'
concerns of their ability to repay loans. A redesigned system could treat all
countries' currencies equally in the sense that all currencies regardless of origin could be used to make national as well as international transactions
[D'Arista 2004, 369–370]. A developing country importer of American goods
could conceivably pay domestic currency for American goods. The importer
gives a check written on a domestic account to an American exporter who
upon deposit gets credited in dollars by their bank. The emerging market denominated check is sent to the Federal Reserve which credits the American
bank's account, and then an ICU comes into play to clear the check between
central banks, ultimately resulting in a debit to the importer's account. The
debiting and crediting are done at the current exchange rate, but no new reserve asset need be created or fixed exchange rates established.

The international economy is subject to liquidity crises because of the construct of the current financial system and central bank policy. Emergency
loans granted by the IMF and governments, and international bank capital adequacy standards,[13] mitigate economic crises and commercial downturns.
Thus official intervention makes the current monetary system work better
than it otherwise would. To some extent this creates a false sense of security.
D'Arista's more egalitarian payments system would further diminish
prospects for crises.

Assuming full implementation of the Davidson proposal, the implied benefits of more radical change to the financial architecture would indeed eliminate the monetary system as the source of economic distress. Exchange rates
would be fixed, capital flows regulated, and current account surpluses expended on the products of nations experiencing deficits. Threats to stability
stemming from trade imbalances, rapid capital outflows, and volatile exchange rates are eliminated or mitigated. Enhanced employment conditions
in deficit nations may be ameliorative to the now growing in-state income
inequalities.

But of course challenges remain in sustaining stability to economic affairs.
Deflationary forces caused by competition-induced over-capacity and business outsourcing remain. Financial liberalization encourages continued risk
taking and speculation. Pro-cyclical finance still amplifies business cycles
that are slowly synchronizing across national borders,[14] and profit squeeze
pressures will necessarily remain. And the implementation of the Davidson
plan does not ensure adequate national attention to domestic demand conditions. Most fundamentally, if the Davidson plan is attempted within the context of the Washington Consensus, the conventional wisdom of the era, public policy would run at cross purposes to the goals of the Davidson plan.

What more can be said about the effects of a de-linkage of finance from funding? There is no evidence or reason to think that market maker trading activity undermines stock and bond markets, or works against a long run upward trend in stock prices. The theoretical model shown above displays an upward trend in equity valuations. Beyond the concerns identified above, there is the potential for outright manipulation of asset prices and for one party to gain at the expense of another. Market making institutions that control large sums of globally sourced money can conceivably manipulate company stock prices or market averages, given their theoretical ability and strategy to trade against overall market trends. The worst case scenario is when market makers who have lending or brokerage relations with a pension or hedge fund trade against the financial position committed to by their client. Using proprietary information established as part of a business contract, market makers can potentially earn more from taking an opposing trading position, gains of which will more than offset loan losses or lost brokerage business from their failed client.[15]

Market makers affect the direction and volume of global capital flows and therefore are responsible for the ebb and flow of global commerce. Market makers may become pessimistic about business conditions or take advantage of public inflows of cash into financial markets. In the former case, market makers can eventually bring down business activity by undermining investment, or in the latter case, make paper financial gains from selling to the public when asset prices rise and buying from the public when asset prices fall. On the one hand, market makers are not the fundamental cause of bull markets turning into bear markets as business cycle effects dominate asset market turning points. And these institutions tend to keep all-out market declines from occurring by buying when the general public is selling. On the other hand, market makers have position and information advantages over the public. Many substantial inequalities pervade the socio-economic landscape of all capitalist societies, and these particular advantages of the market makers simply are examples among a long list of advantages that accrue to small groups throughout the world's economies.[16]

THE FINANCIAL SYSTEM AND GLOBALIZATION

Has the financial system itself contributed to globalization? The answer is certainly yes in that the dollar is the world's transaction and reserve currency. The dollar's central position in global commerce arose historically, commencing with the upheavals of WWI and reaching prominence after WWII. Bretton Woods institutionalized the dollar as the world currency and established a high purchasing power for it relative to other currencies. The dollar's central role and purchasing power facilitated U.S. FDI and import purchases which in turn created growth abroad. Foreign growth encouraged economic integration and adoption of capitalist practices.[17]

But the financial system aided globalization immensely in more subtle ways, and whose root causes were unintended factors of importance for globalization. The first of two factors was Keynesian aggregate demand management policies employed by mid 20th century MDCs, especially the U.S. The second factor has do with the "affluent society" effect throughout western capitalism, but again especially in the U.S.

Acceptance of government responsibility for domestic economic performance and the effectiveness of Keynesian policies became part of the "Keynesian Consensus" following the Great Depression. U.S. foreign policy commitments complemented domestic economic concerns to produce public policies favorable to aggregate demand expansion. Government budget deficits promote commercial profits because government sector spending directly or indirectly promotes business sales. Important research verifies that since WWII the corporate sector has largely run budget surpluses [Godley 1999; Medlen 2005]. Internal funds frequently exceed investment opportunities. The excess cash in American corporations was redirected abroad to expedite their transition as largely domestically focused firms to globally centered transnational enterprises. Excess cash promoted mergers and acquisitions, and facilitated FDI into host countries.

The "affluent society" effect is the second important source for globalization, though unintended as a cause and unnoticed as a source. Beginning with the rise of consumerism in the 1920s, and accelerating after WWII, middle class affluence became a prominent feature of western capitalism. The Galbraith thesis [1958; 1979 (1967)] argues that post-depression policymakers and businesses became obsessed with expanding production through demand to avoid the depressionary pressures of laissez-faire capitalism. Along with supportive public policies, business extended its influence into social life making people into ever unsatisfied consumers of products and services. Corporate planning was employed to create a "dependence effect" where producers created demand for their own production. Prestige and status became obtainable through consumption, and the high consumption of the well-off incited not envy but emulation. Higher debt loads among households gradually replaced saving as a virtue, and upward mobility became the hallmark of successful life. The financial sector's complicity with this social transformation is seen in its ever wider extension of credit and creation of financial products, higher consumption dependency on asset prices, and monetary policy's periodic liquefying of financial markets to head off recession. The transformation to a materialist society became complete during globalization's third wave. Households, again especially in American but elsewhere too, run budget deficits. Household sector deficits produce growing budget surpluses for international business investment and growing savings pools increasingly directed toward global financial markets.

The central role afforded the dollar, Keynesian demand policies, and middle class affluence combine to create a world economic and financial system dominated by American capital and institutions. The relative decline in the U.S. share of world exports and production does not represent American decline but prominence as American capital and capitalism spread across the globe. In earlier stages of capitalism, the middle class was too small to drive much spending, had incomes too low to allow for much use of credit, and government policy was too dominated by Classical thought to pump-prime economic activity. Earlier economic booms required business deficit spending, but since profitability limits the duration of expenditures exceeding income, booms typically collapsed into depressions. This is no longer the case!

And evolving financial arrangements within major economies may dampen credit cycles and make finance less strongly pro-cyclical.[18] With the arrival and deepening of capital markets and growing importance of non-bank financial institutions, credit risk is now distributed across broader and more diverse investors world-wide. Specifically, banks warehouse less credit risk, transferring risk through markets to hedge funds and insurance companies. Conceivably this makes banks more financially resilient and stable, creating stability and confidence in the international payments system which banks dominate. Risk is shifted to institutions with strong risk management skills, and who maintain better matches between asset and liability maturities.[19] These investors also enhance overall liquidity.

Ben Bernanke, Chair of the Federal Reserve, credits industry-led efforts to improve risk management and lessen chances of systemic financial instability:

> According to bank supervisors and most market participants, counterparty risk management has improved significantly since 1998. Some of this progress is due to industry-led efforts, such as two reports by the Counterparty Risk Management Policy Group (CRMPG) that lay out principles that institutions should use in measuring, monitoring, and managing risk. Reviews conducted by bank supervisors in 2004 and 2005 indicated that banks have become more diligent in their dealings with hedge funds. In most cases, substantial resources have been devoted to expanding and improving the staffing of the risk-management functions related to hedge fund counterparties. Dealers universally require hedge funds to post collateral to cover current credit exposures and, with some exceptions, require additional collateral, or initial margin, to cover potential exposures that could arise if markets moved sharply. Now, risk managers can more

accurately measure their current and projected exposures to hedge fund counterparties, and more firms use stress-testing methodologies to assess the sensitivity of their exposures to individual counterparties if the market moves substantially [Bernanke 5/2006].

Moreover, this evolution may reduce the pro-cyclicality of credit. To the
extent that capital markets improve the amount and quality of financial information, non-bank holders of credit risk can potentially act sooner, and in a
more gradual manner, as more timely information becomes available about
changing financial conditions. Gradual pull-backs in credit extension during
business cycle upswings, and the opposite during downturns, could conceivably dampen cycles in commercial activity. Figure 5.4 shows the effect of
IMMC on credit flows which become less volatile compared to historical
swings in credit. See the dotted line beginning at point "B."

The growing cross-border holdings of financial assets help to dampen financial cycles by providing higher portfolio diversification with greater potential returns. While developed country financial markets offer overall lower
risk than in foreign countries and particularly emerging markets, higher returns are possible abroad. Portfolio blending of financial assets, something increasingly realizable and done through professional institutional manage-

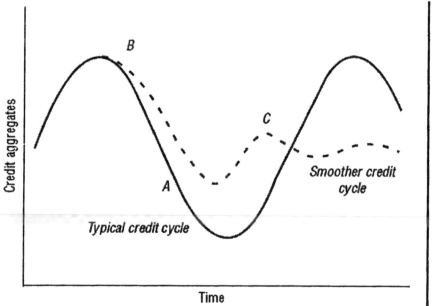

Figure 5.4. Less Volatile Financial Cycles
Source: IMF

ment, offers better risk-return options. In figure 5.5 below the elliptical curve displays the possible tradeoffs.[20] Point "A" could represent only U.S. holdings or only MDC holdings, while point "C" shows the case with only emerging market holdings. Whatever diversification exists initially occurs within those stated holding classifications. As investors move left from point A, diversification increases as MDC stocks are added to the all-U.S. fund or similarly, emerging market assets are added to developed-country holdings. As investors approach point "B," portfolio risk falls because of diversification but return increases as the relatively high growth rates in foreign countries positively affect financial asset valuations. Such an improved risk-return tradeoff can undercut swings in financial cycles by reducing portfolio volatility and hence trading.

U.S. monetary policy importantly affects globalization. Raising interest rates slows down the speed of globalization by deliquifying commerce and creating resistance to asset price increases by slowing spending and profit expectations. Lower rates do the opposite, and facilitate economic integration by promoting foreign investment and lending from the U.S. But not incidental to globalization is the Federal Reserve's impact on income distribution. The Fed shifts income toward labor, thus promoting integration, through an expansionary policy that drives spending, employment, and rising wage income at the expense of interest income. In contrast, restrictive policy shifts income to finance and away from labor, slowing the pace of globalization.

As such, the Fed's policy is conflicted. Its class interest role stands in contention with its larger public responsibility to promote economic prosperity

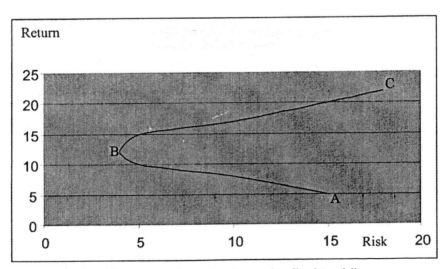

Figure 5.5. The Risk-Return Tradeoff of an Internationalized Portfolio

and stability. On the one hand, the American central bank operates to place a drag on economic activity, thereby restraining globalization and shifting income distribution towards financiers.[21] This policy gets expressed as having a publicly oriented goal of price stability, implying pursuit of a socially beneficial outcome. On the other hand, the Fed accommodates globalization and rising labor and business income with an expansionary policy. But because the forces and trends put into play by globalization create episodes of destabilization and recession, the Fed is forced to ward off such pressures through a gradual easing of credit conditions over time. This facilitates economic boom conditions in the U.S., which in turn promote trade deficits that encourage ever more global integration.[22] Surpluses earned abroad flow back into the U.S. placing upward pressure on asset prices and downward pressure on interest rates. The Fed's policy rate and market interest rates show a declining trend since the early 1980s [Wachovia].

Could a large, permanent fall in the dollar's value interrupt the pace of globalization, or would globalization's drivers simply shift to other MDCs? If the U.S. fails to sustain its engine for globalization, Europe is not a likely substitute driver. The Maastrict Treaty, the Stability and Growth Pact, EU entrance requirements, and ECB monetary policy are too inhibiting of global expansion to make Europe a replacement for American hegemony, despite Europe's contribution to world GDP. Japanese leadership is a possibility given its inclination to pursue expansionary public policies and to intervene in the private sector. But Japanese consumerism must grow to mimic America's affluent society, and firms must outsource and pursue FDI to a greater extent. Otherwise, too little world effective demand will be created to incentivize other countries to integrate and grow. Or perhaps India and China will become the locomotive? These economies are large and growing fast. Domestic growth will gradually increase these countries' imports and their entry into major nation status will prompt more outward investment. The interesting prospect here is the extension and promotion of Asian capitalism to other parts of the world, a variety that differs from Anglo-American institutions.

NOTES

1. Securities, currencies, and commodities all have values derived from the economic performance of those who sold, issued, or produced them.
2. Moreover, ". . . in a savings abundant world, it is conceivable that countries will compete to cheapen their respective currencies, because a cheap currency tends to generate growth and helps liquidate surplus products without introducing inflation. In

an environment of excess savings, the reserve currency is often bid up by the rest of the world, which is trying to stay competitive" [BCA Research 2006, 19].

3. Funding refers here to the actual provision of cash to firms for productive investment.

4. See chapter 6 concerning the profit cycle, business cycles, and economic growth.

5. Top executives have insider knowledge that they pass to market making financial institutions and utilize themselves in making trades that advantage them relative to the general public. Evidence of market maker activity is provided by journalist Alistair Barr for Market Watch, "Insiders didn't Panic in Recent Stock Slump," 3/8/2007.

6. The spreading of financial crises, like growth, from one country to another arises from the increasing finance and commerce linkage, and economic integration, among nation states.

7. This institution is described later in this chapter.

8. And of course these fluctuations are partially induced by the speculators.

9. Politically independent, inflation focused central banks have become part of the Consensus view, furthering the inclination to impose deflationary policies on domestic economies.

10. LDC bonds contain greater risk than MDC bonds; therefore the rate spread is positive.

11. This Post Keynesian theory is well presented by Wray [1989; 1991].

12. The U.S. net international debt to GDP ratio was only 20% in 2004 [Bryson 2006, 3].and 2005 and the U.S. carns a yearly net inflow of income payments. Net debt to GDP in the Euro zone is 15% and 17% in the U.K. in 2005 [WSJ 9/25/06, A9].

13. G10 countries have established the Basel Committee to set forth capital adequacy standards for banks known as the Basel Accords. Basel 1 adopted in 1988 requires that tier 1 capital (equity and retained earnings) and tier 2 capital (subordinated debt and hybrid assets comprising bond and stock characteristics) be equal to 8% of risk-weighted assets. Basel 2 issued in 2004 requires increased bank disclosure of assumed risks and capital standards that are more risk sensitive. See the site: http://en .wikipedia.org/wiki/Basel_Accord

14. The likely result of cycle synchronization is greater swings in world economic activity, and hence the end of the ability for some nation or region experiencing an economic boom to limit the downturn in commerce elsewhere.

15. See BW's [10/09/06, 78] coverage of hedge fund Amaranth's collapse after Wall Street lenders positioned themselves against the financial commitments of their client. Insider financial institutions cooperate on corporate restructurings, purchases, and sales; the same companies may operate as lenders, owners, and underwriters in deals. To get a sense of this, see Market Watch articles July 15, 2006 and October 27, 2006 on the Hertz Corporation.

16. Hence the need for effective laws that require disclosure and regulate economic behavior.

17. While the dollar's value has fluctuated modestly against major trading partners' currencies since the early 1970s, its value relative to all other currencies has sharply risen.

18. See the IMF's Global Financial Stability Report, chapter two, April 2006, pages 62–76.

19. See the BIS sponsored study concerning international bank improvement of risk management systems following the late 1990s financial crises [BIS "On the Use of Information . . ." October 1998].

20. The typical risk-return tradeoff is displayed by segment BC, where higher return can only be had by taking on more risk. Riskier opportunities usually offer potentially greater rates of return.

21. The inference here is that faster globalization requires a more equal income distribution within the U.S. Moreover, public policy can offset the income concentrating effects of a for-profit corporate dominated and led globalization.

22. But stimulative domestic economic policy also makes for more difficult labor market conditions for domestic labor. See the employment-capital outflow model described in chapter seven.

Chapter Six

Business and Financial Cycles

INTRODUCTION

Capitalist economies are inherently dynamic, subject to the ebb and flow in business activity. In the years prior to the 20th century's Great Depression and the rise of welfare states built on activist demand management, boom-bust cycles are the norm in Europe and the West. Strong growth spurts are followed by collapses. Modern fiscal and monetary interventions by the state moderate cycle extremes but do not completely stabilize economic activity. The historical record shows capitalist economies moving through cycles in output, employment, interest rates, and asset prices. Oscillations are driven by changes in commercial profits, financial market volatility, new kinds of technology, and competition for markets.

Up through globalization II, cycles are primarily driven by business investment, which in turn is affected by expectations for profit and financing conditions reflected in financial and banking markets. During economic recoveries from depressed conditions, ample productive capacity exists and prices move up in advance of costs, increasing profitability. The number of investment projects increases and entrepreneurial expectations about risk and profits become favorable. Capital spending picks up, productivity improves, and bank lending accommodates higher corporate and consumer borrowing. Monetary and fiscal policies tend to be expansionary or at least not constricting. Deregulation and the opening of new domestic and international markets bolster optimism and stimulate competition. Net deficit spending and money creation[1] fuel more spending and raise profitability further. While the social and institutional setting can vary substantially from one recovery to the next, private and public policy will attempt to create a positive climate for investment.

Chapter Six

Expansions end when conditions contrary to those that exist at the beginning arise. Capacity constraints develop and interest rates and wages move up as credit and labor markets tighten. Simultaneously, total demand is held back. Acceptable investment opportunities decline and surplus inventories mount, putting downward pressure on prices and investment. Increased income inequality, by raising the amount of savings relative to income, contributes to insufficient effective demand to sustain business sales. Business optimism fades and some reluctance exists to take risks. Rising input costs and declining revenues squeeze profits. Investment and employment fall, eventually creating negative pressure on income and spending.

An economic multiplier adds to cyclical upward and downward momentum. As spending increases during upturns, additions to employment and income create even more spending, furthering increases in jobs and income. Downturns create negative multipliers and reduced spending feeds through to lower employment and income.

Figure 6.1 shows how profitability (P) and GDP move over a typical cycle. The data for both variables are computed as index values over six U.S. business cycles dating back to the 1950s. Each index number represents a value relative to the mean for each of the two series, namely profits and GDP, at nine distinct points or stages across the business cycle. Stage 1 represents the beginning of recovery, stage 5 is the peak of the cycle, and stage 9 represents the end of recession. The empirical evidence on profitability demonstrates that profits rise in early and mid economic expansion, peak in stage 4, one stage before the peak in GDP, and profits fall throughout recession which begins in stage six. Evidence demonstrates that GDP always ends the cycle

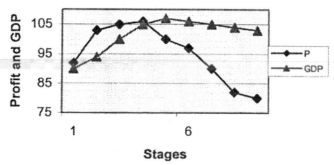

Figure 6.1.   The Profit and Output Cycle

higher than it began, but profits can fall substantially, even below where they began the cycle.

Concurrent with these swings in commercial and consumer activity, capitalist economies up to the current age are impacted by financial cycles. Finance can promote and destabilize an economy. First, finance affects business by determining the cost of external funds. As financing costs fall relative to business cash flows, investment is promoted, but rising costs can curtail investment. Commitment of banks to business matters, as strong commitment is expressed in easy loan terms and willingness to refinance. Finance can affect long-term investment yield projections made by business. Stable and rising stock prices tend to boost investment because they suggest higher expected future returns on capital investment. Stock market volatility and declining share prices undercut investment by creating pessimistic return expectations. If the financial community is bent on speculation and trading, and has force in corporate governance, it can destabilize investment. When volatile equity market valuations of firms supersede the more entrepreneurially generated assessments of investment profitability, investment may be misdirected and reduced. Keynes [1997 (1936), 158] writes of the importance of both business confidence and financial conditions for creating healthy economic conditions.

> So far we have had chiefly in mind the state of confidence of the . . . speculative investor (entrepreneur) and . . . tacitly assuming that, if he himself is satisfied with the prospects, he has unlimited command over money at the market rate of interest. This is, of course, not the case. Thus we must also take account of the other facet of the state of confidence, namely, the confidence of the lending institutions towards those who seek to borrow from them, sometimes described as the state of credit. A collapse in the price of equities, which has had disastrous reactions on the (rate of return), may have been due to the weakening either of speculative confidence or of the state of credit. But whereas the weakening of either is enough to cause a collapse, recovery requires the revival of both.

Investment must be financed and firms opt for internal funds first because they are the least costly.[2] Typically debt financing is employed next with equity finance the most costly source selected last. Firms in a hedge financing position are in a relatively low risk position because cash flows exceed financing costs. A more risky situation is called speculative finance, where a firm's financing costs exceed, in the short run, its cash flow. The company borrows to meet spending commitments. The worst position is ponzi finance where a firm must increase its borrowing each period to meet spending and debt commitments. Debt financing becomes an ever-larger portion of investment and cash flows are not expected to cover payment commitments over the long run.

Debt and equity financing costs rise as firms move from hedge to ponzi positions. The pace of investment quickens as deficit spending drives profitability, improving the economy's overall fortunes. Rising property values and stock prices increase business access to credit, further promoting investment. Aggregate corporate financial situations determine whether general macroeconomic conditions are robust or fragile. In early and mid expansion, most firms in the economy are in hedge or moderately speculative positions, imparting stability to the economy. But as the typical cycle proceeds, downward pressure on profitability curtails cash flows. Rising interest rates, elevated by private creditors and central bank policy, begin to add to the carrying cost of bank loans and new bond issues. Equity prices continue to rise well into late expansion but eventually turn down, raising external financing costs further. The general economy moves progressively from a hedge to a speculative and onto a ponzi financial position. This changing financial fortune in the business sector feeds back onto the financial sector, as more banks and finance companies possess greater leverage and depressed stock prices.

Deteriorating financial conditions and commercial profitability force down investment, creating a decline in economic activity. This in turn intensifies credit demand and desires to liquidate asset positions to generate cash. Collateral values decline, depressing investment and reducing access to credit and falling business profitability undermines companies' ability to pay dividends and interest expenses. Banks and other financial institutions raise loan standards and costs, often prompted by business bankruptcies that increase portfolio risk. The central bank continues to hike rates to stem inflation. These actions push more firms into speculative or ponzi financial conditions; defaults, layoffs, and a drop in spending create recession.

Complicating capitalist downturns prior to the second era of globalization was deflation. In the days preceding public policy efforts to support demand and income, recessions and depressions sometimes fostered deflation as goods prices fell in absolute terms [Atkeson and Kehoe 2004]. The international gold standard contributed to deflation by restricting money growth and insufficiently providing illiquidity in times of intense increases in money demand. Deflation exacerbates profit squeeze and financial fragility by lowering sales revenue for business, undermining investment, while increasing loan repayment burdens; indebtedness burdens increase as debtors must pay fixed commitments to banks as they experience revenue declines from lower prices for what they sell. This deflation-depression link disappears largely after WWII, as active government demand management comes into play. During globalization III, deflation reappears as asset price declines. Financial crises in emerging markets induce financial asset price deflation with recession, and the most important episode of recession occurring simultaneously with asset price deflation in an MDC is Japan during the 1990s and early 2000s.

Active aggregate demand management and public intervention in the economy arise following the Great Depression in developed nations during the second wave of globalization. These tools are effective at lengthening cycle upturns, moderating cycle amplitudes, and avoiding deflation. However, business investment remains the important driver of cycles. The historical instability of investment, arising from genuine long term uncertainty over eventual returns, remains a public policy concern. Profit squeeze and financial fragility continue to interrupt economic expansions and stability.

CYCLE STABILITY AND NET WORTH

With time comes evolution in systems, and as globalization III comes of age, business cycle dynamics change in leading capitalist nations. Cyclical activity in commerce remains typical, but commercial swings are more stable, economic upturns increase in duration, and financial fragility wanes in importance. The forces driving globalization are powerful and will remain in force. Contemporary policy encourages free trade and capital flows. Technology increases the capacity for private enterprise to go global. The profit motive is enhanced as product and labor markets quickly expand. Globalization integrates nation states as FDI, financial capital flows (portfolio investment), and U.S. military actions grow.

Business cycles, as noted above, are more stable in this current era but why? First, household consumption replaces business investment as the principal driving factor. Consumption varies less than investment and is less subject to collapse. Second, increases in consumption sensitivity to higher wealth allows for consumption growth to exceed income growth for sustained periods. Third, exports become more important too as integration proceeds, both for MDC and LDC nations. Emerging market economies are especially dependent for growth on exports as incessantly increasing Anglo-American current account deficits fuel their surpluses. Economic success in emerging markets invites continued integration and openness. Fourth, public policy has a two-fold effect on cycles. Policy remains in support of effective demand as in the prior period of globalization, but it also expedites internationalization via free trade agreements and cooperation with other nations to open their economies. The fifth factor for MDC cycle stabilization has to do with the structural change away from capital goods to service sector prominence.

Service spending varies less than consumption of durable goods, and fewer inventories are required in service industries. The "affluent society" effect in some countries and the rising proportion of upper middle class income earners create a perpetual spending machine within the household sector. A final element in cycle stabilization is International Money Manager Capitalism itself. As explained in chapters three and five, this institutional development imparts a financial stability to the business cycle.

Globalization III benefits of course from a more stable business cycle and longer economic expansions. As addressed in chapters two and three, the augmentation of household net worth in Anglo-American economies is a critical development in promoting momentum for and success of globalization. Tempered cyclical dynamics puts upward pressure on net worth. Economic activity stays strong longer and economic risk lessens, so more money is funneled to asset markets.

But an array of variables is responsible for the upward pressure on net worth, not just a stabilized business cycle. One such variable is the growing FDI across the globe. FDI seeks out low production costs, and incorporates improved technology and supply chain management to increase labor productivity. As output per labor hour increases and production costs fall, profit flows to business increase. Expanding consumer markets and growing middle class incomes further improve profit prospects, resulting in higher share prices.

A second variable is portfolio investment. Given capital mobility and difficulties connected to pegged exchange rates of emerging market economies, the international financial system is constructed around a flexible exchange rate system. Governments do manage relative exchange rates, and the current regime favors developing country goods exports. The U.S. hegemonic economic status, as reflected in sustained current account deficits, amplifies growth abroad. Surpluses in many nations flow back to the U.S. and other MDC economies, facilitating expansionary financial conditions in capital markets and job producing FDI in labor markets. A contributing third variable comes from U.S. military actions and commitments. Hegemonic foreign policy pumps additional money into the global economy and attempts to push more of the world into adopting integrating economic and political institutions. Both the current trade-capital flow regime and U.S. military posture put upward pressure on Anglo-American household net worth.[3]

A final important variable is MDC asset markets themselves. More people in developed economies see themselves as mini-capitalists. They have long run financial needs that must be met through investing in capital and real estate markets. Income from work and traditional savings vehicles simply are inadequate to meet the needs of an upwardly mobile and ownership minded public. Capital gains are promoted by regular inflows of money through big institutions geared to long term performance outlooks.

CYCLE DYNAMICS AND NET WORTH

So there are multiple factors underpinning business cycle stability and multiple variables, including cycle stability, supporting household sector net worth. Rising net worth creates the possibility for collateralized deficit spending by consumers. No longer is current income and interest expense alone the major contributors to consumption as in past periods. Globalization III has its growth given momentum through upward pressure on the wealth of people in Anglo-American economies. The foundational context for globalization comes from policy, technology, and the profit motive. Its sustainability comes from relentless pressure on net wealth to rise.

The theoretical model of globalization III is outlined below. As noted, the foundation for globalization stems from public policy, technology, and the profit motive, all of which "permit" integration to go forth. The cause and effect dynamics described above give globalization its needed momentum. Consumption (C), exports (X), public policy (PP), the service sector (SS), and international money manager capitalism (IMMC) together promote business cycle stability (BCS). In turn, cycle stability combines with FDI, the trade-capital flow-exchange rate regime (Regime), foreign policy (FP), and asset markets (Asset Mks) to affect net worth (NW) in developed economies. Net worth importantly affects the extent to which MDC household sectors deficit spend. Net spending then affects world economic growth, and by implication unemployment, and growth feeds back into consumption, exports, policy, and money manager capitalism that define our age.

In Figure 6.2, net spending is the difference between demand (D) and income (Y), and a net deficit exists when the change in D exceeds the change in Y, which occurs to the right of zero. A net household sector surplus exists to the left of zero. Net worth (NW) is measured on the vertical axis, and an economy's household effective demand (ED) function is a positively sloped line as increasing household budget deficits, stimulated by rising net worth, raise overall effective demand. It takes a net worth of at least NW* to generate net household spending; otherwise households tend to increase their spending by less than their income, generating surpluses. The higher the net spending or effective demand the lower the unemployment rate. For example, a net worth of NW1 produces an effective demand of ED1, creating low unemployment.

Foundation

Public Policy

Technology   ---------------> Globalization -------> Nation-State Integration

Profit Motive

Figure 6.2.   The Theoretical Model of Globalization III

Cause and Effect Dynamics:

1. Business Cycle Stability (BCS) = f (C, X, PP, SS, IMMC)
2. Net Worth (NW) = f (BCS, FDI, Regime, FP, Asset Mks)
3. Effective Demand (ED) = f (NW)
4. World Economic Growth = f (ED)
5. C, X, PP, SS, IMMC = f (World Economic Growth)

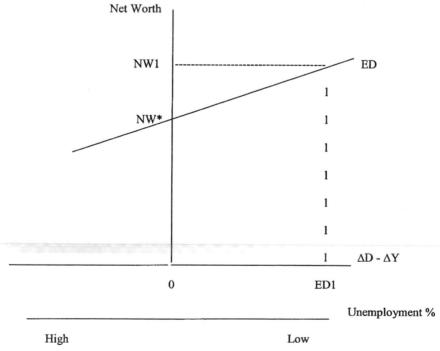

Figure 6.3.   Effective Demand, Net Worth, and Unemployment

What weak points exist for globalization in terms of cyclical stability? Chapter Three addresses a host of potential problems, of which income distribution shifts and the public policy orientation could jeopardize the march toward full integration. Rising inequality could conceivably undercut effective demand if inequality gets "too large." In the graph above, a growing income concentration would shift the ED line leftward, so that lower effective demand, at the same net worth, creates more unemployment. Greater inequality could simply generate too much savings and too much price volatility in financial asset markets that household spending could not hold up, leading to a less robust economy. Alternatively, if policy turns too Classical or too restrictive, again demand could be undercut and ED shifts left. Either of these events could lower net spending directly for any given net worth level, or indirectly by first lowering net worth, and thus undermining the ability to deficit spend. If demand falters but asset prices hold up (a shift in ED occurs only with no change in NW), conceivably growth and employment are less negatively influenced.

A failure of the financial system or the central bank to sustain sufficient money growth, or if households reach debt saturation, the ED function will shift left. Over the very long run, the gradual ending of capitalism's final frontier will put downward pressure on net worth, and therefore the economic vitality induced by private sector consumption, a problem that public policy will then be forced to address.

While normally more financially stable, IMMC is potentially subject to severe financial instability if all of the right conditions exist. The broader use of financial derivatives and the increased trading in financial assets could, under certain synchronized circumstances, produce a financial instability that spills over into the commercial economy and hence affects the business cycle. Adapting the concept of negative convexity for bond price curves to general financial stability aides in explaining what could happen.

Negative convexity in bond prices occurs when interest rate changes have varying effects in magnitude on bond values, not constant effects. As rates decline, callable bonds are more likely to be called so that the issuer can refinance at the lower rate, thereby reducing the old bond's duration and hence the investor's return. Bond prices rise but increasingly less in magnitude as rates decline because the likelihood of a call increases. Rising rates produce accelerating falls in bond prices as increasing duration stretches out interest and principal payments, and because the likelihood of delinquency and default increases. Therefore interest rate changes produce curved bond price functions as shown in Figure 6.4.[4]

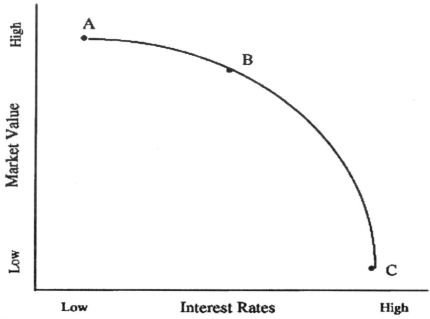

Figure 6.4. Market Value of a Convex Bond under Changing Rate Scenarios

The concept of convexity applies to the broader financial markets and how asset valuations respond to changing interest rates, returns, and risk. Asset valuation curves (AV), as shown below, display positive convexity under increasingly favorable financial conditions and negative convexity under increasingly unfavorable financial conditions. The "Sharpe ratio" (SR) is included with interest rates on the horizontal axis, and financial asset valuation is measured on the vertical axis. Sharpe measures the difference between business investment return (r) and the risk-less return on short term government debt (i), all divided by risk as measured by the standard deviation in possible return outcomes (SD).

$$SR = (r-i) / SD$$

First consider increasingly unfavorable financial conditions for business investment. Unfavorable conditions are shown on the right side of the graphic below where AV displays negative convexity. As rates rise, and the Sharpe ratio declines from rising risk[5] or falling investment returns (a movement to the right on the horizontal axis), economic conditions become more and more difficult. The increasingly unfavorable situation induces destabilizing, syn-

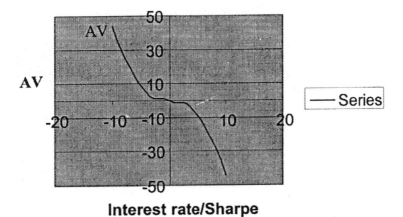

Interest rate/Sharpe

Figure 6.5.   The Asset Valuation Curve

chronized financial activity. The key ways in which instability can arise are summarized below:

(1) *dynamic hedging and feedback*: This occurs when portfolios are continually rebalanced in reaction to changing economic and political factors, and the effects of rebalancing create further portfolio shifts in the same direction.[6]

(2) *increased asset trading*: Deteriorating economic conditions can prompt more trading activity and greater volatility in asset values. More trading and volatility increase the perceived risk in holding financial assets, inducing more trading and selling.[7]

(3) *short selling*: Falling asset prices or the perception that asset prices are likely to fall, encourages more outright stock sales and more short selling. As interest in short selling increases, more stock is borrowed and sold, putting downward pressure on market prices.

(4) *negative carry trade*[8]: Rising rates and changing country economic fortunes can create a reversal in carry trades. First, higher borrowing rates squeeze interest margins. Second, higher rates in countries where borrowings originated redirect capital away from countries where loans were made, and the combined effect of capital outflow and better business conditions in the low rate countries, causes exchange rates to fall in higher rate nations, accelerating the capital outflow. Traders are subject to interest rate and exchange rate risk simultaneously.

(5) *concentrated holdings*: While derivatives potentially transfer and disperse risk, concentrated holdings imply that losses on derivatives are con-

centrated and may prompt liquidation. Forced liquidation can create
destabilizing unwinding of positions that create greater overall risk in financial markets.

(6) *momentum buying*: **Money** flows follow returns, and rising or high returns beget ever increasing inflows of cash to markets from investors
seeking to duplicate past performance. Stock and commodity markets become over-bought and company merger and buyout prices come to exceed the underlying economic fundamentals of the involved businesses.
Rising capital flows chase a shrinking pool of commercially viable endeavors. Once identified, excessive asset valuations prompt repeated
rounds of selling that cause prices to collapse.

If some of these destabilizing financial activities become more prominent as
rates rise and the Sharpe ratio falls, downward pressure on asset values increases, creating an accelerating price decline. It is the increased rapidity of
price declines that produces the negative convexity in AV, surely impacting the
phase of the business cycle and ultimately net worth and effective demand.[9]
The converse case is where economically favorable conditions, arising from
falling rates and a rising Sharpe ratio, induce financial activity that forces up
asset valuations in an accelerating manner. Therefore there is the positive convexity of AV on the left side of the graph, and the implied stimulus to effective
demand, that reinforces the original favorable economic conditions.

Moreover, the financial industry can encourage risk-taking by developing,
marketing, and selling more complex products or products offering potentially higher returns. The industry makes profits from selling more products
and services, and earns more off of higher risk products. Consider the quote
below from a prestigious financial analysis firm:

> Financial institutions have huge incentives to come up with new products that
> meet investors' desires for higher returns. Thus, in a world where the level of
> bond yields and spreads offer little appeal, the trick has been to create new ve-
> hicles that use complicated derivative strategies and/or increased leverage to
> create more exciting potential returns. The fact that risks are commensurately
> higher has not been an impediment to the success of these securities [BCA Re-
> search 12/06, 4].

DERIVATIVES AND FINANCIAL INSTABILITY

Financial derivatives could have the opposite effect than intended, inflicting
macroeconomic damage to an economy. Investment banks construct derivative products for investors like hedge funds that apportion the liabilities of

companies into risk categories called tranches, and then sell off the tranches separately. The senior level tranch contains the least risk while the junior tranch contains the most risk. As shown in Figure 6.6, short term liabilities such as commercial paper typically have relatively low risk and therefore become part of one of the two lower risk classifications. Equity holdings involve the most risk and take a junior status. If corporate bonds are rated below investment grade, they receive a junior ranking; otherwise, bonds are placed in the lower of two mezzanine tranches.

Investors expect that the derivative values of these tranches move in a coordinated fashion. If some event causes the equity tranch to fall in value, the other tranches should move in the same direction value wise. Investors may therefore be "long on" the equity tranch and "short" the mezzanine tranch as

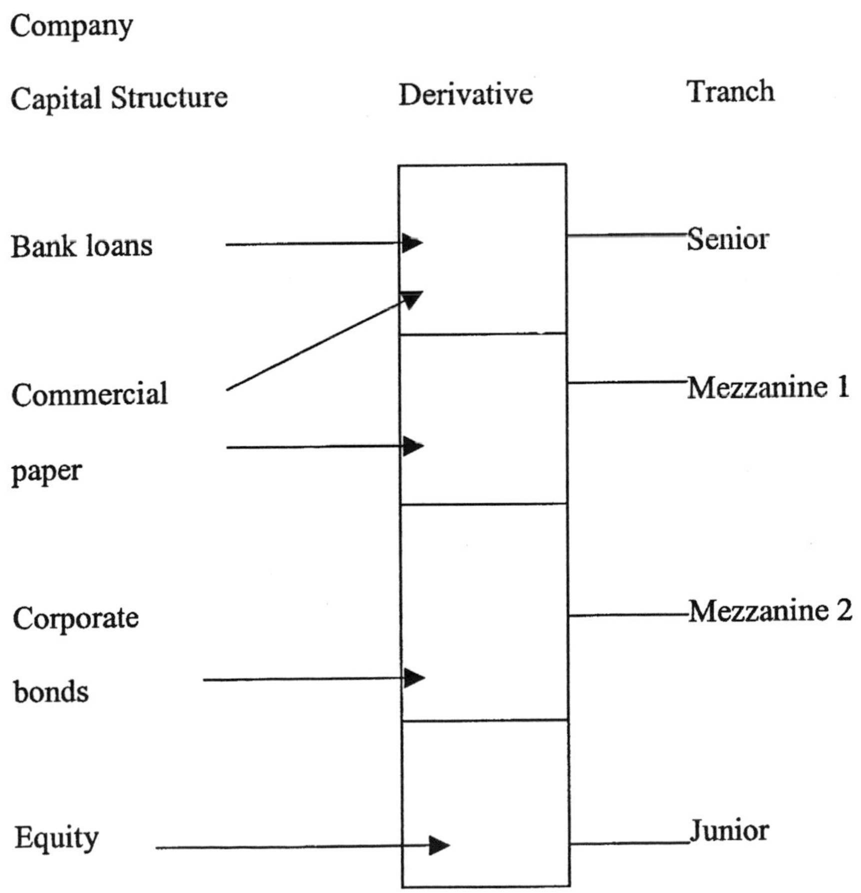

Company

| Capital Structure | Derivative | Tranch |

Figure 6.6.   Breakdown of a Derivative

a hedge. But what if the mezzanine tranch unexpectedly rises in value?[10] And what if there are numerous and heavily invested positions in the manner described?[11] Investors would be subject to losses on both positions taken, perhaps prompting a disorderly unwinding of the positions. Financial asset values could collapse, particularly if aggravated by the illiquidity of markets for complex derivative products and feedback effects among markets. Large trading losses would negatively affect net worth and effective demand. The business cycle phase could abruptly shift from expansion to contraction!

Derivatives come in many varieties and a common play is where the derivative seller takes a financial position exactly opposite the buyer. The derivative seller gets paid a fee for origination plus can garner a capital gain when an asset's price varies from some initial value but in the opposite direction than the position taken by the buyer. Someone must lose from this derivative contract and the question for financial stability is whether the losing party or parties can fully meet their obligation is a timely, orderly way.

The point is that any substantial change in the underlying business conditions of an economy can, if certain kinds of financial activity then take place simultaneously, create an explosive or parabolic effect on financial market prices, and consequently feedback onto the vitality of commercial conditions. The responsibility here of government or central banks must be to extend proprietary exams of banks to all financial institutions, particularly hedge funds and private equity funds. These enterprises are the recipients of the vast wealth created during the current phase of globalization, not unlike investment banks being the outlet for concentrated industrial wealth created during the 19th century.

A theoretical conundrum presents itself in that while macroeconomic instability has decreased during the most recent globalization period, financial asset price volatility has increased. Rogoff [2006] offers empirical evidence and citations of other works which confirm a decline in output volatility across MDC economies [13–15]. He also confirms an increase in financial asset and housing price volatility [15–16]. Rogoff's explanation for the disconnect has more to do with why asset price inflation has occurred than why asset price volatility has increased [16–17]. Drawing from this chapter, higher financial asset price volatility is most likely due to a combination of factors associated with the current age. The rising concentration of globally sourced money capital, negative convexity of prices, and synchronized, potentially destabilizing financial strategies are all relevant to global finance. The confluence of these three forces is the likely cause of greater financial market volatility. And the association of substantial financial asset price inflation with an increase in the variation of returns simply conforms to the long known positive risk-return correlation so fundamental to financial economics.

PUBLIC POLICY

During the globalization I era, Keynes understood that the system's vitality depended on the sufficient dispersal of income to effective demand, otherwise the system was subject to stagnation. Keynes reasoned that the greater the income and wealth, the greater the gap between the economy's potential output and the current level of effective demand. Employment could not increase further if business investment did not grow at a rate sufficient to absorb the community's savings at the current employment level [Keynes 1997, 28–30]. Keynes elaborates on the system's tendency toward economic difficulties:

> This analysis supplies us with an explanation of the paradox of poverty in the midst of plenty. For the mere existence of an insufficiency of effective demand may, and often will, bring the increase of employment to a standstill before a level of full employment has been reached. The insufficiency of effective demand will inhibit the process of production . . . Moreover the richer the community, the wider will tend to be the gap between its actual and its potential production; and therefore the more obvious and outrageous the defects of the economic system. For a poor community will be prone to consume by far the greater part of its output, so that a very modest measure of investment will be sufficient to provide full employment; whereas a wealthy community will have to discover much ampler opportunities for investment if the saving propensities of its wealthier members are to be compatible with the employment of its poorer members [30–31].

The current system has a similar problem. It must continually find a way to broadly share the fruits of economic development, not only in terms of widely allocating income across the globe, but importantly in fostering a wide distribution of property ownership and broadly rising asset values. A broadly distributed upward pressure on household net worth,[12] especially in MDC economies, is essential for continued economic prosperity and consequently, political stability.[13]

Whereas Keynes called for a "socialization of investment" [376–378], our current age demands a kind of "socialization of private property." A type of capitalism known as "Finance Capitalism" marked the second half of globalization's first era. The Keynesian critique of that era centered on the frequent potential for financial markets to undermine business investment. Keynes identified four factors inhibiting investment: volatility of stock prices, high interest rates, financial markets' assessments of business profitability dominating entrepreneurial assessments, and the revocability of stock and bond commitments relative to the irrevocable commitments to long term projects by businesses. Therefore Keynes writes,

> In conditions of laissez-faire the avoidance of wide fluctuations in employment
> may, therefore, prove impossible without a far-reaching change in the psychol-
> ogy of investment markets such as there is no reason to expect. I conclude that
> the duty of ordering the current volume of investment cannot safely be left in
> private hands [320].

Adjustments to tax rates and interest rates are offered to contend with the
problem of inadequate effective demand.

In the contemporary age, built as it is on the notion of a property conscious
society, effective demand is more dependent on an on-going symbiotic relationship between developed and less developed economies, and on a rising
importance of net worth in household spending decisions. A socialization of
private property does not mean to shift ownership and control to the state, but
to widely distribute privately held assets across the population. The state will
most certainly assist in this, implementing policies to off-set the inherent inclination towards private ownership concentration. What policies might come
into play here?

(1) *A state commitment to domestic full employment.* Activist aggregate de-
    mand management directed at maintaining high employment keeps pri-
    vate sector spending high and puts upward pressure on labor income.
    Greater income equality is achievable as labor income growth accelerates
    and more small business opportunities arise, while high incomes are
    taxed more heavily to fund government spending. Financial asset prices
    are sensitive to profit growth, a factor benefiting from economic growth.
    Consumer debt saturation is avoided.
(2) *A continuance of tax incentives promoting home ownership.* Tax incen-
    tives allow more people the financial wherewithal to purchase and main-
    tain residential property. Real estate assets provide diversification to port-
    folios and increase wealth and income security. Governments should
    continue their support of secondary mortgage markets to maintain liquid-
    ity and lower interest expense for borrowers. Property ownership creates
    a broad-based popular buy-in to the economic system.
(3) *A New Deal employee benefits policy.* As recommended in the conclusion
    chapter, government can assist MDC country firms to compete against
    any LDC country firm, no matter that business' cost structure, by taking
    over entirely employee pension and health care benefits. But public pol-
    icy commitment to funding basic benefits has a positive effect on net
    worth and thus the ability to net spend. Public funding of basic benefits
    extends social insurance across the population regardless of employment
    status and creates a floor to living standards, thus instilling a sense of se-

curity to the labor force. Ample public commitment to income security in an age of great change induces more risk taking by, and offers more pre-tax income for private wealth building to, the general public.[14]

(4) *A commitment to rigorous examinations of financial institutions.* Central banks and government agencies must require the reporting of income and balance sheet data of all financial institutions above a certain asset size. Disclosure of short positions, use of dynamic hedging, and employment of derivatives is a must. Authorities should compute the concentration in holdings and assess the riskiness of operations. The BIS could act as a central repository for national data and evaluation concerning the global ramifications of financial institutional practice. This policy allows for the regulatory oversight necessary to monitor financial activity and to avoid instability arising from the financial sector.

(5) *A government commitment to a full functional finance fiscal policy.* A fiscal policy truly informed by functional finance establishes budget priorities solely on meeting the social needs of the population and does not impose a funding constraint on spending. The size of the budget deficit is positively correlated with the level of private sector unemployment. Moreover, in this view, money is any asset that can create a claim on resources and acts as a means of payment. All modern money is the state's money in that the state determines the asset that functions as money and gives that asset value by demanding tax liabilities to be paid in that money.[15] The purpose of bond sales and taxes is to drain money from bank accounts that were credited as money flowed into these accounts as a consequence of the government's spending. Budget policy affects the level of effective demand by regulating the money flow through the economic system. Wray [2006] addresses the supposed budget constraint of government and identifies the instrumental value of functional finance in the passage below:

> . . . the notion of a government budget constraint only applies ex post, as a statement of an identity that has no significance as an economic constraint. . . . it is certainly true that any increase of government spending will be matched by an increase in taxes . . . or an increase of sovereign debt. But this does not mean that taxes or bonds actually "financed" the government spending. Government might well enact provisions that dictate relations between changes to spending and changes to tax revenues; it might require that bonds are issued before deficit spending actually takes place; it might require that the treasury have "money in the bank" before it can cut a check; . . . These provisions might constrain government's ability to spend at the desired level. However, economic analysis shows that they are self-imposed and are not economically necessary—although they may well be politically

necessary. What is the significance of this? It means that the state can take advantage of its role in the monetary system to mobilize resources in the public interest, without worrying about "availability of finance." [13].

Because governments don't have short run profitability constraints, long run social objectives are more easily pursued than in private enterprise. Promoting modern infrastructure and critical new industries helps to keep a country's economy globally competitive in the long run, and expanding demand in the short run. This kind of spending encourages MDC exports and an expansionary economic system, thus creating upward pressure on asset values and wealth, thereby driving effective demand.[16]

But actually implementing policies one and three require governments to accept non-Classical economic principles because conventional notions object to employment targets over inflation targets and state intervention levels necessary to take on the costs of extended social benefits. Adoption of functional finance budget policy necessitates not only a different philosophical perspective, but an alternative institutional make up as well. Under current institutional arrangements, profit oriented private banks and creditor dominated central banks significantly influence the circulation of money in economies. The separation of monetary policy from fiscal policy and central bank independence from the political process are institutional arrangements which reinforce the private control of funding economic development.[17] A full functional finance system overturns these arrangements, expediting the achievement of social objectives by ending imposed private constraints on public spending. Government spending and taxation would now actually influence the quantity of money in circulation and interest rates because the emission of new money becomes in part a public responsibility driven by politically supported goals.[18]

NOTES

1. Growth requires that the change in spending exceed the change in income (net deficits) and that new money finance the deficits, a role played by the banking sector.

2. The following is a succinct account of Minsky's [1986] Financial Instability Hypothesis.

3. The fact that many nations of the world are early in their maturation and modernization, the three factors just noted above should impart upward pressure for a long time on asset valuations and commercial profitability.

4. See the site http://www.tiff.org/TEF/glossary/convexity.html for an explanation and diagram of negative convexity.

5. Financial market volatility increases during business downturns as asset returns become more uncertain. For discussion and evidence of this, see BIS Papers #29, August 2006.

6. Static hedging occurs when a fixed position is taken in some assets whose expected performance will offset any negative change in valuation of some already held asset position.

7. Goldman Sachs' trading revenues in fiscal 2006 were 67% of its total revenues [BW 12/25/06, 32].

8. Carry trades arise when traders can borrow in currencies where rates are low and lend in countries where rates are high.

9. Regulatory concerns exist with the paucity of public information on hedge funds, and the liquidity and systemic effects of hedge fund activity. To get at these problems, some propose that regulatory authorities maintain a confidential database of hedge fund positions to monitor the potential buildup of risk. Authorities could also maintain a non-confidential database on hedge funds [Bernanke 5/2006].

10. Financiers could reason that while future expected profits of a firm are likely to decline, the balance sheet and future viability of a firm look solid, so demand increases for the company's debt.

11. As in other assets, concentration in hedge fund holdings exists. In a hedge fund industry of 7,000 funds, 80% of the industry's assets are held by 125 funds, which represent just 2% of the total industry [WSJ "Hedge-Fund Managers Make Midair Pitches" 9/29/06, pC1]. Also see WSJ, 4/19/07, page C1 "Big Hedge Funds Get Bigger, . . ."

12. And this is best measured by rising median household net worth not simply higher average net worth.

13. Rising MDC net worth fosters the growing export surpluses and FDI required to integrate and make prosperous LDCs.

14. While national taxes are higher, these taxes are progressively structured and some firms will pay higher wages with no benefits expense responsibilities. The general population should be less concerned with basic post–tax health care and pension expenditures and more fixated on building wealth in the form of pre-tax funding of financial assets and real estate.

15. A complete exposition and defense of the functional finance view is provided by Wray [1998].

16. The modern New Deal policy and functional finance is geared towards helping businesses in high living standard MDCs to compete against businesses in low living standard LDCs during the modern era.

17. These institutional arrangements were put into place following the collapse of the gold standard which acted as a major constraint to spending, tying the supply of money to the quantity of gold held.

18. Fiscal policy based on functional finance shares responsibility with household consumption in keeping effective demand rising.

Chapter Seven

The Discontents
of Contemporary Globalization

This text has tried to accomplish much in the fewest pages possible. This next chapter is importantly devoted to assessing the current globalization wave and carefully reflecting on the themes and arguments contained in the book. This chapter revisits and furthers the discussion points laid out in earlier chapters. But first a book summary is provided to highlight some of the central ideas and themes addressed earlier. A summary of this chapter is provided at the end.

CHAPTER SUMMARIES 1–6

Chapter One

This chapter contains an overview of the entire book where the main concepts and arguments are identified.

Chapter Two

The economic institutions of societies evolve over time, and therefore societies change in character and in economic performance. Modern globalization has occurred in three distinct waves, the first beginning in the 19th century, the second arising out of WWII, and the third most recent wave began around 1980. Each era is characterized by a hegemon that is the impetus to world integration and by a particular financial system and public policy. The nature of the firm changes with each age. Systemic defects and instability in the period up to the 1930s, induced both by institutions and war, lead to mid-century reforms. These reforms shift power away from the financial sector and support management dominated firms, unionization, and welfare states. The economic difficulties of the 1970s permit a resurgence in conservative economic doctrine and conventional public policy. These changes shape the modern wave of globalization. In addition to the end of Bretton Woods, new macroeconomic and employment policies come into play in Anglo-American countries. Finance again comes to dominate economic life evidenced by attention given to financial measures of well-being and financial strategies employed by new kinds of financial institutions. Along with unprecedented technological change, emerging markets, dollar denominated transactions, and money management characterize the third era of globalization. This chapter on history ends with a table comparing the key differentiating traits of each era of globalization.

Chapter Three

It is not colonization and racial superiority, as in the first wave, nor fighting communism and promotion of democracy, as in wave two, that drives the third wave of globalization. Era three is distinguished by a "clash between civilizations," a contention and struggle over identity defined by modernization and capitalism versus one of tradition and non-capitalist economics. All three eras share an effort to extend Western business and financial practices and institutions abroad. The United States has used a combination of government tax and foreign policy, the Washington Consensus as expressed through U.S. government departments and the IMF, and growing U.S. current account deficits to foster an Anglo-American directed new world order. These trade deficits are instrumental in invigorating world economic conditions and reaffirming the centrality of American economic policy, geo-political position, and diplomacy in effecting global conditions and outcomes. Anglo-American economies stimulate surpluses and growth in other countries, encouraging adoption of free market institutions and policies, and encouraging integration into a growing capitalist world system. Consequential to globalization three are stabilizing institutions and conditions that confront trends that threaten continued stability and growth. Positive and negative income and employment effects, potential rebuke of the current income distribution system, and upper class excesses create public policy challenges that may not be fully appreciated by governments in economically dominate countries. And these governments face the challenge of balancing the promotion of pro-business incentives and free trade while maintaining conditions of political-economic stability. An equally challenging problem is for governments to decide on how internationally engaged they desire to be and the degree of private economic influence they permit or succumb to as public authorities.

Chapter Four

There is a growing uniformity in central bank rhetoric about the practice of monetary policy throughout the world, underscored by Classical economic doctrine. Stated policy is heavily geared toward fighting inflation despite negative effects on growth, employment, financial stability, and income distribution. The European Central Bank exemplifies a monetary policy and rhetoric most closely associated with monetary restriction and inflation control. Defects are exposed in the construction of The Economic and Monetary Union which compound restrictive Bank policy. Proposals for alternative central bank policies and structure exist that give more weight to democratic input and financial stabilization over inflation control, which some economists believe is not really possible anyhow through interest rate manipulation. Globalization produces five important policy conundrums for central bankers, and persistent problems relating to financially induced crises pressure Banks to compromise desired policy settings for ones that ease credit conditions and rescue troubled economies.

Chapter Five

Along with the development of long term problems noted in chapter three, the current international financial and economic system confronts a series of more immediate problems. Economic imbalances, deflationary forces, capital flight and pro-cyclical finance are examples. Theoreticians and policymakers argue for structural reforms which include a global currency, a world central bank, a more efficient payment and clearing system, or alternatively, moving away from new or increased state intervention to no intervention. Concerns revolve around destabilizing exchange rate adjustments, capital mobility, and speculation. But these concerns have not compelled institutional change in a world where ongoing daily commerce seems unencumbered and government/central bank financial rescues appear to work and allow the system to continue without reform. And not all economic problems of the current age are located in financial practices or arrangements. Moreover, some governments are committed to enhancing domestic demand which assists the progress of global integration, and some financial activity such as use of derivatives may enhance economic stability. If the U.S. engine for globalization weakens, responsibility for growth and management may shift to Asia.

Chapter Six

This chapter covers business and financial cycles and how they interact. Cycle stability has increased since mid twentieth century and consumption has replaced investment as a key driver of profits and growth. Financial conditions can be conducive or undermining to business vitality, and the state of investor confidence is critical in maintaining prosperity. Overall, evolution in both the commercial and financial sectors facilitates economic stability and growth. Most forces in today's economies place upward pressure on household net worth, a factor of critical importance to sustaining effective demand. This chapter presents a theoretical model of contemporary globalization and then discusses factors that potentially could work to undermine the symbiotic prosperity between developed and developing nations characteristic of today's world. There are potentially important destabilizing financial activities and financial products that could generate accelerating asset price declines that negatively affect effective demand. The section ends arguing that if policymakers reject Classical economic theory and are open to institutional change, public policy can be a force promoting a wide distribution of private property, and thereby help to sustain world-wide economic prosperity and the political stability required to allow international integration to continue.

THE GLOBAL MARKET ECONOMY MYTH

Transnational businesses like to characterize the global economic system as a collection of competitive interdependent markets. This makes the study of international economics about market forces, and economic problems must be analyzed from a demand and supply framework with no institutional context. The world economy is viewed as comprised largely of enterprising individuals engaged with one another in competitive commerce, all tied together through markets. Business, workers, and consumers react to market signals and markets produce efficient outcomes because people must earn a profit at what they do or otherwise they will fail. Consumers are the main beneficiaries, reaping volumes of low cost, quality products.

The main, though not only, problem with this view is that it abstracts away from real world institutions and their policies. All outcomes stem from impersonal market forces, not institutions. Absent in this story is responsibility, power, and conflict. The world political economy is actually structured around institutions which are organized economic vehicles used to achieve financial objectives. Multi-billion dollar corporations and banks, amassing and employing huge amounts of resources and people, are specifically responsible for economic development and performance. Transactions take place in markets but the prices that are displayed, and the productive capacity and output that are confronted, result from a long line of industry decisions and planning.

Two kinds of markets prevail in capitalist economies, one created through contracts and one that exists for traders to price goods known as commodity markets. Overwhelmingly, the economy is built around contract markets [Davidson 1996]. These markets arise to sell goods and services where contracts specify the prices to be paid and other obligations of the signing parties. Once the goods and services reach retail, it's a take it or leave it situation. But in commodity markets, speculative trading takes place where commodity values vary frequently over the course of a day. Buyers and sellers speculate on the economic (demand and supply) facts of the industry, for which the industry (the collection of firms) is responsible. Market prices are the consequence of industry-member businesses and speculators basing trades on known and suspected industry conditions.

By comprehending world commerce merely as numerous transactions among individuals, no thought can be seriously given to power and conflict. Globally positioned corporations and financial centers cannot impinge on the market but must comply with consumer demands. The agglomeration of property, people, resources, legal talent, and political connections somehow has no relevance in a global market economy. Conflicts need not be contemplated because market forces compel property owners to serve consumers and take care of workers to assure the ability to compete.

An institutional view however invites consideration of not simply inter-firm rivalry for growth and dominance but intra-firm struggle over the revenues earned by the enterprise; just what income distribution should prevail among the contributors to the firm's production and sales? Those with the most power tend to prevail and the key source of power is manifested in the way the institution is structured. Moreover, conflicts exist among a nation's most important companies and the state as disagreements readily occur over the location of business, corporate decisions and actions, and the direction of investment. Government and corporations fight over the pricing and production of essential services, particularly where public regulation or supervision already exists.

And now that International Money Manager Capitalism has created a stock-holding middle class, a substantial fraction of people rely on firms for employment and capitalist income. And it's their connection to the stock exchange and to wage labor that they have committed their wellbeing. When overall economic performance is good, millions of new committed corporate capitalists are created. But downturns in employment or asset values can threaten a serious revision in thinking and reversion to reformist views as in past eras.

Two points of importance reveal themselves. Markets alone cannot be safely let to regulate distribution since they largely reflect outcomes of institutional power and competition, not impersonal causal forces. And second, populist politics can break out in capitalist nations when issues of inequality and fairness are solely left to unregulated private economic outcomes.

MARKETS AND EFFICIENCY

Speculative trading activities have increased during modern globalization. More firms nowadays make most or all of their revenue from trading for their own accounts or trading for clients. In addition to the traditional liquid markets in stocks, bonds, and farm products, country currencies, oil, and derivatives of financial assets are routinely traded.

Free-market fundamentalists and classical economists argue for market determined outcomes partly predicated on the notion of efficiency. Buying and selling are done on demand and supply factors, and the resulting market prices require no centralized body to determine valuations or to balance demand with supply. Decentralized pricing and pricing that captures traders sentiments concerning economic benefits and costs are said to be efficient. Economics is importantly about efficient resource allocation, and the market mechanism is the vehicle that produces desired outcomes.

While markets continually match buyers with sellers and prices change according to trading pressures, competitive, auction-like markets produce continually fluctuating prices. Trades are made on facts and relevant experiences of those involved. But trades are also made on misinformation, personal interpretations of facts, human emotion, and expectations of possible future events and policy. Outright volatility is not necessarily and always the outcome, but perpetually changing prices are normal.

If the "right price" is a market determined price, is it necessarily the case that speculative market trading gets us the right price? Speculative trading is done to exploit price discrepancies at a point in time or on asset valuations to generate capital gain. Speculators seek capital gain. Profit driven buying and selling is characterized by all of the factors noted above, activity disconnected from commercial need.

Perceived profit opportunities beget trading which in turn can create more fluctuation in prices that tempt more trading because the fluctuations create more potential profit opportunities. IMMC has increased the variety of assets available for speculation and technology has made these markets liquid and fast. When upward trends in asset valuations are established, risk-taking increases, driving prices beyond what fundamentals call for, a situation known as an over-bought market. Risk-taking changes to risk-aversion and market corrections occur.[1]

Derivatives are financial assets that allow businesses and speculators to hedge against losses that could arise from their current financial position. The derivative offers an off-setting, oppositely correlated financial gain to whatever downside risk is currently held. Hence derivatives are created to hedge against risk stemming from price fluctuation, but moreover derivative assets are traded, and derivatives of derivatives are created to protect against derivative price fluctuation. All of this invites more speculative trading.

It is reasonable to conclude from this that markets affected by speculative trading are not necessarily producing the "right price" and foster economic activity not based on material provisioning but gambling. Price fluctuations make corporate planning more difficult and investment more risky. Speculation represents the diversion of economic resources away from productive affairs. So it seems that Globalization Three has imbued the international economy with a dimension of inefficiency.

BANKING, DEBT, AND INSTABILITY

Banks are responsible for injecting new money into the system through lending. Both banks and central banks largely accommodate private money demand by supplying new money, given whatever demand exists at the banking system's loan rate mark-up over the central bank's policy rate.

Firms in the economy compete for money. They compete for consumers' dollars and they compete for finance. Money acquisition is the measure of commercial success. Firms that establish a competitive advantage attract more finance at lower cost and earn more from consumers. Less competitive companies earn less and attract less finance at more expense.

Since any given bank only loans X amount of money yet expects to be repaid X plus a premium, there must be a continuous injection of new money into the economy by the banking system.[2] Firms and consumers must engage in new-money financed deficit spending to grow the economy. Economic growth generates the growth in earnings necessary to repay claims created when financial firms provided credit. Equity financed investment creates the same kind of claims because stockholders demand capital gains on their shares. Company dividend payments and stock repurchases help create capital appreciation. Capitalism is not healthy unless it's growing, and growth warrants deficit spending financed by debt and money creation. Financial sector health is evidenced by rising bond and stock markets. Continuous economic growth requires rising private sector debt loads, and financial market strength depends on commercial success. These basic relations are identified below:

$$\text{Total Spending} = \text{Total Income} = \text{GDP}$$

Private spending can be funded from income (Y) plus intermediated savings[3] (S) plus new money (M) borrowings. This sum equals GDP.

$$Y + S + M = \text{GDP}$$

To grow GDP, the economy must net deficit spend.[4] Net deficits will equal the change in GDP. The sum of all deficits is the economy's debt load.

$$\text{Net deficits} = \text{DGDP}$$
$$\text{S deficits} = \text{debt}$$

Deficits and debt must increasingly rise to sustain sufficient GDP growth to sustain financial asset appreciation. With growth and prosperity come increasing financial sector claims on commercial and consumer income. Rising financial claims to income affect income distribution dynamics. If workers are sufficiently weak in claiming income from the total revenues of firms but finance presents strong claims, income inequality will increase, favoring property interests. If labor's claim is powerful, income equality tends to increase. Inflation may result if sustained upward pressure on labor income prompts property owners to partially offset labor's share increase through price and interest rate hikes.

   While a new money-debt financed spending system is a prerequisite for growth, where continually higher spending is needed to achieve on-going growth in income, this very process sets in motion economic upturns that are not sustainable by the private system alone. One of two effects may arise. First, debt limits or credit saturation can be reached that lead to economic downturns. An inability to service debt or an inability to access more debt stops spending from growing. Financial fragility could create a financial crisis and recession, or economic stagnation could simply develop. If the latter is the case, the economy doesn't contract but is unable to grow, slowly undermining business creation and employment. These consequences can arise from a second source, namely the mismatch of income gains and those who took on the most debt. Sometimes the firms and consumers who take on the most debt wind up in more difficult budget circumstances because their debt-financed risks don't pan out. Defaults occur and growth stops.

Two means exist to address private sector proneness to financial crises. A more egalitarian income distribution would mitigate fragility and debt dependence by expanding access to credit to more borrowers and by reducing the concentration of and control over society's savings. Large and growing middle classes in capitalist states would ensure a growing effective demand for business output. Upward pressure on labor and small business income, and progressive taxation of incomes, generate greater domestic demand and lessen the degree of speculative trading. Wealth taxes on concentrated savings inhibit the development of a leisure class and speculative trading. This is the policy undertaken by Western capitalist nations during and after the Great Depression.

A second preventive is to shift complete monetary authority to governments and away from upper-class-based central banks. Under conditions of private sector unemployment, national governments would inject more money through spending into the economy than they drain through taxation, thus regulating the flow of funds to meet employment and growth policy objectives. Governments' responsibility would be to run deficits to augment aggregate demand instead of relying on borrowed money from capitalists, and adjust deficits to a size sufficient to drive their respective economies to full employment. This fiscal policy approach breaks the private hold over money now in force, and uses public sector budget deficits to build surpluses in private sector budgets, a preventative of financial fragility. Cash flow surplus households and businesses would not require high debt levels to acquire material needs and wants.[5]

MACRO STABILITY, MICRO INSTABILITY

During globalization three, a number of MDCs are experiencing prolonged upturns in economic activity, and display increases in macroeconomic stability. Some EU countries and Japan represent exceptions, though their economics are more often stagnant or slow growing than in outright contraction. Despite heighten macro stability, microeconomic instability is higher. There is more volatility in sales, profits, and employment than in the earlier era [Samuelson 2/20/06].[6] Why so?

Government deficit spending in the UK and US, and gradually improving credit conditions since the early 1980s, has assisted overall growth. Fiscal and monetary policies in China and India are stimulative. US trade deficits are helping to stabilize the German and Japanese economies. Various emerging market economies are growing through export surpluses. And when financial crises develop, international institutions intervene to turn around these economies, avoiding negative spillover effects elsewhere. Complementing these public policy measures are the stabilizing private sector structural changes addressed in chapter three and improvements in national business cycle stability discussed in chapter six. These factors together explain the enhanced macro and global economic stability observed during this age of globalization.

Microeconomic instability is higher however, and this is consistent with the increased dynamics imparted through rapid technological change, deregulation, and altered economic flows. Old patterns of economic flows, business structure, and employment opportunities are overthrown as economies reconfigure themselves in the global economic age. Microeconomic flux exists within macroeconomic stability. Instability, and the uncertainty, anxiety, and insecurity[7] that attends to this, play out in the following specific ways:

(1) Global companies are increasingly disaggregated networks of operations, a consequence in part of technology and free trade. Workers can be readily employed and unemployed anywhere and anytime necessary as firms continually strive to find the lowest cost, most productive, or most talented labor pools. Off-shoring and outsourcing are thought to be "transformational" in that firms use these options to remake themselves into competitive powerhouses [BW 1/30/06, 50–58, 64, 122].

(2) Very flexible labor markets exist in the U.S., and pressures are mounting for Europe to model itself after the U.S. Traditional long term contracts that provide employment and benefit security are being replaced by short term contracts or no contracts in some European countries. These measures are applied to younger workers and non-union labor, freeing business to hire and fire, and to reduce benefit commitments. Chinese law that once placed employees ahead of creditors in receiving payments from bankrupt companies now puts creditors ahead of labor.[8] The 2000s economic upturn in the U.S., like that of the 1990s, took extra time in generating net job growth and concentrated job creation in just a few private sector industries.[9] Employment flexibility has grown with employer resistance to private sector unionization and from employer escape to Sunbelt states for new investment.[10]

(3) Capital flows run increasingly to emerging market economies and employment growth shifts to new and globally competitive industries located outside of MDCs. More and more service and professional employment is outsourced to LDCs. Higher and/or different educational requirements to meet MDC business demand place income and family life pressures on labor to keep up with what business needs, or risk permanent un-employability. Income distribution shifts toward profit and

granting of stock options to a small group of highly paid employees, and away from wages. Employment growth lags and is less correlated with output growth, because firms can globally source labor as needed and use productivity growth to limit hiring [Silva 2005].

A model of labor's predicament is in Figure 7.1. MDC wage growth (w) is measured on the vertical axis above the origin and capital outflow (ko) is measured below the origin. The horizontal axis measures foreign labor (L) hired by developed country transnational companies. The employment curve (E) displays the quantity of foreign labor hired given wage growth in developed countries. As wage growth increases, more foreign labor is hired. The employment curve relevant for Era 2 is given by E2. Low wage growth does not induce hiring of foreign labor but growth above w2 does. The steep E line indicates that high wage growth is necessary to induce much hiring abroad. Wage growth w3 induces the hiring of L1 foreign labor, which in turn produces a minimal encouragement of world integration (WI) measured by low capital outflows equal to ko1. Economic systems in Era 2 were built around nation-state economies, domestic production and employment, capital controls, and trade largely involving only MDC linkages. Limited capital mobility, the state of technology, and public policy worked to support an emphasis on domestic economic vitality, domestic business investment, unions, and income supports. World integration occurred but mainly tying together developed countries.

But the third phase of modern globalization creates more difficult economic circumstances for domestically oriented business and labor. Now low wage growth induces foreign hiring and outward investment, so the new employment curve becomes E3, one of much lower slope. Any given increase in w creates a relatively larger increase in foreign hiring; w3 produces L2 (much greater than L1) and capital outflow ko2 (much greater than ko1). Free trade policy is connecting nearly the entire world. New technologies and the profit motive encourage cross-border commercial and financial ties. Globalization pressures prompt dispersal of company assets, flexible labor markets, and more mobile capital. And a self reinforcing mechanism becomes engaged here. As MDC wage growth encourages more foreign hiring, more imports, and more FDI and portfolio investment, there is a loss of bargaining power and more anxiety among labor and domestic business. As more domestic business builds an international dimension to themselves, and labor confronts more flexible labor markets, even relatively low wage growth induces even more foreign hiring and more outflow of money. In the model, the E and WI curves pivot downward, increasing economic pressure on domestic business and workers.

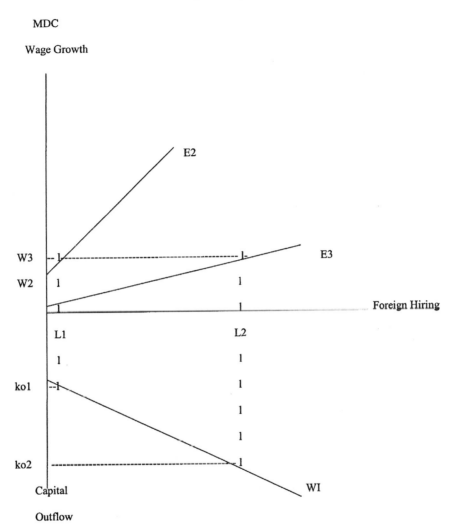

Figure 7.1.   **Globalization and Employment-Wage Effects**

Public policy issues arise here having to do with intra-country income distribution and domestic aggregate demand management. With respect to the
former, certain classes of workers and property owners reap much financial
gain from globalization. Upper middle class professional incomes rise, and
business profits and stock prices rise. Class economic advantage arising from
globalization induces political pressure to expedite the current economic
trend through policy and creates economic incentive for internationalizing
business and finance. With respect to the latter, policy makers are stuck with

Table 7.1.   Fiscal Policy Options and Consequences

Policy Variable	Fiscal Policy Stimulus	No Fiscal Stimulus
Wage growth	Substantial upward pressure	Little pressure on wages to rise
Unemployment	Falling unemployment rate	Rising unemployment rate
Globalization	Rapid pace of globalization from stimulus, trade policy, profits, and technology	Slow pace but promoted by trade deals and technology
Inequality	Rising intra-nation income and wealth inequality	Rising intra-nation income and wealth inequality
Interest rates	Rising rates but tempered by inward capital flows and financial crisis potential	Falling rates to jump start depressed economic conditions
Net Worth	Upward pressure on stock prices and real estate values	No policy support for asset prices

a dilemma. Fostering domestic activity lowers unemployment and puts upward pressure on wages but rising wage growth encourages the kind of hiring and capital outflow that gradually undermines the demand stimulus. Alternatively, allowing the private economy to languish dampens momentum toward fast globalization but also greatly limits domestic wage growth and produces higher domestic unemployment. Either way, policymakers confront political pressures to alter course.

Table 7.1 displays the two policy options confronted with the likely economic outcomes they generate. Policymakers are inclined to choose a fiscal policy that stimulates domestic aggregate demand, and indeed Anglo-American governments have taken this option. Domestic labor and business are helped some in that wages and profits receive a boost, unemployment is low, and asset prices are propelled higher. The pace of globalization is accelerated, prompting transnational corporate support. Monetary policy may run at cross purposes however. To the extent that central banks restrict credit to fight inflation, their freedom to lift rates substantially is limited given the potential for financial crises in this era and their incomplete control over the yield curve.[11] On the contrary, if central bankers employ a financial policy over a traditional monetary policy as advocated by reformers of Classical central banking, central bank policy would not contravene fiscal policy.

While overall economically and politically better than option two of no stimulus, the first option splits the workforce along lines of who is better positioned for globalization or who can transition quickly to meet the demands of the age. Inequality rises from both policies but more opportunities avail themselves from option one. Perhaps there is a third policy, a way out completely from this political and policy dilemma? Employing Palley's [1998] proposal that developed countries simultaneously pursue expansionary policies would direct more of the economic stimulus outwardly directed from globalization back into economies employing stimulative domestic fiscal policy. Conceivably, improved domestic business conditions and less inequality are outcomes of coordinated nation-state policy action.

GLOBALIZATION AND GROWTH

Globalization advocates argue that all countries should pursue an outward orientation to economic development and growth. Statistics reveal that growth is positively correlated to openness. Export oriented industrialization strategies (EOI), as in East Asia, and efforts to modernize, as in India and China, demonstrate their effectiveness in generating growth and reducing poverty [Bhagwati 2004, chapter 5].

Countries which pursue outward and open trade policies succeed in part because openness invites additional commercial connections and more potential economic activity because more players exist to trade and transact. But what is critical to achieving growth is that the country or region opening itself to economic integration is seen as a new frontier or new market, initiating capital flows from already developed nations. High 19th century US growth rates occurred because West Europeans saw the U.S. as a new investment frontier offering new profitable outlets for capital. Frontier expansion allowed Midwestern and Western farms and businesses to grow, selling to Europeans and Americans in the East. The same circumstance explains the growth success of contemporary emerging market economies. Europe, Japan, the U.S., and other MDCs make EOI strategies into success stories by creating high demand for emerging market goods, resources, and people.

One should not infer that EOI strategies are invariably good for any country at any time. Circumstances matter. Success requires an outward looking and growing MDCs that seek and need new investment outlets to resuscitate domestic profits. New frontier emerging market economies are successes because such circumstances exist in this era. In fact, there would be no "new era" were it not for FDI and the import needs of MDCs, and policies that foster capital outflow from MDCs.

And as Keynes [1997] argued in the 1930s, during a time when finance dominated the economy not unlike today, the positions conveyed favoring moderately high interest rates then and now are flawed. The conventional position advocates high rates to stimulate risk taking and to foster savings to fuel growth. High rates are as well seen as a means to prevent a boom from collapsing into a depression. On these points Keynes speaks to our current age of international money manager capitalism:

(1) Risk taking is best exemplified by the entrepreneur not the finance capitalist who receives a reward based on the scarcity of capital, for which no intrinsic reason exists, and for which there is "no genuine sacrifice" made [376]. It is the long term investor who willingly makes irrevocable commitments, prompted by constructive impulses, who "most promotes the public interest" [chapter 12].

(2) Savings in the aggregate cannot be increased by incentivizing people to save more out of current income. A few individuals may successfully save more by restraining consumption but if done more broadly across the population the result will be to reduce effective demand creating a decline in business sales and income. In the aggregate, less will be saved. For Keynes, "up to the point where full employment prevails, the growth of capital depends not at all on a low propensity to consume (high savings rate) but is, on the contrary, held back by it" [372–373]. Moreover "the extent of effective saving is necessarily determined by the scale of investment and that the scale of investment is promoted by a low rate of interest" [375].

(3) Keynes opposed using high interest rates to prevent a boom from occurring, particularly because he never observed investment to be high enough to create full employment in a laissez-faire system of minimal public intervention. Low rates not only encourage strong economic growth but allow a boom to proceed. "The right remedy for the trade cycle (business cycle) is not to be found in abolishing booms and thus keeping us permanently in a semi-slump; but in abolishing slumps and thus keeping us permanently in a quasi-boom" [322].

Besides these enduring reasons to maintain low rates, policymakers must tailor policy to the needs of the age. The current economic system and globalization require the continuance of private sector deficit spending and asset price appreciation. High rates undermine the ability of financial and real estate markets to advance asset prices. High rates discourage borrowing and raise debt servicing costs. An important part of people's wealth accumulation stems from capital gain, promoted by low rates of interest, not savings accumulated out of current income. Furthermore, high interest rates are not essential to maintain a high U.S. dollar value given the ongoing central role of America in world affairs. Policies based on these recognitions are best for global growth.

Anglo-American governments and American-dominated international institutions have pressured emerging market economies to dramatically open their economies to global trade and capital flows. This trade liberalization argument is embedded in the Washington Consensus which makes the case that open global competition and market forces are the best basis to encourage growth in developing economies. But a wholesale acceptance and implementation of this policy has often failed to generate the kind of performance promised by the policy's adherents. While some openness to the world economy and institutional modernization are helpful in injecting dynamism and growth into relatively poor developing countries, their economies typically lack important structural characteristics to ensure broad-based economic success and independence. Developing countries require strong indigenous commercial and banking sectors to support the kind of internal employment and spending that create positive multiplier effects.[12] These countries need a relatively diverse economy so that overall economic performance is not undermined by single industry troubles. And importantly, a robust domestic sector helps to maintain freedom from too much outside transnational corporate influence and to ensure sufficient domestic economic influence on developing countries' politics and policies.

Kregel [2003] writes about the failure of Latin American economies to sustain any measurable economic success following implementation of trade liberalization policies. These countries have failed to produce sustainable economic growth and have experienced stagnation in wages and per capita incomes. The distribution of income is now more unequal. Opening to the world and liberalization has subjected these economies to rapid flows of financial capital that affect interest rates and their external balances are affected more by debt service payments. For Kregel, free trade must raise domestic value added if it to be seen as successful policy, and the benefits of free trade are only had if the economy is already at full employment. The Latin American experience has generally not raised domestic value added and liberalization occurred under conditions of unemployment.

The work of Greenwald and Stiglitz [2006] is compatible with the notion that emerging market economies should not quickly open their economies to full scale competition from abroad. Some Asian economies, west Europe, and the U.S. all represent case studies in the use of development strategies that protected domestic economies. The argument here is that technological change exerts a real positive force on domestic growth if countries allow for the development of an indigenous manufacturing base that promotes technological spillovers into more traditional economic sectors. To Greenwald and Stiglitz industrial sectors are sources of innovation where knowledge is produced and disseminated. These authors argue for tariff protection that is broadly based enough to avoid the creation of special industry-interest groups and self limiting in that when prosperous domestic industries reach world-class status and begin to export, commercial protection is removed.

PUBLIC REGULATORY INFRASTRUCTURE

The policies that emerge out of crisis prone and social problem plagued 19th century nation-state capitalism provide the foundation for the prosperity of 20th century economic development. But history repeats itself. Currently and relentlessly, the third wave of globalization and its policymakers are creating a modern variant of the unencumbered free market, laissez-faire economic system that predates the rise of state intervention and income support programs. Washington Consensus type policies, coupled with increased competition world-wide, tend to concentrate opportunities and stratify economic outcomes within nations. Two observations are warranted here.

(1) First, the current globalization trend produces visible prosperity in part from inheriting an institutional structure and policy activism that foster stability and growth. During globalization II, welfare states were erected and state spending increased. Large middle classes developed and income supports were implemented. These structures and policies remain largely in place, albeit with some erosion. Therefore, the gradualism with which globalization proceeds, while tending towards a more laissez-faire system, is nonetheless supported by a successful institutional structure. The legacy of globalization II is a supportive foundational base that limits the vicissitudes of open competition.

(2) Second, as argued by Palley [Blog 1/18/06], globalization raises the "specter of destructive competition" across the globe, and that the pursuit of profit can lead to "sub-optimal outcomes." Policymakers must develop "a perspective (that) leads to the idea of regimes of competition," and policy should aim to create a competitive environment in which working families prosper. "The challenge is to design regulatory institutions (regimes) that balance the Keynesian need for stable flows of demand and income with the capitalist need for economic incentives." Palley argues that these regimes prevent excessive economic fluctuations, monopoly, and labor exploitation. For Palley, "what appears to maximize well-being from an individual perspective can be sub-optimal once the competitive inter-play of actions is taken into account." Properly designed institutions ensure that material welfare is well shared across classes and society. Palley [1998] advocates a regime consisting of social tariffs, capital flow restrictions, and a "Common Markets" based international trade.[13]

A conundrum arises from Globalization III. By advancing trade flows and economic connections, by stimulating investment and employment, globalization is spreading material improvement, and even prosperity, world-wide. A certain excitement about economic life and prospects for improvement spread across the globe as economic activity increases. Conventional measures of outcomes from globalization largely reveal a rather wide distribution of success. Levels of unemployment, numbers of new business formations, income and output growth, are moderately to very good in many countries. Financial crises are quickly reversed and recessions short lived.

Yet, there are negative attending effects to globalization that are ill measured or hidden from view. Negative social outcomes result from the same processes that generate benefits. While employment and career stability are down, the duration of unemployment and employment dislocation are up. Capital mobility is forcing greater labor mobility, and hence less community continuity. While increased competition has beneficial consequences on technological innovation and risk taking, competition also produces many losers. More risk is shifted to the individual as public income supports deteriorate, and disruptions to income flows are more frequently experienced. Volatility in economic life, or the mere threat of it, undermines people's efforts to commit to long term financial and family plans.

The puzzle for policymakers is to somehow continue the good effects while softening and responding to the social downsides. Moreover, they have a responsibility and ethical obligation to not ignore the downsides or pretend they don't exist. So too with the executives and capitalists directly responsible for the attending challenges to family life brought about by their decisions. Executive decisions have human consequences that obligate attention and redress.

Perhaps what is needed in the advanced countries is a modern "New Deal?" Larger middle classes, higher living standards, greater tax and regulatory costs, and highly valued currencies on world markets are modern comforts that subject MDC labor to extensive competition based on cost differences. Exploiting these cost differences creates huge profits for international business. If we are to let cost-driven competition persist, why not create a New Deal style framework that supports middle class economic standards by removing an important component to business costs? Let globalization proceed apace but ensure that no degradation of wellbeing occurs. What would such a framework entail? Essentially all that is required is for the state to socialize employer-provided benefits funded by those most benefiting from the current policy.

Complete state takeover of healthcare and pension costs throughout the economy will significantly diminish business expenses and allow American-based companies to be cost and price competitive globally. Since asset price appreciation is an important component in fostering private spending and the "ownership society" notion, wealth taxes paid yearly and estate taxes paid at death become the state's main financing tool. Progressive income and profit taxes could round out the bulk of governments' tax receipts. In accord with "functional finance," any required government deficits are to be funded from money creation.

NATIONAL SECURITY STATE

Globalization waves are driven by a hegemonic power. Britain drove the first wave of globalization, and the U.S, drove the second wave and is currently driving the third wave of world commercial and financial integration. In all three globalization periods, the hegemon pursues leadership not just through economic and diplomatic ties, but through a global military reach. Global economic objectives are sought and achieved in part through national security and military strategies. In fact the notion of national security is inextricably linked to growth in international trade and a world military presence. Economic success for the hegemon, and for globalization in general, requires open communication and transportation lanes, access to inexpensive energy, and adoption of common regulations and institutions across countries. Military presence is for maintaining stability and coercing compliance with the hegemon's principles and goals. The global hegemon pushes free trade ideology and open trade policies.

In the second half of the 19th century, the British occupy Egypt, conquer the upper Nile valley, and consolidate their holdings in central, south, and east Africa. The British control India and Burma, New Zealand and Australia, and Canada. Other European empires and the Japanese divide up the world with the British, driven by nationalism and the pursuit of economic advantage. The Powers also sought economic and social stability to secure business opportunities. The British sought influence in South Africa to secure gold to bolster their currency. Their efforts in Egypt are directed to securing British creditors and securing the Suez Canal route to India. Armed force is often used to bring about the influence necessary to achieve economic and territorial ambitions. By dominating global networks, the European Powers impose on foreign lands a system of rigidly bound territories [Bayly 2004, 228–234]. The consequence of imperialism is seen in the growth of a Western-dominated world economic system, where governments become key economic actors in forging formal trading arrangements [238].

U.S. global leadership and the Cold War characterize the second wave of globalization. The American dominated Bretton Woods system promotes stable, expansionary trade and capital flows. American trade policy opens the

U.S. market to all nations rejecting alliance with the USSR. Western culture and economic ways spread across the globe. American military posture contains Soviet expansion and fights hot wars in Third World states. The U.S, strives to create Third World capitalist democracies and free economic systems. Military bases and the Navy promote social and economic stability, and keep commercial trading ties open. Access to foreign oil sources is maintained through alliances with democratic and non-democratic states.

While the fixed exchange rate monetary system and the division of the world into Cold War camps end, U.S. world hegemony is maintained and expands in the third wave of globalization. The IMF, the WTO, and the U.S. government impose onto or encourage the adoption of economic Neo-liberalism and democratic governance among a growing number of nations. Mid-east and Russian energy sources, and oil competitors China and India, become ever more serious foreign policy concerns for Western interests. As the American military reach becomes global, interventions in non-capitalist areas increase and efforts are directed at stabilizing and integrating globally disconnected states.

Does globalization require an aggressive military policy by the hegemon? Can the historical link between globalization and militarism be broken without hindering globalization? The British and some other European powers conducted a multi-century military policy of intervention throughout the world. United States foreign policy combating the spread of socialism and communism lasted almost a century. The "White Man's" burden justified European aggression and atheistic- totalitarianism justified the Cold War. The integration-blocking cultural and economic divide between radical and fundamentalist Arab-Islamic interests and Western Anglo-American interests is now the arena for global contention. High level policymakers currently in power in America warn of a possible 30 to 70 year war against "global terrorism," the argued manifestation of the current contention.[14]

Sweeping and costly global military commitments require justification to permit interventionist policy to be ongoing and uninterrupted. Some U.S. foreign policy elites do try to characterize all events and disagreements with non-capitalist, non-modern nations as somehow threatening to security interests or disruptive to a global economic advance that benefits everyone. As addressed later in this chapter, intervention, whether commercial or military, can create resistance and the impression of a security or economic threat. That perceived threat in-turn "invites and warrants" hegemon intervention.[15] But forced whole-sale transformation of parts of the globe into integrated modern capitalist states necessitates long run human sacrifice of all involved. And as well, the U.S. decision to move forward on such an adventure, as experienced by earlier hegemons, is really a choice to engage in a long term "war," not an obligation or compulsion to do so.

Coercion is not essential for successful globalization. Lack of hegemonic coercion may slow integration, may slow adoption of certain capitalist institutions, but not out-rightly prevent growing world commercial relations. Less nation-state uniformity may prevail but the existence of such does not necessarily block some trade, cooperation, dialogue, and peaceful coexistence. If the U.S. really wants to export freedom, it must allow other cultures to be free to be not like Americans.

What does the historical role of global leadership suggest for the U.S.? There appears to be an historical connection among a nation's security interests, its military projection, and its economic needs. Arguably these three variables are mutually interdependent, each reinforcing the other. A hegemon and secondary global rivals thus view these three variables as bound up into one overarching national challenge, necessitating an integrated strategy to realize some perceived or expected nationally optimal outcome. What this creates is a perpetual, unrelenting concern about economic prosperity and national security. This concern becomes a worry or even fear about decline or loss of national prestige, wealth, and sovereignty. Amplifying the worry is the competitive economic order that is now global in context. Not every nation "can win" all the time or to the same degree. We therefore get "democratic" nations running aggressive military-political-economic policies, justified as necessary for the welfare and preservation of liberty and opportunity. While governments and economic elites are behind such policies, the human and financial sacrifice is spread widely.

Globalization and the global oil economy intersect with national security quite clearly. Rapid economic growth and development of modern systems depend critically on oil. Oil has become a tradable commodity during the current globalization period. The final price of oil is set by commodity markets, and commodity markets are subject to trades made daily based on current and expected industry conditions. Asset appreciation in America and some other countries is a critical driver of spending that keeps world economies stimulated, and to that end, policymakers pursue courses that foster demand for assets. Pushing globalization forward through market integration fosters transactions in assets and upward pressure on asset values. Keeping the world energy supply accessible and inexpensive is of paramount important in the hegemon's foreign policy, and necessary to the continuance of national wealth creation.

Policies to raise asset values intersect national security concerns when transactions in assets involve states, or companies from states, which are adversarial. Promoting globalization has public purpose for good and ill. No country, however integrated into the new world economic order, should promote or acquiesce to all and any asset transactions that involve security implications. Successful globalization does not necessitate permission of foreign interests to own any asset or company in a country when national security concerns are apparent. Some limitations to what is foreign owned are prudential in that limits create a balance between security and commercial deals. Nations must manage globalization and not simply let private profit opportunities determine the path of economic development and ownership. Nor would prevention of a few deals having national security implications discourage momentum towards integration, especially since integration offers many economic benefits and creates greater security through nation-state interdependency.

Another issue confronting national security in the twenty-first century and a direct by-product of globalization is the existence of multiple regional blocks of allied nations. World integration is increasingly creating many economically prosperous nations that are aligning themselves into regional, or spatially dispersed but linked, economic trading zones. Mutual commercial benefits, assisted in some cases by common political values, are causing nations to develop these zones. The question for the Anglo-American hegemon is what security policy is most appropriate in relation to these zones. Commercial and political alliances create zones of influence and hegemonic policies directed at specific nations may be undermined by the alliances. For example, economic and diplomatic pressures to force compliance with some hegemonic goal may fail because economic alliances offer financial independence from coercion, and political alliances offer military or diplomatic independence, to nations that resist American pressures. Will these situations be perceived by the U.S. as national security threats? If so, the American government will be involved in perpetual global conflicts as globalization bolsters the economies of aligned nations not desirous of succumbing to American domination.

PEACE, PROSPERITY, AND CONFLICT

Globalization is understood as the progressive and relentless process of nation-state economic integration and interdependency. Security benefits of world peace and material benefits associated with trade   and technology are frequently touted and empirically verified. Why is it one must ask that the period following the end of the Cold War and coinciding with the current wave of globalization has brought so much conflict throughout the world? The end of the Cold War marked the success of Globalization Two to assimilate some LDCs and most of the USSR's allies into the Western fold. The present global transformation is defined by the arrival of India, China, and other east Asian nations as major capitalist competitors. The trajectory of globalization for the coming decades will be to attempt an integration of the remaining non-capitalist nations to create a truly integrated world capitalist system. The line of political and military conflict going forward is defined by the boundary between the modern, western capitalist and the more traditional, mid-eastern non-capitalist world. Why is this the case?

Globalization Three offers the prospect of global economic prosperity and global peace [Barnett 2004; Friedman 1980, 50–52]. Increasing interdependence of association among nations promotes a friendliness and awareness that make war unthinkable. The cost of conflict is substantially higher too if nations go to war. They would create simultaneous and mutual physical destruction and economic interruption, recognition of such greatly discourages conflict.

But globalization's ultimate success in getting the world to a peacefully prosperous place depends critically on its ability to spread the wealth wide enough to create acceptance among the people affected by it. The question is will an Anglo-American driven globalization sufficiently share material prosperity to garner broad approval or will transnational corporations and banks reap and retain most of the benefits? The quote below from Tom Palley is instructive:

> What really matters is what happens to real hourly wages and median household income—which is the income of a real world household situated in the middle of the income distribution. Here, the data for the last four years are clear. Real hourly wages have been essentially flat, and median household income actually fell from $46,058 in 2000 to $44,389 in 2004—a decline of $1,669. The reason is that all productivity growth is going to profits, and none to wages. Chinese wage competition, China induced manufacturing job loss, and the persistent threat of off-shoring are part of the explanation. . . . More importantly, there is the question of what happens if this arrangement breaks down (the trade pattern between China and the U.S.). In that event, what will be the cost to the US economy and standard of living of a high dependence on imports combined with an atrophied manufacturing sector? [Palley Blog "The China Effect: . . ." 2/3/06].

To some extent of course, it will be public policy that determines whether wealth is adequately distributed. Governments can assist their populations in transitioning to a global economic system. Governments must provide the means to compete and sufficient income protections, and be willing to make those who gain the most from globalization pay for society's adjustment and protection. But equally important, economic elites must step forward to ease the transition and properly reward labor for its critical contribution in making the global economic system successful. Capitalists are forcing rather dramatic, unsettling change onto people who don't have the property or political-economic connections to protect themselves, and who have not initiated nor directed the current course of events called globalization. Again from Palley,

> . . . the trade debate tends to focus on growth, but increased welfare rather than growth is the real goal of economic policy. Growth is necessary for rising welfare, but it is not sufficient. There is also need to attend to the character of growth and ensure that it is inclusive. This concern with character is especially important with regard to development and poverty reduction [Palley 1/18/06, 2].
>
> Changes in the structure of the U.S. IT industry are being driven by corporations, which are intent on maximizing their own profits. In a nationally based economy, such as was the case in the 1950s and 1960s, profit maximization by companies tends to maximize national income. In a global economy, that is not the case. Instead, profit maximization promotes the maximization of global income rather than national income. Companies are happy to outsource because they earn the profits on outsourced production, but that does not maximize national income. This fundamental insight is not yet appreciated within Washington policy circles. . . . The debate over globalization is not about the benefits of IT, and opposition to globalization does not mean opposition to technology. Instead, the debate is about the character of globalization—the absence of labor standards, the absence of rules for exchange rates, the implications of outsourcing for workers, and changed power relations that enable corporations to set economic policy and collar productivity gains for their top management and owners. . . . the benefits of IT would have flowed regardless of expanded globalization, and for working families they might have been even larger under an alternative globalization [Palley Blog "Globalization and IT . . ." 10/12/06].

People understand who they are by, and hold allegiance to, a "way of life" and they hold a "world view." These perceptions define who they are. Government, economics, and culture are the manifestation of a people's way of life. History demonstrates the frequent desire for some nations to extend their way of life beyond current borders and other nations to defend encroachment by an alternative way of life or view. Global capitalism is a way of life with an accompanying perspective, and its expansive and competitive nature makes it an engine capable of transforming alternative social systems.

The non-capitalist developing world, what Barnett refers to as the "Non-Integrated Gap" [Barnett 2004], does not share the institutions and culture, the "way of life and view," of the developed capitalist world. The nations that make up the latter, Barnett's "Functioning Core" countries, represent the modern, currently integrated capitalist societies. These nations share many common institutions and belief systems, and while they differ some in cultural norms, there exists a cultural understanding and acceptance among the peoples.[16] Economic integration and political ties are cemented by a cultural acceptance that promotes not only commercial connections but a "way of life" that bonds people. Similar political-economic institutions and aspirations make ongoing integration easier than when such commonality is not present.[17]

Conflict between very different kinds of societies requires a catalyst; the mere existence of difference creates no animosity or enmity. Stage Three global capitalism provides the needed catalyst for conflict. The penetrating, transforming power of integration necessarily must create conflict as differing ways of life and views confront one another. Global capitalism desires assimilation and the creation of facilitating political-economic institutions by Gap countries. Along with such dramatic change comes cultural transformation. One way of life is threatened by another. Capitalist expansion creates conflict as it presses in upon a way of life and viewpoints incompatible with capitalism's needs.

International Money Manager Capitalism can drastically alter a Gap country's way of life, and does so in many ways. Flows of foreign financial capital affect borrowing costs and liquidity, and subject an economy to booms and financial panics. By depressing asset values, emerging market economic crises invite foreign penetration and ownership,[18] and thus increase foreign political-economic influence in domestic affairs. Given the dollar's world currency status, the Federal Reserve has influence over the world money supply and borrowing costs, and because MDC currency has high relative value, corporate investment into LDCs is inexpensive. And it is FDI that has the most dramatic influence. FDI brings a particular form of corporate governance, accounting and financing rules, and commercial and banking law. New consumer products and services enter the country, preceded by new management practices and technology. Such investment affects host country economic ownership and development patterns, and orients the public sector's policy toward regulation and promotion of foreign investment and control. Integration may entail immigration flows, will certainly involve openness to new ideas about cultural mores and political governance, and encourage tourism.

Research shows that high Federal Reserve policy rates are associated with falling or flat developing country stock markets and vice versa [BCA Research 2006, p23]. Also see the empirical evidence of American policy influence on emerging market currency values in chapter two's discussion on financial crises during globalization's third era.

Publicly funded international organizations assist transformative MDC penetration into emerging markets. An example is the cooperative effort by the IMF and the World Bank known as the Capital Markets Consultative Group (CMCG).[19] This partnership establishes an informal private sector contact network to discuss FDI in emerging market countries. The group consists of executives from 40 private companies and financial institutions. The purposes are to make assessments of capital flows to emerging markets and to seek input for policy advice on FDI and the business climate in these markets. Most basically, the effort disseminates the views of multinational corporations (MNCs) to emerging market governments concerning the kind of environment conducive to FDI and capital flows into developing countries. The IMF and World Bank work with member countries to create the business and political climates that attract foreign capital. MNCs seek assistance from various IMF and World Bank groups in obtaining financing, in obtaining assessments of economic conditions to aid company risk management, in securing structural reforms to regulatory and tax systems, and in the promotion of host country capital markets and improved infrastructure.[20]

While the World Bank funds antipoverty efforts throughout the world by directly supporting governments, it has a private investment arm known as the International Finance Corporation (IFC). World Bank member country governments fund the IFC to partner with private firms to make equity investments into emerging market private sector projects. The IFC augments private capital to spur private sector economic development. The block quote below comes from an IFC news release:

The International Finance Corporation, the private sector arm of the World Bank Group, will invest up to $45 million in equity in Banco del Bajio, S.A., a regional bank in Mexico that focuses on small and medium enterprises, agribusiness, and commercial banking. . . . IFC's investment, through the subscription of new common shares of Banco del Bajio, will help the bank expand its lending activities, allowing it to play a more effective role in the development of the private sector. This is especially important since smaller businesses' access to credit in Mexico is limited. The investment is still subject to approval from the Mexican authorities. . . . Banco del Bajio, based in the city of Leon, is the eighth-largest bank in Mexico and the largest regional bank in the country. It has significant presence in the northern, western, and central regions of Mexico. . . . IFC's strategy for Mexico focuses on enhancing the international competitiveness of the country's private sector, especially by further deepening the financial sector, promoting investments where the private sector could play a larger role, and promoting sustainable social and environmental development and good corporate governance [August 23, 2006].[21]

And given that a hegemon or competing hegemonic nations have driven all prior eras of globalization, a military presence is likely or an indirect hegemonic influence through international institutions may result. In fact, both are occurring in the current age. U.S. military presence and action is prevalent world-wide, and the IMF and U.S. have used economic crisis in emerging market countries to push economic reforms consistent with the Washington Consensus. Privatization, deregulation, and free market competition are often conditions imposed on crisis stricken countries to receive aid.[22] America's energy dependence forces an interventionist foreign policy into oil-rich parts of the world.

The Overseas Private Investment Corporation (OPIC), a self-financed government agency,[23] funds FDI, provides political risk insurance, and operates as a tool of U.S. foreign policy. Its intention is to promote growth and development in emerging markets and in areas critical to U.S. strategic interests such as Africa, the Middle East, and Southeast Asia. Its efforts are directed at channeling the flow of private capital and equity control to the developing world by complementing these flows with financial assistance. Recent work has encouraged investment into Pakistan and Afghanistan, and business opportunities in Iraq. OPIC is partnering with the Iraq government to build infrastructure and to promote Iraq-U.S. business ties. The Agency contributes money to private equity funds that invest directly into private companies. OPIC seeks to create political stability and free market economics by facilitating increased U.S. business and banking ties with foreign countries.

Despite the fact that state-directed domestic development policies have proved useful and efficacious, and that a number of current economic powerhouses employed such efforts early in their development process, the WTO is restricting measures taken within LDCs to boost domestic industry. The WTO's dispute settlement mechanism is used frequently by MDCs to restrict or prohibit domestic development efforts. WTO adjudication has curtailed the use of tariffs, subsidies, import controls, local content rules, and patents. Non-oil producing developing countries rely significantly on tariff revenues to fund government social and development programs, and the current trend to progressively restrict internal development options means reducing an important funding source. And a lack of domestic industry vitality and diversity implies a probable over-dependence on a few agricultural or natural resource products offering comparative advantage.[24]

Globalization therefore must mean to any Gap country the adoption of a new way of life and acceptance to some extent of a new world view. Resistance is inevitable and can come in three forms. One form comes from resistance by the current government that fears loss of power or economic privilege. The second form is in resistance by classes harmed economically from the revolution in their economic structure and modern technologies that displace traditional forms of employment. The third form of resistance comes from those threatened by competing cultural and religious ideas that upset norms and conventions. Economic dislocations can result in efforts to protect the prevailing economic structure, or more violently in efforts to overthrow the current government that is allowing commercial globalization to coerce change. The extent to which political and cultural dislocations play out violently depends on the degree and rapidness of change, and the extent to which the affected constituencies have input into change. The more the perceived upsetting of long ingrained positions of political and cultural privilege and power, the more socially disruptive the consequences for all countries involved.

Threat to globalization does not just come from conflicts surrounding challenges to ways of life and views of emerging market economies. A threat exists within developed capitalist nations where the income distribution system heavily favors high level corporate insiders and money managers. In those economies economic change disproportionately benefits the few, where income is not associated with individual productivity, and whole new classes of elites are created, are countries ripe for social conflict. Ongoing media, academic, and regulatory attention to extremes in pay differentials and job losses create public disenchantment over bias and favoritism built into the system. Corporate scandals, back-dating stock options [WSJ 3/18/06 pA1,A5], million dollar severance packages and restricted stock grants [BW 4/3/06 32–35], lower tax rates on property income than wages, etc., can infuriate the masses in democratic societies.[25] Continuing critical commentary on these matters can potentially undermine the public support so essential to globalization's progress. If elite political power is perceived to be unchecked or grossly unbalanced, and if riches are perceived to be limitless when economic insecurities are growing for most people, further integration is threatened, despite the benefits.

Such disproportionate gains come in part from the democratization of technology, finance, and information in the context of free market integration that allow people to sell into a single, unified global economic system [Friedman 2000, chapters 4 and 14]. But Friedman's use of the expression "democratization" does not adequately do justice to what actually happens to people confronting economic upheaval. Put alternatively, large income inequalities arise from the global economic structural shifts underway. As industrial and financial MNCs reposition enterprises across the globe, wholesale turnovers occur in workforces but not in control and ownership. Business insiders redeploy their assets to capture lower production costs and efficiencies, while simultaneously replacing one group of workers with another. Greater capital mobility produces social costs. Profit margins and stock prices rise as employment security and wages weaken in countries losing the investment. This reality must be addressed by governments in a socially responsible way; failure to do so has higher long run costs than making the requisite expenditures now to humanely transition people into the new global order.

GLOBALIZATION AND NATIONALISM

As the hegemon and major beneficiary of globalization, the U.S. will have to accept some restraint on its ability to be nationally independent in policy-making. Nation states will certainly maintain a distinct identify as they globalize. But integration and interdependency necessitate the creation of supranational institutions and multilateral cooperation. Regional or intra-state conflicts, and international financial crises, require proactive cooperative nation-state responses. Trade and immigration disputes require nation-state diplomacy, compromise, and agreements. Environmental and health issues have global effects, and call for world-wide national commitments and cooperation.

Leadership from the hegemon means addressing global problems, which stem from the advance of nation-state integration, and facilitating cross-border participation. It means supporting international institutions. And it means accepting some internationally promulgated regulations and expectations that impinge on national self direction. The U.S. cannot have it both ways always. It cannot drive globalization yet act unilaterally on matters that have dimensions whose scope extends beyond national borders. If the U.S, does not acquiesce to WTO, UN, and World Court rulings, if it is an uncooperative member of such organizations, America will lose its authority or legitimacy to foster and mold globalization.

Leadership also obligates American capitalists and elites to run globalization as fiduciaries of the global economy. Leaders must be willing to protect the integrity and credibility of the system. Elites and the privileged, those who have constructed and benefited the most from the current system, must act as trustees. Proper fiduciary responsibility entails taking proactive correction when defects surface as to the functioning of the economic system.[26] And it means sacrificing immediate gain and wealth, not taking any and all means to exploit people and the environment, and to ensure an amply broad distribution of gains across all classes of people. Successful globalization is just as much about a robust sharing of material and social benefits as it is about nation-state integration, free markets, and resource allocation efficiency. Especially where negative social externalities develop across borders, such as environmental impact or consumer product safety issues, private enterprise must not lapse back into nationalistic arguments that legal codes only apply domestically. Private interests cannot have it both ways, arguing for global integration when it promotes profit and arguing for national independence when integrated commerce has real socio-economic cross-border consequences.

As critical as a broad distribution of material gains are for broadening support for the current evolution in economics, U.S. advancement of a "universalism" is essential. Universalism is the idea that what the cultures of the world have in common is our humanity. Despite differing and competing convictions and practices, people commonly throughout the world seek personal fulfillment and health. Advancement of globalization must not undermine these common needs and objectives. This calls into question a globalization that encroaches on a society in advance of some indigenous approval or one that harms the health of people affected by the advance.

Moreover, it is a must that the hegemon exemplify a universalism within its own borders; if so, encouraging such abroad will be easier. A foreign policy supported by a domestic universalism means that the U.S. can dialogue with nations where understanding and acceptance of differences is encouraged. It means at times some accommodation of other nation's interests, even if such accommodation does not expedite globalization or other U.S. interests. Accommodation does not necessarily represent weakness. Dialogue, diplomacy, and personal interaction with other people work in the service of peace and prosperity, and therefore aide in moving modernization and free economics to traditional societies. Practicing internally what is preached externally will do more to accomplish integration goals than force and intimidation.

IMMIGRATION

The United States, the driving force of globalization, is responsible for growing world integration and interdependency. Ever larger amounts of goods, technology, and capital are flowing in and out of the American economy. The reshuffling of commercial location and competitiveness throughout the world has heightened employment instability. While few American laborers emigrate to work in other countries, the pull of job opportunities within the U.S. and the material desperation of foreign workers are increasing immigration into the U.S. This flow of people is a mixture of legal and illegal immigrants, and is causing contention over wage effects and assimilation issues. Globalization is breaking down national borders, opening countries to flows of all kinds including people.

Immigration becomes a cultural and economic issue increasingly so in nations integrating into the global economic system. Increased people flows are just another reflection of globalization.[27]

If the U.S. or any other country wants to reduce the flow of illegal immigrants into their economy, a policy designed to discourage hiring and reduce the need to emigrate must be implemented. Government can require employers to hire only citizens; that is, the burden must be placed on employers to document the citizenship of their workforce, and thereby simply follow the law. But employers have much more clout than anyone else and part of the reason to let more immigrants in, whatever their status, is to satisfy demand by higher income people to have low cost people available to subsidize their lifestyle. And by pressing for rapid immigration, business gets to forgo relocation and living expenses that they would otherwise make to bring unemployed Americans to the Sunbelt to work.

The second element of policy must be to apply domestic expansionary Keynesian policies in the poorer country or countries from which people are emigrating. High job and income growth domestically would eliminate the necessity for people to search out economic opportunities outside their nation or commit crimes in their own country to meet material needs. A monetary policy of low interest rates and liquidity and a functional finance fiscal policy can do the job. This will take some convincing on the part of U.S. leaders for example if they want to truly address their nation's illegal immigration problem sourced south of the border. And Mexico cannot only rely on export led growth, but must take responsibility for its own internal economic challenges if contention with the U.S. over immigration is to be settled.

One might think there is no connection between exchange rates and immigration. But there is a relationship. Exchange rates affect national commercial competitiveness, and ultimately who sells what and who buys what. Some East Asian countries maintain pegged exchange rates with the U.S. dollar in an effort to drive their domestic growth through export surpluses. These relative currency values contribute to the American immigration problem by indirectly affecting Mexican economic performance. Palley writes:

> A final way in which China's under-valued currency has impacted the U.S. economy is through China's impact on Mexico. For the past several years the business press has been full of stories of manufacturing firms leaving Mexico and going to China where wages and labor standards are even lower and the exchange rate is under-valued. The closure of Mexican factories and the loss of Mexican manufacturing jobs have in turn increased illegal immigration into the United States. This has increased the labor supply, and contributed to additional downward wage pressures at the low skill end of the labor market [Palley Blog 4/13/06 "Pressure China to Change"]

Immigration pressures will remain at the forefront of concern due to shifting national cost competitiveness arising from implementation of additional free trade policies and continued nation-state integration into the larger global order. As developing nations lose their relative commercial position to other developing nations, unemployment and disgruntlement with worsening domestic conditions will compel movement of people across borders.

THE POLITICS OF GLOBALIZATION

Economics is about resource allocation, wealth, and power; politics and public policy are important means to address these economic matters. Globalization produces benefits but drawbacks as well, and affects people differently and to different degrees. There are therefore class contentions to consider.

Economic conservatives and elites tend to defend globalization and its consequences. Arguments are frequently framed in one of two ways, either to disguise class effects, as if globalization's consequences are uniformly felt across a population, or to split labor's or the general public's perceptions of differentially felt consequences. Consider some examples:

Immigration

Increased flows of people are a dimension of contemporary globalization. One perspective on this matter is to divide the immigrant class into those who desire assimilation and those who don't. The deserving immigrants of American freedom and prosperity are those who play by the rules and are legal admits, while the undeserving are those illegally in the U.S. This approach to the immigration issue politically splits legal from illegal immigrants, and splits the public by directing attention to legal status and patriotism. Employer class responsibility for employment law violation or awareness of Mexican poverty and unemployment are not in focus from this approach.

Unionization

Cost-based competition and emerging market integration during the current globalization era pits an expanding labor pool of relatively low cost workers against high wage workers in MDCs. Unionization is undermined as MDC employers seek low wage, unorganized labor alternatives globally. Conservative argument typically avoids mentioning unionization, directing attention to the efficiencies of labor market flexibility and the strong work ethic of foreign labor. If unionization is referred to, organized labor is blamed for making U.S. based companies uncompetitive and for an unwillingness to innovate production methods.[28] This approach to unionization politically splits organized labor from the unorganized, high from low wage labor, and splits those in white collar management positions from organized labor since work rules only apply to contracted labor not labor in management. Such an approach diverts attention away from capitalist class lobbying efforts to bring the world's labor into competition and away from the resulting income distribution shift to profits and executive pay.[29]

Foreign Policy

In every era of globalization, the hegemon has employed a foreign policy to assist the expansion of foreign economic ties. But foreign policy by definition for a globalizing hegemon cannot be noninterventionist. To justify an ever active foreign policy, the U.S. government must frame its actions as devoted to extending America's virtues of freedom and self determination to people abroad. Interventionism is expensive, in lives and treasure, and it is always difficult for an elected government to justify such public sacrifices. And intervention invites resistance. Extension of economic and political power, often through military means, must not be seen by the public for what it really is, but must be framed in an way that appeals to people's higher instincts and hopes, or their fears. For example, U.S. policy elites disassociated the Cold War from multinational corporate interests and the Iraq War of our modern age with industry and strategic interests to access oil reserves and create oil price stability. Fear and security dominate the debate, domestic support for American troops is an issue, bringing freedom and opportunity to the oppressed is a stated intention, not power or money.

The point of all of this is that the public must understand that there is a genuine political dimension to globalization. The challenge is to comprehend the politics in all of its manifestations, and not only in those ways expressed by globalization's ardent defenders and beneficiaries. Healthy skepticism is called for when arguments pose only cross-class benefits or create division within non-elite classes that in effect undermine political adhesion and hence an opposing power bloc to elite interests.

In turn, elites and direct beneficiaries of globalization must understand and accept the legitimacy of opposition. Dissent will almost universally reflect a loyal opposition where opponents represent patriotic supporters of a country yet object to some of globalization's effects. Elites who suppress dissent or characterize criticism as disloyal, implying that all critique undermines and weakens national security or prosperity, will ultimately pay a high price. The high price comes in the form of an aggravated, inflexible opposition whose efforts to redress some ill effects of change mutates into hardened objection to all change. Complicating the situation is the rightward political party drift on economic policy in Anglo-American countries that drive globalization. The concern here is that too much agreement in the two leading parties on economic policy and trends provides no effective political expression to aggrieved interests. These interests now have no party, and the two dominant parties compete over how extreme pro-globalization policies should be.[30]

Thomas Friedman has written extensively about globalization [2000; 2005], and addresses important national and global political aspects. He sees the world flattening where national borders are broken down creating increased economic opportunity for connection and collaboration [2005, 205–213]. He sees globalization changing rules, roles, and relationships more quickly than before, and creating new social, political, and business models that arise from the pressures of competition, technology and rising productivity [44–47]. Unease among populations stems from the rapidity of change and dislocations connected to modern globalization. Success in the new world requires leadership, flexibility, imagination, and the ability to adapt to rapid change; the pressures and disruptions of the age do not create "an orderly transfer of power from the old winners to the new winners" [46].

Friedman argues that globalization levels the competitive playing field, expedites the search for fellow collaborators, and that technology allows more people to do more globally. "Everywhere you turn, hierarchies are being challenged from below or transforming themselves from top-down structures into more horizontal and collaborative ones" [2005, 45].

He speaks of the democratization of technology, finance, and information [2000, chapter 4]. Falling entry costs and open, global trade offer more business opportunities for average people, and technology allows greater access to customers and greater customer impact on what business produces. The democratization of decision-making and the de-concentration of power and information undercut slow moving bureaucracies and "most of the information needed to answer most of the problems now rests in the hands of people on the outer edges of organizations, not the center" [2000, 86].

Governments can no longer isolate their citizens from world events, information, and knowledge of how others live [2000, 66–68]. This reality creates pressures on developing country governments to reform their macroeconomic policies and commercial infrastructure, and ultimately open to world trade and capital flows. Governments must adopt good governance practices [2000, chapters 8, 9].

Globalization can impact the politics of developed nations as well. American politics could be reshuffled as social conservatives align themselves with unionized workers, and multinational business interests align themselves with social liberals. The first group desires protection from increasing integration and the second group benefits from furthering integration [2005, 221–222]. For Friedman, the contending political forces are between those who desire separation versus integration internationally, and between those who advocate for laissez-faire policy versus those who desire maintaining social safety nets [2000, 437–440].

While there is much truth in Friedman's observations, make no mistake that globalization entails the quest for global domination of markets, industries, and profits. Competition eventually leads to concentration in most areas, and while there is increased access to information and money and wide application of technology, the creation, production, and control of technology, finance, and resources take place largely within rivalry among transnational enterprises. Bureaucracies are shaken up and market shares altered but there remains a list of globally dominant players located in the leading economic nations who run globally oriented, complex systems. The whole economic infrastructure of the world is built and managed by the leading global enterprises working in concert with the major governments of the world. There is no de-concentration of power or undermining of hierarchies in any meaningful political-economic sense. Also, Friedman is right about the contemporary domestic political breakdown. But in time, as globalization wears on, the separatists will wane and disappear as a political force, replaced by contest between the integrators pushing for global governance and those who will try to maintain the current nation-state regulatory framework. The latter arrangement now in force of course gives the greatest opportunity for private economic interests to mold the world unmolested.

SUMMARY OF CHAPTER SEVEN

This chapter addresses political economic discontents. The first part of the chapter addresses markets. While markets have their analytical role in economics, it is essential that they do not become the focus of attention to the exclusion of institutions. Power, initiative, and innovation are all imbedded in institutions that organize economic action. Markets reflect economic outcomes and decisions made within institutions, and social change comes from institutional reform, not through market reform. Transactions based on demand and supply conditions determine prices but whether markets are efficient depends on how much psychology, emotion, and ignorance influence trading decisions.

Themes of growth and stability are addressed next. Private sector deficit spending drives growth and places upward pressure on asset prices, but over the longer run this source of economic stimulus is limited by credit saturation and defaults. A number of factors operate to improve national macroeconomic and global stability but microeconomic conditions engendered by globalization display increased volatility. The chapter addresses the effects on labor from industry instability and argues that world integration pressures create momentum for continued job churning. Comments on export oriented growth policy are made and adoption of complete trade liberalization schemes by developing countries is discussed. If the U.S. and other developed country growth engines fail at some point, a policy of either reverting to 20th century Keynesian policy of building growing middle classes of stable spenders or innovating away from restrictive monetary policy and adopting functional finance deficit spending by government is required. The current global free market system is really operating on supportive institutional structures inherited from the last century. A modern New Deal program is suggested for developed economies to contend with cost-based global competition.

The final part of the conclusion confronts various and important foreign policy issues that have interplay with economic issues. Hegemonic aggression occurs in each era, and there is a link among national security concerns, military operations, and economic interests. Global or regional conflicts arise as the integrated western capitalist economies confront non-integrated states, the latter feeling threatened by opposing world views and differing ways of life. Globalization is transformative to nation-states. Government and business elites must take a fiduciary leadership role to manage and improve global economic performance so that the benefits of expansion and integration are broadly shared. A foreign policy of universalism is advocated. Final words are directed at the politics of globalization and how electoral division is fomented to prevent socially necessary reform. Elites need to recognize that criticism of an aggressively pursued globalization reflects a loyal opposition expressing the need for legitimate correctives. National politics will in MDCs be centered on economic concentration issues and how best to govern world commerce and finance in the public interest. The chapter ends with an assessment of Tom Friedman's work on globalization.

NOTES

1. I've adopted here the language from a presentation entitled "Turmoil in Financial Markets" by Enrique Sanchez, delivered to the Charlotte World Trade Association on June 8, 2006.

2. Korten [1999, 34–35, 197] acknowledges this and points to this as a source of capitalist instability.

3. That is, borrowing from someone else.

4. GDP is the total value of all newly produced final goods within a nation in a year. Net deficits refer to the condition where the total deficits created in the economy are larger than all of the surpluses generated in the economy.

5. This is called a "functional finance" fiscal policy and is also addressed in chapter six above. Functional finance is one way to implement Keynes' call for a "socialization of investment" [Keynes 1997 (1936), chapter 24].

6. For more empirical verification of instability at the firm level, see Comin et al [2/06]. http://www.newyorkfed.org/research/staff_reports/sr238.html

7. Reduced worker bargaining power is admitted to by financial strategists and Federal Reserve policymakers. See The Economist [9/30/06, 88] and Greenspan [1997].

8. With the rise of democratic politics in Indonesia in the late 1990s, pro-worker labor law was passed greatly improving severance pay and minimum wages. But company desires for flexible markets and de-facto capital mobility are working to reverse the legislation, despite the fact that the country's economic difficulties stem from a variety of variables unrelated to favorable labor law [WSJ 12/7/06, pA8].

9. On these themes, see the following: WSJ "Amid Europe's Gloom, Spain Blossoms with Short-Term Jobs" 9/28/05 page A1, WSJ "China Approves Bankruptcy Law . . ." 8/28/06 page A4, BW 9/25/06 pages 55–62.

10. The American Sunbelt states offer fewer and weaker unions, and a less regulatory business environment.

11. In the given era, MDC central banks have significant difficulty in push up long term rates by elevating short term

12. A positive multiplier occurs when a new round of spending increases income which in turn fosters more spending and income increases.

13. A social tariff is a tax on imports that funds worker retraining and education programs. The common markets concept is policy that elevates LDC living standards and social protections to diminish the huge gaps that prevail in social conditions across countries.

14. Fashioning the argument this way makes it appear the hegemon is only acting defensively.

15. Such intervention may be seen by a global power as purely defensive in scope or security enhancing, yet in effect promotes an unending chain reaction of conflict where further resistance justifies further intervention. Mid-east conflicts involving British, Israeli, and American intervention exemplify chain reaction conflict.

16. When acceptance or tolerance is weak or nonexistent, there is no interest in knowing or leaning about another culture.

17. American dominance in world affairs is exploited to refashion communitarian capitalist MDCs along Anglo-American lines. Pressures exist on European and Japanese economies to adopt versions of American employment, corporate finance, and income distribution practices. See the WSJ January 16, 2007 edition page A2 for articles on Germany and Japan, and the article " Fund Challenges Japanese Steel Deal" on page C2.

18. For a study of foreign bank penetration into Latin America, see Peek and Rosengren [2000, 145–170].

19. See the IMF's "Global Financial Stability Report" April 2006, pages 26–27, and the "Foreign Direct Investment in Emerging Market Countries" September 2003, a report of the Working Group of the Capital Markets Consultative Group at www .imf.org/external/np/cmcg/2003/eng/091803.htm.

20. The World Bank produces an annual publication series entitled Doing Business that assesses developing country reforms pertaining to contracts, employment law, credit access, registering property, investor protection, and taxes.

21. The World Bank's Multilateral Investment Guarantee Agency supports MNC investment by providing insurance against expropriation and breach of contract, guaranteed loans to reduce interest expense, and mediation of disputes.

22. As explained by Yeldan [2006, 208–210], indirect U.S. influence through the IMF can affect a nation's "political apparatus."

23. The self financing dimension helps to avoid possible political tensions if Congress had to keep renewing funding for OPIC. See OPIC's web site: http://www.opic .gov/about/contact/index.asp.

24. See the following: DiCaprio and Gallagher [2006] and Gallagher [2007].

25. That no real competitive market exists for elite positions fosters contempt as well. A system closed to genuine outside competition protects those in the system and keeps their income very high. I thank colleague Dr. John Plecnik for this insight. Also see the end of chapter 3 for many examples of ethically questionable behavior of leaders.

26. And it means admission that human designed systems always have flaws and therefore laissez-faire policies are irresponsible socially.

27. Western Europe is contending with immigration from southern and eastern Europe, and China is struggling to integrate rural Chinese into the eastern developing urban areas of China.

28. Highly compensated organized labor was the result of American company profitability and world dominance, and an internal corporate income distribution system awarding productivity improvements to labor. The current American company un-competitiveness results not from high paid labor per se but from corporate directed opening of all economies to cost-based competition.

29. What if there was a global market for executives instead of a rather closed, rather small, nationally based group of people groomed through elite social circles to take executive positions? Probably there would be a different kind of and pace to globalization. It would be interesting to see eight-figure income American executives compete with four or five figure income emerging market executives for employment!

30. Also read Palley's [2007, 5] discussion of the political contentions arising from globalization.

Chapter Eight

Conclusion

DISCUSSION ON PUBLIC POLICY RESPONSIBILITY

An intent of this book is to clearly show the complexity of the phenomena of globalization. World integration has its merits and demerits, and affects people differently and some in multiple ways. Globalization has political, commercial, financial, social, and cultural dimensions. The current wave of integration differs in many respects from the two preceding waves, but they all share an imperial hegemon, an economic gain causal factor, and common effects such as war and the spread of capital. Aspects of the current era's institutional design impart economic stability but other aspects create, or potentially can create, political and financial instability. Today's globalization challenges national independence, the existing dominant industries and technologies, and cultural identity.

One very important conclusion from all of this is that if globalization is to continue apace, governments ought to accept the social responsibility to guide economic evolution and make social outcomes as beneficial as possible for the broadest numbers of people. Indeed, this should be the function of all good government in modern life. Therefore nation-state integration must be regulated and supervised to assure that globalization takes a socially humane course, both in terms of ameliorating socio-economic outcomes and avoiding global conflict. As in other respects, the words of Keynes about the tension between economic need and political responsibility apply to current times:

> There are valuable human activities which require the motive of money-making and the environment of private wealth-ownership for their full fruition. Moreover, dangerous human proclivities can be canalized into comparatively harmless channels by the existence of opportunities for money-making and private

wealth, which, if they cannot be satisfied in this way, may find their outlet in cruelty, the reckless pursuit of personal power and authority, and other forms of self-aggrandisement. . . . it is not necessary for the stimulation of these activities . . . that the game should be played for such high stakes . . . Much lower stakes will serve the purpose equally well, . . . The task of transmuting human nature must not be confused with the task of managing it. . . . it may still be wise and prudent statesmanship to allow the game to be played, subject to rules and limitations, so long as the average man, . . . is in fact strongly addicted to the money-making passion [Keynes 1997 (1936), 374].

An accomplishment of this book is that it lays out the wide variety of problems and challenges faced by nations undergoing integration, change, and upheaval, with reasonable and doable policy responses. Table 8.1 identifies each problem with the attending necessary policy reaction.

The public authorities and economic elites responsible for globalization and for the welfare of their citizenry must take a pro-active approach to regulation. This means not only responding to crises but attempting to head them off. It is much better for all involved for policymakers to prevent calamity and to understand that the history of capitalism justifies intervention. While regulators are aided by the system's stabilizing forces and policymakers benefit politically from the favorable consequences of globalization, prudence and

Table 8.1. Policy Problems and Responses

Problems and Challenges of the Current Age	Proposed Policy Responses and Recognitions
Excessive Income Inequality	Progressive Income Taxation
Excessive Wealth Inequality	Yearly Wealth Tax
	Estate Tax
Domestic Unemployment	Low Interest Rate Monetary Policy
	Functional Finance Fiscal Policy
	Full Employment Target
Domestic Inflation	Incomes Policy
	Influenced Globally
	Not Under Central Bank Control
Corporate	Modern New Deal
Cost Competitiveness	
Foreign Conflict	Universalism
	Supranational Institutions
Financial Instability	Central Bank Financial Policy
	Financial Institution Exams
	Foster Wide Distribution of Property Ownership
Maintain Popular Support	Limiting Economic Excesses
For Globalization	Fostering Proportionate Benefits

honesty dictate public sector activism to curtail or prevent the socialization of the ill effects of pursuit of private profit.

A recurring theme throughout the text is income distribution, partly because it is affected in myriad ways from globalization and public policy, but also because of the politics surrounding distributional issues and what an economic distribution signifies about a society. Times of great economic change typify periods of income concentration if state regulatory policy and activism subside concurrently with the change. Distributional outcomes tend not to be very divisive however if the new opportunities and churning that take place are seen to create substantial financial rewards for entrepreneurial and worker efforts. Being productive, innovative, and catering to the material needs and desires of consumers justify compensatory gains to leaders and key people responsible for generating an economy that services human welfare.

But when people are seen to make great gains merely from property ownership or from the structural manipulation of productive enterprises, widening income dispersion and growing wealth concentration become politically and potentially socially disruptive. The more removed income is from work or product innovation the more questionable any income distribution becomes. And globalization and global governance are concomitantly complicit in fermenting political agitation in the current age. Moves in Anglo-American economies to free up capital and reduce economic regulation, and the implementation of the Washington Consensus in developing nations, have increased opportunity to achieve unprecedented wealth through asset manipulation.[1]

The current path of economic development allows tens of thousands of companies across the globe to potentially integrate or shuffle assets among one another to potentially create capital gains from the shuffling. Mergers and acquisitions, leveraged buyouts, initial or new public offerings, and company breakups followed by asset redeployment are the practical ways that productive firms are reconfigured to "unlock" value.[2] But it is not the reconfiguring or manipulation that actually creates value but whether or not the new company has embedded in it the productive, creative, and entrepreneurial abilities to make for a prosperous firm. The state has a social responsibility here of some sort. Policy options may include the following:

(1) It must require by law that there is some kind of democratic approval of affected constituencies for asset reconfiguring and that gains or losses be similarly shared,

(2) Or it must require by law that any capital gains be distributed across all economic agents,

(3) And that no outsized income gains be awarded to top insiders or outside controllers from reconfiguration based on spurious claims about the talent, knowledge, or incentives needed to bring such business outcomes to fruition.[3]

How governments across the world handle this political economic problem will go a long way in determining how smoothly globalization develops.

But is globalization stoppable or reversible? Probably not given that technology and the profit motive are important drivers. And there are technological and economic benefits to globalization that would be missed otherwise. But policy has a role too and it can be fashioned in a way to direct or guide globalization along a certain path. Despite the broader economic stability of the age revealed in aggregate data, the microeconomic volatility impinging on families and small business is of social importance. Life is made more uncertain and planning is made more difficult. Changing material fortunes create more frequent change in lifestyles and financial plans as people are now more subject to extreme swings in economic outcomes. Class is relevant here as those with substantial property holdings can not only withstand more easily shifting economic conditions but partake in creating the greater micro instability in the first place. Therefore one of the arguments of the text bears repeating, namely that public policymakers and economic elites within integrating countries must fully embrace a social responsibility ethic to care for the ill affected.

And history teaches much in importance. Beginning with the Roman Empire, on up through to today, the hegemon of the period has always confronted opposition from societies who differ economically, politically, and culturally in practice. Hegemons, despite their own moral justifications for power extension and despite some genuine benefits spread to other societies, have inevitably faced resistance. The threatened overthrow of established mores and laws, or revolution in economic institutions with the resulting reordering of power relations, has often created severe and violent opposition. We know when hegemonic overreach has occurred in history when the intensity of opposition accelerates. And hegemons feel vindicated in responding aggressively because of the mounting violent or persistent opposition.

So what might slow, redirect, or temporarily stop globalization? Perhaps an insurgent upper middle class revolt within the Anglo-American alliance as the spread of western capital and culture causes repetitious violent reaction with the attending human costs experienced from outside and from within the boundaries of the hegemon. When the economic welfare or security interests of a class of people are threatened who have the means to take concerted, organized action, a consensus could develop to do just that. Such a power block could alter the course of globalization and the distribution of its costs and benefits.[4]

ETHICS AND GLOBALIZATION

Globalization supporters argue for free capital flows, free trade among all, and economic opening of economies to competition. Transnational interests like this paradigm because it provides access to untapped markets and enhances competition among the world's labor for jobs. It undermines national protections imposed by unions and government regulations as increased capital mobility reconfigures competitive balance, and reallocates economic opportunity and prosperity, across nations. Consequently, labor's security is reduced and the dependence on capital increased, thus shifting political and economic power within economic relations.

A defining aspect of this manuscript is its insistence on ethical conduct on the part of those leading the globalization process whose financial rewards must be directly tied to their own productivity, and for a public policy that has as its intention to broadly spread the benefits of globalization. An addendum to this must be included. Conservative economists and elites must not employ any argument that sets up a double standard across classes or one that selectively advocates policy geared toward helping one class over another. Once recognized by the larger population and policymakers, double standards and selectivity will only undermine efforts at world integration.

When trade restrictions are roundly rejected during trade negotiations except for intellectual property protections or assurances against expropriation, it is clear that restrictions are not so much the issue as is protection of capital. Similarly, capital flow restrictions are seemingly objected to as a general principle except when emerging market companies and stock markets, advantaged by globalization, take income and markets away from developed-country capitalists. In these cases it is clear that freedom is not so much the issue as is the distribution of income and opportunity among global capitalists.

Recognition and public acknowledgement by leading economic interests that global economics require some restrictions, regulations, and management, will go a long way in sustaining popular support for integration and modernization throughout the world. Terminating the selective use of principles and making efforts to construct class neutral policies openly arrived at will create a real sense of fairness about globalization. Maintaining and following high ethical standards within business and finance will further the ac-

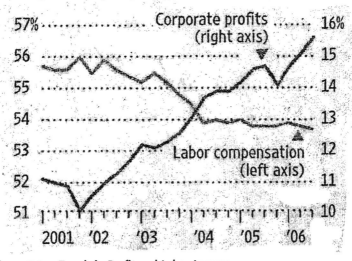

Figure 8.1.   Trends in Profit and Labor Income
Sources: National sources; Morgan Stanley research
Source: WSJ 1/25/07, pA10

ceptance of a world order very much designed by and benefiting global capitalists.

An ethically run globalization is all the more pressing given the shift in economic class fortunes during the current era. As shown graphically in Figure 8.1, class incomes as a share of economic output have moved in favor of property interests. While more workers now receive property income, and such income is a bigger proportion of total labor income, property income remains concentrated and income inequality has increased.

CLASS POWER

So what economic agent or group occupies a position of power during the current age of globalization? Which class is most influential in effecting outcomes? While there is more than one way to measure class power, examining the economic health of institutions and income trends of classes is revealing and easily assessed.

Labor's position in the developed world has on the whole weakened though segments of this class are prospering. Organized power is reduced as old-line unions are committed to industries facing restructuring, productivity advances, off-shoring, and downsizing. Being far less mobile than capital and rooted in communities, labor organization remains in gradual decline. Middle class opportunities and income shrink, and economic life becomes more insecure. In fact, most labor faces higher insecurity and more personal risk. Somewhat offsetting is the rising proportion of upper middle class labor who are well positioned or become better positioned to take full advantage of global business and work opportunities. These workers are part of the "ownership society," their affluence reflected in greater property holdings and whose consumption is more sensitive to upswings in wealth.

But as in all earlier economic periods, the propertied classes garner the most power to affect political-economic outcomes. Decision-making authority is lodged in institutions which organize property, resources, and people to produce outputs. These class incomes depend not just on work, but on the use and manipulation of property and the power granted to property over labor.

It would seem that the internationalization of domestic money manager capitalism, one important development of the current age, must mean that finance capital is ascendant. And indeed great power is had here evidenced by rising income shares, the prominent place accorded finance and financial strategies, the high profile status of financial institutions, and the magnitude of financial and currency reforms undertaken across nations.

Yet while all earlier periods in developed capitalist countries are periods dominated by either commerce or finance, the age known as globalization three is noted for its shared domination by both commerce and finance. Corporate businesses are running yearly budget surpluses, and enjoying record profits and elevated profit margins despite increased competition. Interest costs are low, credit conditions expansionary, and corporate financial liabilities carry inflated prices. Surplus cash conditions allow for healthy balance sheets and stock repurchases among the larger multinational enterprises. Public dependence on business investment and philanthropy has given the corporation preeminent social status. Of course world political-economic conditions can change and events in a world of genuine uncertainty cannot be fully anticipated. Systemic economic instability possibilities remain and private property's inclination toward anti-social behavior persists, and hence these potentially serious problems require attention by policymakers. Nevertheless, the corporation as an institution is the most dominant economic vehicle for commerce and finance, and the incomes flowing to its controllers and manipulators are making capitalists richer and more powerful than in any other age.

Alternatively, power is evidenced through the ease at which classes can organize and use organization to conduct economic strikes. Labor organizing efforts don't exist in emerging market nations and in the developed world have come under increased employer resistance. As labor organization weakens, amplified by capital mobility, the effectiveness of worker strikes wanes.

The converse is true for both sets of capital. The concentration of business and money capital into ever larger global organizations enhances the ability to inflict economic damage through strikes.[5] Commercial capital strikes when it withdraws investment and job creation from economies, given public policies or labor agitation that it opposes. While the resultant economic consequences are somewhat gradually negative as it takes time for reduced spending flows to affect employment and income, financial capital's strikes are immediately felt in financial markets. Rapid outflows of money depress currency and asset values as liquidation requires selling that drives down market prices; contraction in bank lending intensifies the strike, gradually affecting business and employment conditions. Given the greater volatility and interconnectedness of financial markets relative to other sectors, finance capital strikes are more frequent, more broadly felt, and add a greater element of uncertainty and insecurity to economic life.

MONETARY POLICY AND FINANCIAL MARKETS

The prominence of financial markets and the needs of global growth constrain monetary policy action. The necessity to sustain financial market stability and ample global liquidity limit interest rate management flexibility. An upper ceiling to rate hikes is imposed on policymakers despite their hawkish rhetoric concerning inflation.

The current era of globalization is marked by growing income inequality within nations, the dominance of non-bank financial institutions, and frequent central bank and government interventions to ward off financial crises and recessions. The result of these factors is a global financial system awash in liquidity, which in turn has pushed up asset prices, lowered interest rates, and fueled debt-driven consumption. Global growth and world commercial integration benefit. But for this benign scenario to continue, financial markets and capital flows must remain stable, and liquidity conditions must remain ample. This puts a ceiling on how high monetary policy can push rates, and the global system of era three has required (or at least has adjusted to) ever lower rates and more liquidity. A gradual fall in global interest rates will likely continue due to the factors raising liquidity. Therefore the interest rate ceiling will continue to fall as well, limiting the flexibility central banks prefer to have to moderate increases in inflation and growth rates. In fact, there may develop a "policy rate squeeze" where the lowering of rates to stimulate activity gets ever closer to the zero interest rate policy floor, below which policy cannot push rates to resuscitate economic activity.[6]

A NOTE ON THE FIRM

How will the twenty-first century remake the firm? The 1980s and 1990s witnessed the development of large corporate multinational enterprises where the production and distribution of goods and services, logistics, and finance became fully internationalized. And these firms blended financial and industrial capital within the corporate structure, enabling firms to earn profit from commercial and financial endeavors. From this point on, firms will be remade as cross-border mergers and acquisitions combine assets of nationally dominant enterprises, a process eventually producing world-wide oligopolies. But what might be of more interest than oligopolization is the change in the institutional financial investor class who owns the multinationals incorporating more and more government run sovereign investment funds into their ranks. Their assets exceed those of hedge funds [Economist 5/26/07, 79–80], and their acquisition of financial power comes from two sources. Emerging market economic growth is one source as increased incomes translate into more taxes paid to national governments. The second and more important funding source stems from reserve accumulations of leading country currencies. As domestic emerging market firms earn these currencies, they swap them for domestic currency from their government or central bank. And as sovereign funds establish greater financial and ownership linkages with multinational firms, earnings from these asset holdings can be reinvested back into the same or different corporations.

What are the implications of this trend? First, the rise of financial institutional ownership has made big private companies more like public firms in that their ownership base is very wide and that they employ and affect many people. Sovereign funds are furthering this process of making private companies into essentially public ones. And this process will fully internationalize multinationals by globalizing their ownership. Second, given the longer time horizons typically characteristic of governments, sovereign funds should bolster the financial sector's commitment of funds to capital investment, thereby underpinning economic stability. This likelihood reinforces the process already underway with the growth of large private financial institutions. The third implication concerns how sovereign funds may be used by governments. Will the broader social global concerns of nation states, the issues and problems that cut across borders, compel states to pursue public objectives over commercial profit or will it work the other way? Will corporate multinationals be turned to the social good, making profit margins and stock prices mean less in enterprise, or will these funds push for maximum returns in order for governments to more completely pursue nationalistic objectives?

In large measure, the answer to this question depends on how cooperative or coercive the integration process of globalization plays out to be in the century.

WAR OR PEACE?

At this point it is reasonable to ask again, Will globalization on balance foster world peace or conflict? While globalization is expressed in various ways, two critical aspects seem most important to answering the question at hand. Peace or war heavily depends on how the economic and cultural effects of globalization play out. Countries are integrating financially and commercially. Simultaneously, and largely the result of economic integration, there is growing cultural contact among people. The economic and cultural effects could potentially work either way, fostering war or peace. The schematic in Figure 8.2 shows the possibilities.

Conceivably, economic integration can produce peaceful relations. Integration promotes an economic interdependence as nations tie their material fortunes to cross investment and financial flows. As economic ties become stronger, cross border activity works to foster a mutual prosperity evidenced in growing output and employment, and rising incomes, within the block of

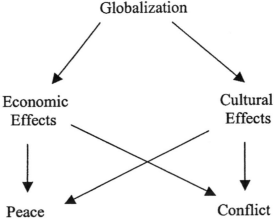

Figure 8.2. War or Peace from Globalization?

nations connected. This benign scenario could unravel or fail to develop if the institutional economic arrangement strongly favors a given class within nations or one nation over the others in the group. High inequality in resource control or economic outcomes would create dissention and opposition to the current order and undermine the potential harmony from trade.

Moreover, the cultural dimension of globalization can produce either a harmonious or conflictual outcome. Growing cultural contacts and blending will create nation-states of greater diversity but when occurring among countries that subscribe to a universalistic notion of humanity, diversity will occur within socially peaceful conditions. The problem for the twenty-first century will be whether the major religions of the world pursue ecumenical efforts and acceptance of differing faith traditions. But Christianity and Islam have strong evangelical and proselytizing dimensions given their religious texts, and hence desire to win over people of other faiths. Competition between these two religions for world domination can only create tension, reaction, and opposition. Cultural hostility can undermine harmonic relations arising from economic ties, hence causing a clash of civilizations.

If policymakers take the initiative to create strong economic institutional structures, and are willing to change and regulate these structures as necessary to meet stability and equity concerns, global economic integration is likely to produce peaceful human relations. The more serious worry lies on the cultural front. Regulators in the economic arena have now a substantial history of successful regulation and effective response to crises. Religious leaders have little such experience to draw upon, despite a much longer history. And given the strong human identities associated with cultural and particularly religious practices, world religious leadership can very easily harness these identity commitments to face off against other faiths in a competitive struggle for members and influence. If religious leaders, or politicians playing to the religious vote, opt for using the identity commitments of people to foster competitive rivalry, globalization produces more world conflagrations, as cultural enmity wins out over mutual economic advantage.

THE NEXT AMERICAN CENTURY

It is time to reflect on the meaning of the title of the book The Next American Century. Just how could it be that the twenty-first century will be the second century of American dominance and greatness when the European Union, Japan, India, China, or all of Southeast Asia, look like powerhouses? America's greatness in the twentieth century is exemplified by the winning of world wars and a cold war, its anti-colonial stance, the Marshall Plan and the

United Nations, its Middle East peace efforts, and through the encouragement of adopting liberal and modern political and economic institutions. America's world dominance is reflected in the relative size of its economy, its influence in Bretton Woods and post-Bretton Woods institutions, the reserve currency status of the dollar, the substantial intervention in foreign country affairs, and the world-wide positioning of its military. But in the current century, America's preeminence will not be from a singular nation-state dominance of the world but be measured by the growing relative political economic importance of many nations that copy much of what America does. Much of the earth will, in some variation or form, identify with and practice an American consumerism, revere private property ownership, employ a secular republican government, and adopt capitalist economics. The evolutionary process of globalization is strengthening other nations relative to the U.S. but simultaneously creating more uniformity in business and government practices because integration is based on the American model. So it is that while nation-states become an ever greater mixture of people, ideas, and cultures, the dominant inter-continental political and economic values will largely reflect a high level of conformity. And despite America's gradual decline as the pre-eminent superpower, analysts of globalization will continue to explain international integration and development within the context of American economic performance and public policy.

NOTES

1. Technology, the profit motive, and policy drive globalization, which in turn increases competitive sales and cost pressures, in turn creating more distressed and bankrupt companies, creating more opportunities for speculative restructuring, which results in more wealth concentration. See the short case study by the WSJ on the restructuring of the American auto parts industry [12/21/06, A1].

2. Colleague Dr. John Plecnik has observed that the business law principle that a benefit of the corporate structure is infinite life is false. Corporations are frequently killed and new ones created through capital mobility and capital structure reconfiguration.

3. The ultra-high incomes awarded to executives and financiers who shuffle assets should not be misunderstood as a necessary incentive to create potentially more competitive enterprises. The high incomes aren't needed to induce creative thinking about asset makeup but are the effect of those in a position of power to access or extract more money from a newly created profitable firm. The shufflers are not responsible for improved economic performance but get the authority to shuffle from ownership rights.

4. The ideas expressed in the last three paragraphs arose from conversations with colleague Dr. John Plecnik.

5. The permissive merger and acquisition environment conducive to capital organization contrasts with the declining organizational effectiveness of labor. The concept of strike is applicable across classes since theoretically any economic agent or class can withhold its productive contribution. What matters is whether effectual organization exists to empower the strike.

6. The Japanese economy may already be there in that sixteen years of falling and ultra-low interest rates have failed to fully resuscitate economic activity. The economy remains exposed to mild deflation.

Bibliography

Angell, W. "Virtue and Inflation." *Wall Street Journal*, (June 24, 1994): A10.

Agnew, John. *Hegemony*. New York: W.W. Norton, 2005.

Aretis, Philip and Malcolm Sawyer. "European Integration and the Euro Project." *Policy Note*, Levy Economics Institute, (2002/2003):1–8.

Atkeson, Andrew and Patrick Kehoe. "Deflation and Depression: Is There an Empirical Link?" American Economic Review *Papers and Proceedings*, (May 2004): 99 103.

Autor, David, Lawrence Katz, and Melissa Kearney. "The Polarization of the U.S. Labor Market." American Economic Review *Papers and Proceedings*, (May 2006):189–194.

BCA Research. *Global Investment Strategy*, (September 29, 2006).

BCA Research. *The Bank Credit Analyst*, (December 2006).

Barnett, Thomas. *The Pentagon's New Map*. New York: G.P. Putnam's Sons, 2004.

Barro, Robert. *Getting It Right*. MIT Press, 1996.

Barro, R. and Gordon, D. "Rules, Discretion and Reputation in a Model of Monetary Policy," *Journal of Monetary Economics*, (July 1983):101–121.

Barro, R. and Gordon, D. "A Positive Theory of Monetary Policy in a Natural Rate Model," *Journal of Political Economy*, (August 1983):589–610.

Bayly, C.A. The Birth of the Modern World. Malden: Blackwell Publishing, 2004.

Bell, Stephanie. "Do Taxes and Bonds Finance Government Spending?" *Journal of Economic Issues* 34, no. 3 (September 2000):603–620.

Bernanke, Ben. "Hedge Funds and Systemic Risk." A speech at the 2006 Financial Markets Conference sponsored by the Federal Reserve Bank of Atlanta, May 16, 2006.

Bernanke, B. and Frederick Mishkin. "Inflation Targeting: A New Framework for Monetary Policy." *Journal of Economic Perspectives*, 11 (Spring 1997):97–116.

Bhagwati, Jagdish. *In Defense of Globalization*. Oxford: Oxford University Press, 2004.

Bibow, Jorg "Reflections on the Current Fashion for Central Bank Independence." working paper 334, Levy Economics Institute, (July.2001)

——. "Europe's Quest for Monetary Stability: Central Banking Gone Astray." working paper 428, Levy Economics Institute, (August 2005).

BIS Papers #29. "The Recent Behavior of Financial Market Volatility." Monetary and Economics Department, (August 2006).

BIS sponsored study "On the Use of Information and Risk Management by International Banks." (October 1998): http://www.federalreserve.gov/boarddocs/surveys/RiskMgmt/riskmgmt.pdf

Bivens, L. Josh. and Christian Weller. "The Job Loss Recovery: Not New, Just Worse." *Journal of Economic Issues* 40, (September 2006):603–628.

Bluestone, Barry and Bennett Harrison. *The Deindustrialization of America*. New York: Basic Books, 1982.

Blustein, Paul. *The Chastening*. New York: Public Affairs, 2003.

Brawley, Mark. *Turning Points*. Ontario: Broadview Press, 1998.

Bryson, Jay. "Is the U.S. Current Account Deficit Sustainable?" *Economic Commentary*, (May 30, 2006):1–5.

Business Week (BW). Various issues.

Canterbery, E Ray. *The Theory of the Bondholding Class*. Singapore: World Scientific, 2000.

Clark, T. "U.S. Inflation Developments in 1995." *Economic Review*, Federal Reserve Bank of Kansas City, (First Quarter 1996):27–42.

Comin, Diego, Erica L. Groshen, and Bess Rabin. "Turbulent Firms, Turbulent Wages?" Federal Reserve Bank of NY, Staff Report no. 238, (February 2006).

Cornwall, J. and W. Cornwall. *Capitalist Development in the Twentieth Century: An Evolutionary-Keynesian Analysis*. Cambridge: Cambridge University Press, 2001.

Cox, W.M. "Two Types of Paper: The Case for Federal Reserve Independence." *Annual Report*, Federal Reserve Bank of Dallas, (1990).

Cukierman, A. *Central Bank Strategy, Credibility, and Independence*. Cambridge:The MIT Press. (1992)

D'Arista, Jane. "Dollars, Debt, and Dependence: The Case for International Monetary Reform." *Journal of Post Keynesian Economics* 26, (Summer 2004):557–572.

Davidson, Paul. *Post Keynesian Macroeconomic Theory*. Cheltenham: Edward Elgar, 1994.

——. *Economics for a Civilized Society*. Armonk: M.E. Sharpe, 1996.

——. "Globalization." *Journal of Post Keynesian Economics* 24, (spring 2002):475–492.

——. "The Future of the International Financial System." *Journal of Post Keynesian Economics* 26, (summer 2004):591–605.

——. "A Post Keynesian View of the Washington Consensus and how to Improve it." *Journal of Post Keynesian Economics*. 27, (winter 2004–2005):207–228.

Dhawan, Rajeev and Karsten Jeske. "How Resilient is the Modern Economy to Energy Price Shocks?" Federal Reserve Bank of Atlanta. *Economic Review*, (Third Quarter 2006):21–32.

DiCaprio , Alisa and Kevin P. Gallagher. "The WTO and the Shrinking of Development Space—How Big is the Bite?" *Journal of World Investment and Trade* 7, no. 5, (October 2006). http://www.wernerpubl.com/frame_inves.htm

Dotsey, Michael. "A Review of Inflation Targeting in Developed Countries." *Business Review*. Philadelphia Federal Reserve, (quarter three 2006):10–20.

Economic Commentary. "The Bernanke Era Begins." Wachovia (February 13, 2006):1–8.

Economist. "The World's Most Expensive Club." May 26, 2007, 79–80.

Edwards, Franklin. *The New Finance*. Washington: AEI Press, 1996.

Economic Quarterly. "The Fiftieth Anniversary of the Accord." Federal Reserve Bank of Richmond 87, Winter 2001.

Financial Markets Center (FMC). New Fed Governors' Financial Disclosures. March 16 2006.

Federal Reserve Bulletin. Various issues.

Fischer, David. *The Great Wave*. Oxford: Oxford University Press, 1996.

Friedman, Milton. "A Monetary and Fiscal Framework for Economic Stabilization," *American Economic Review*, (June 1948):245–264.

———. *Essays in Positive Economics*. Chicago: University of Chicago Press, 1953.

———. "The Role of Monetary Policy," *American Economic Review*, (March 1968):1–17.

———. "The Case for a Monetary Rule." *Newsweek*, (February 7, 1972).

———. *Free To Choose*. New York: Harcourt Brace, 1980.

Friedman, Milton and Anna J. Schwartz. *A Monetary History of the United States 1867 – 1960*. Princeton: Princeton University Press, 1963.

Friedman, Thomas. *The Lexus and the Olive Tree*. New York: Anchor Books, 2000.

———. *The World is Flat*. New York: Farrar, Straus and Giroux, 2005.

Gallagher, Kevin. "Measuring the Cost of Lost Policy Space at the WTO." International Relations Center, Americas Program Policy Brief, www.irc-online.org. (March 20, 2007):1–6.

Galbraith, James. "Endogenous Doctrine, or, Why is Monetary Policy in America so much Better than in Europe?" *Journal of Post Keynesian Economics* 28, (Spring 2006):423–432.

Galbraith, John K. *The Great Crash 1929*. Boston: Houghton Mifflin Co., 1997.

———. *The New Industrial State*. Boston: Houghton Mifflin, 1979.

Global Financial Stability Report. IMF. April 2006, and September 2005.

Godley, Wynne. "Seven Unsustainable Processes: Medium-Term Prospects and Policies for the United States and the World." Levy Economics Institute, 1999.

Goldstein, Jonathan. "The Simple Analytics and Empirics of the Cyclical Profit Squeeze and Cyclical Under-consumption Theories." *Review of Radical Political Economics*, (Spring 1999):74–88.

Goodfriend, M. "Monetary Policy Comes of Age: A 20th Century Odyssey." Federal Reserve Bank of Richmond, *Economic Quarterly*, (Winter 1997):1–22.

Goodfriend, Marvin and Jeffrey Lacker. "Limited Commitment and Central Banking." Federal Reserve Bank of Richmond. *Economic Quarterly* 85, (Fall 1999).

Gordon, David. "Chickens Come Home to Roost: From Prosperity to Stagnation in the Postwar U.S. Economy." In Bernstein's and Adler's *Understanding American Economic Decline*. Cambridge: Cambridge University Press, 1994, 34–76.

Greenspan, Alan. "Testimony before the Committee on the Budget." U.S. Senate, Federal Reserve Board, January 21, 1997.

Greenwald, Bruce and Joseph Stiglitz. "Helping Infant Economies Grow: Foundations of Trade Policies for Developing Countries." American Economic Review *Papers and Proceedings*, (May 2006):141–146.

Hawley, James and Andrew Williams. "The Emergence of Universal Owners." *Challenge*. Vol.43, (July/August 2000):43–61.

Henretta, James, W. Brownlee, David Brody, and Susan Ware. *America's History Since 1865*. Chicago: The Dorsey Press, 1987.

Herman, Edward. *Corporate Control, Corporate Power*. Cambridge University Press, 1981.

Hetzel, R. "A Quantity Theory Framework for Monetary Policy." *Economic Quarterly*, Federal Reserve Bank of Richmond, (Summer 1993):35–47.

——. "The Case for a Monetary Rule in a Constitutional Democracy." *Economic Quarterly*, Federal Reserve Bank of Richmond, (Spring 1997):45–65.

Huntington, Samuel. *The Clash of Civilizations and the Remaking of World Order*. New York: Touchstone, 1996.

IMF. Public Information Notice (PIN). External Relations Department. PIN # 06/90 "IMF Executive Board Concludes 2006 Discussion on Common Policies of Member Countries with the Central African Economic and Monetary Community." 8/7/2006.

IMF. "Foreign Direct Investment in Emerging Market Countries." A report of the Working Group of the Capital Markets Consultative Group, September 18, 2003.

Journal of Post Keynesian Economics (JPKE) symposium on the Washington Consensus, (winter 2004–2005).

Journal of Post Keynesian Economics (JPKE) symposium on central banking 28, (summer 2006).

Kambhu, John. "Trading Risk, Market Liquidity, and Convergence Trading in the Interest Rate Swap Spread." FRB of NY, *Economic Policy Review*, (May 2006):1–13.

Kelly, Marjorie. *The Devine Right of Capital*. San Francisco: Berrett-Koehler Publishers, 2001.

Keynes, John Maynard. *The General Theory of Employment, Interest, and Money*, Amherst: Prometheus Books, 1997.

Kindleberger, Charles. *Manias, Panics, and Crashes*. NY: Basic Books, 1978.

King, Philip and Sharmila King. *International Economics and International Economic Policy*. Boston: McGraw-Hill, 2005.

Korten, David. *When Corporations Rule the World*. San Francisco: Kumarian Press and Berrett-Koehler Publishers, 2001.

——. *The Post-Corporate World*. San Francisco: Kumarian Press and Berrett-Koehler Publishers, 1999.

Kregel, Jan. "The Perils of Globalization." Center for Full Employment and Price Stability. Seminar paper no. 13, (April 2003):1–13.

Krugman, Paul. *The Return of Depression Economics*. New York: W.W. Norton, 2000.

Kumar, Anil. "Did NAFTA Spur Texas Exports?" *Southwest Economy*. Federal Reserve Bank of Dallas, March/April 2006.

Kydland, F. and Prescott, E. "Rules Rather than Discretion: The Inconsistency of Optimal Plans." *Journal of Political Economy*, (June 1977):473–491.

Lacker, Jeffrey. Speech delivered at West Virginia University, February 14, 2006. http://www.richmondfed.org/news_and_speeches/presidents_speeches/index.cfm/2006/id=81

Lane, Philip and Gian Maria Milesi-Ferretti. "Existing Financial Imbalances." *Finance and Development* 43, IMF. (March 2006).

Lechner, Frank and John Boli. *The Globalization Reader*. Oxford: Blackwell Publishing, 2004.

Lenin, V.I. Lenin: Collected Works. Volume 22. Moscow: Progress Publishers, second printing, 1974.

Lissakers, Karin. *Banks, Borrowers, and the Establishment*. New York: Basic Books, 1991.

Mahn, Chris. "Exchange Rates and Capital Flight Controls: Three Economists Perspectives." Belmont Abbey College senior economics thesis, 2005.

Market Watch. www.marketwatch.com.

Markham, Jerry. *A Financial History of the United States*. Armonk: M.E. Sharpe, 2002.

Mayer, T. "Replacing the FOMC by a PC." *Contemporary Policy Issues*, (April 1987):31–43.

McCallum, B. "Robustness Properties of a Rule for Monetary Policy." Carnegie-Rochester Conference Series on Public Policy, (Autumn 1988):173–204.

———. Monetary Economics: Theory and Policy. New York: Macmillan, 1989.

Medlen, Craig. "Two Sets of Twins? An exploration of Domestic Saving-Investment Imbalances." *Journal of Economic Issues* 39, (September 2005):551–577.

Mihailov, Alexander. "Operational Independence, Inflation Targeting, and UK Monetary Policy." *Journal of Post Keynesian Economics* 28, (Spring 2006):395–421.

Minsky, Hyman. *Stabilizing An Unstable Economy* . New Haven: Yale University Press, 1986.

Mitrusi, Andrew and James Poterba. "The Distribution of Payroll and Income Tax Burdens, 1979–1999." *National Tax Journal* 53, (September 2, 2000):765–794.

Moore, Basil. "The Endogenous Money Supply." *Journal of Post Keynesian Economics*, 1988, 372–385.

Moore, Basil. "A Global Currency for a Global Economy." *Journal of Post Keynesian Economics* 26, (summer 2004):631–653.

Mosler, Warren. "Soft Currency Economics" www.mosler.org 1995.

NPR. National Public Radio. Market Watch Morning Report. Commentary by Robert Reich. November 22, 2006.

O'Rourke, Kevin and Jeffrey Williamson. *Globalization and History*. Cambridge: MIT Press, 2000.

Palley, Tom. *Plenty of Nothing*. Princeton: Princeton University Press, 1998.

——. "Restoring Prosperity: Why the U.S. Model is not the Right Answer for the U.S. or Europe," *Journal of Post Keynesian Economics* 20, (Spring 1998):337–354.

——. "China, The Global Economy, and the Contradictions of Export-led Growth." Research Section, Working Paper, Palley Blog. (October 2005):1–13. http://www .thomaspalley.com/

——. "Economics and Politics of Trade Deficits." Palley Blog. (November 13, 2006).

——. "Thinking Outside the Box about Trade, Development, and Poverty Reduction." *Foreign Policy In Focus*. Blog. (January 18 2006):1–12.

——. "The Economics of Outsourcing." *Public Policy Brief*. Levy Economics Institute, no. 89A, 2007, 1–6.

Peek, Joe and Eric Rosengren. "Implications of the Globalization of the Banking Sector: The Latin American Experience." in Building an Infrastructure for Financial Stability. Federal Reserve Bank of Boston conference proceedings # 44, June 2000.

Phillips, Kevin. *The Politics of Rich and Poor*. New York: Harper Collins, 1990.

Piketty, Thomas and Emmanuel Saez. "The Evolution of Top Incomes: A Historical and International Perspective." AER *Papers and Proceedings*. May 2006, 200–205.

Reich, Robert. *The Work of Nations*. New York: Vintage Books, 1992.

Rodrik, Dani. "Has Globalization Gone Too Far?" Institute for International Economics. (March 1997): http://bookstore.petersoninstitute.org/merchant.mvc?Screen= PROD&Product_Code=57

Rogoff, Kenneth. "Impact of Globalization on Monetary Policy." Paper for the Federal Reserve Bank of Kansan City symposium The New Economic Geography: Effects and Policy Implications, August 24–26, 2006. See http://www.kc.frb.org/ publicat/sympos/2006/pdf/rogoff.paper.0829.pdf

Samuelson, Robert. "Anxiety Amid The Prosperity." *Newsweek*. (February 20, 2006).

Samuelson, Robert. "Will America Pass the Baton?" Newsweek. (March 6, 2006). http://www.msnbc.msn.com/id/11567353/site/newsweek/

Sargent, T. and Wallace, N. "Rational Expectations, The Optimal Monetary Instrument, and the Optimal Money Supply Rule." *Journal of Political Economy*, (April 1975):241–254.

Sherman, Howard. *The Business Cycle*. Princeton: Princeton University Press, 1991.

Silva, John. "Employment: The Economics Behind the Financial Market's Most Important Statistic." *Economic Commentary*. (July 19, 2005).

Stiglitz, Joseph. *Globalization and its Discontents*. New York: W.W. Norton, 2003.

Stockhammer, Engelbert. "Shareholder Value Orientation and the Investment-Profit Puzzle." *Journal of Post Keynesian Economics* 28, (Winter 2005–2006):193–215.

Symposium. *Maintaining Financial Stability in a Global Economy*. Federal Reserve Bank of Kansas City, (August 28–30, 1997).

Tager, Michael and William Van Lear. "Fiscal and Monetary Policy Rules Revisited." *The Social Science Journal* 38, no.1, (2001):69–84.

Taylor, J. "Discretion versus Policy Rules in Practice." Carnegie-Rochester Conference Series on Public Policy, (December 1993):195–214.

The Economist. "Economics Focus: Curve Ball." (September 30, 2006):88.

The Economist. Various issues.

Thurow, Lester. *The Future of Capitalism*. New York: Penguin Books, 1996.

Thurow, Lester. *Head To Head*. New York: Harper Collins, 2003.

Tymoigne, Eric. "Asset Prices, Financial Fragility, and Central Banking." Levy Economics Institute, working paper 456, (June 2006).

Underwood, Mike. "Six Sigma: The Emergence of the New Quality System of the 21st Century." Senior thesis. Belmont Abbey College. February 2006.

Van Lear, William. "Profitability in Business Cycle Theory and Forecasting." *Review of Radical Political Economic,*. (Spring 1999):46–60.

Van Lear, William. "A Review of the Rules Versus Discretion Debate in Monetary Policy" Eastern *Economic Journal* 26, (Winter 2000):29–40.

Van Lear, William. *A Populist Challenge to Corporate Capitalism*. Singapore: World Scientific Publishing Co., 2002.

Wachovia. Wachovia Economics Group. *Economic and Financial Commentary*.

Wall Street Journal (WSJ). Various issues.

Wallbank, T. Walter, Alastair Taylor, Nels Bailkey, and George Jewsbury. *Civilization Past and Present*. 5th edition, Glenview: Scott, Foresman and Co., 1985.

Whalen, Charles. "Money Manager Capitalism and the End of Shared Prosperity." *Journal of Economic Issues*, (June 1997):517–525.

White, William. "Procyclicality in the Financial System: Do We Need A New Macrofinancial Stabilization Framework?" BIS Working Papers #193. (January 2006):1–25.

———. "Is Price Stability Enough?" BIS Working Papers # 205. (April 2006):1–18.

Wolfson, Martin. *Financial Crises*. Armonk: M.E. Sharpe, 1994.

Wray, Randall. "A Keynesian Presentation of the Relations among Government Deficits, Investment, Saving, and Growth." *Journal of Economic Issues* 23, 1989, 977–1002

———. Savings, Profits and Speculation in Capitalist Economies. *Journal of Economic Issues* 25 (December 1991):951–976.

———. *Understanding Modern Money*, Cheltenham: Edward Elgar, 1998.

———. "The Fed and the New Monetary Consensus." *Public Policy Brief*. Levy Economics Institute. No. 80, 2004.

———. "Banking, Finance, and Money: A Socioeconomics Approach." Levy Economics working paper # 459, (July 2006).

Wynne, Mark. "EMU at 1." in *International Economics and International Economic Policy*. edited by King and King, Boston: McGraw-Hill Irwin, 2005, 305–321.

Yeldan, Erinc. "Neoliberal Global Remedies: From Speculative-Led Growth to IMF-Led Crisis in Turkey." *Review of Radical Political Economics* 38, (spring 2006):193–213.